Data File
by Lynne Blesz Vestal

to accompany

Sociology

Eighth Edition

John J. Macionis

PRENTICE HALL, Upper Saddle River, NJ 07458

©2001 by PRENTICE-HALL, INC.
PEARSON EDUCATION
Upper Saddle River, New Jersey 07458

10 9 8 7 6 5 4 3 2

ISBN 0-13-018497-7

Printed in the United States of America

Contents

Chapter 1

The Sociological Perspective

I. The Sociological Perspective.
 A. Sociology is the systematic study of human society.
 B. The sociological perspective helps us to see general social patterns in the behavior of particular individuals.
 C. It also encourages us to realize that society guides our thoughts and deeds — to see the strange in the familiar.
  1. APPLYING SOCIOLOGY BOX—What's in a Name? How Social Forces Affect Personal Choice. U.S. citizens with "foreign" names frequently change them to sound more English.
 D. Sociology also encourages us to see individuality in social context.
  1. For example, Emile Durkheim's research showed that the suicide rate was strongly influenced by the extent to which people were socially integrated with others.

II. The Importance of Global Perspective.
 A. Sociologists also strive to see issues in global perspective, defined as the study of the larger world and our society's place in it.
  1. WINDOW ON THE WORLD—Global Map 1–1: Economic Development in Global Perspective. There are three different types of nations in the world.
    a. The world's high-income countries are industrialized nations in which most people have relatively high incomes.
    b. The world's middle-income countries have limited industrialization and moderate personal income.
    c. The world's low-income countries have little industrialization in which most people are poor.
  2. GLOBAL SOCIOLOGY BOX—The Global Village: A Social Snapshot of Our World. Think of the population breakdown if the world were a village of one thousand people.
  3. Global thinking is an important component of the sociological perspective for three reasons:
    a. Societies the world over are increasingly interconnected, making traditional distinctions between "us" and "them" less and less valid.
    b. Many human problems faced in the United States are far more serious elsewhere.
    c. Thinking globally is a good way to learn more about ourselves.

III. Applying the Sociological Perspective.
    A. Certain situations like the following promote a sociological way of viewing reality.
        1. Experiencing social marginality, the state of being excluded from social activity as an "outsider." People at the margins of social life are aware of social patterns that others rarely think about.
        2. Living through periods of social crisis like the Great Depression or the 1960s.
    B. Benefits of the sociological perspective.
        1. The sociological perspective helps us assess the truth of "common sense."
        2. The sociological perspective helps us assess both opportunities and constraints in our lives.
        3. The sociological perspective empowers us to be active participants in our society.
        4. The sociological perspective helps us to live in a diverse world.
    C. The application of sociology is evident in the role that sociology has had in shaping public policy and law in many ways. A background in sociology is also good preparation for the working world. An increasing number of sociologists work in all sorts of applied fields.
        1. APPLYING SOCIOLOGY BOX—The Social Imagination: Turning Personal Problems into Public Issues. The power of the sociological perspective lies not just in changing individual lives but in transforming society.

IV. The Origins of Sociology.
    A. Auguste Comte believed that the major goal of sociology was to understand society as it actually operates. Comte saw sociology as the product of a three-stage historical development:
        1. The theological stage, in which thought was guided by religion.
        2. The metaphysical stage, a transitional phase.
        3. The scientific stage.
    B. Three major social changes during the seventeenth and eighteenth centuries are important to the development of sociology.
        1. The rise of a factory-based industrial economy.
        2. The emergence of great cities in Europe.
        3. Political changes, including a rising concern with individual liberty and rights. The French Revolution symbolized this dramatic break with political and social tradition.
    C. Auguste Comte and Karl Marx are well-known political pioneers of sociology. Other sociological pioneers who made important contributions include Harriet Martineau, Jane Addams, and William Edward Burghardt Du Bois, all pushed to the margins of society.

V. Sociological Theory.
    A. A theory is a statement of how and why specific facts are related. The goal of sociological theory is to explain social behavior in the real world. For example, SEEING OURSELVES—National Map 1–1 shows suicide rates across the United States.

B. Theories are based on theoretical paradigms, sets of assumptions that guide thinking and research. Sociologists ask two basic questions: What issues should we study? How should we connect the facts? There are three major sociological paradigms:

1. The structural-functional paradigm is a framework for building theory that sees society as a complex system whose parts work together to promote solidarity and stability.

    a. It asserts that our lives are guided by social structures (relatively stable patterns of social behavior).

    b. Each social structure has social functions, or consequences, for the operation of society as a whole.

    c. Key figures in the development of this paradigm include Auguste Comte, Emile Durkheim, Herbert Spencer, and Talcott Parsons.

    d. Robert Merton introduced three concepts related to social function:

        1) manifest functions, the recognized and intended consequences of any social pattern

        2) latent functions, largely unrecognized and unintended consequences and

        3) social dysfunctions, undesirable consequences of a social pattern for the operation of society.

    e. Critical Evaluation: The influence of this paradigm has declined in recent decades.

        1) It focuses on stability, thereby ignoring inequalities of social class, race, and gender.

2. The social-conflict paradigm is a framework for building theory that sees society as an arena of inequality that generates conflict and change. Most sociologists who favor the conflict paradigm attempt not only to understand society but also to reduce social inequality.

    a. Key figures in this tradition include Karl Marx and W. E. B. DuBois.

    b. Critical evaluation: This paradigm has developed rapidly in recent years. It has several weaknesses.

        1) It ignores social unity based on mutual interdependence and shared values.

        2) Because it is explicitly political, it cannot claim scientific objectivity.

        3) Like the structural-functional paradigm, it envisions society in terms of broad abstractions.

    c. APPLYING SOCIOLOGY BOX—Sociology at Work: Understanding the Issue of Race. DuBois, one of sociology's pioneers, wanted to apply sociology to solving the problems of his time, especially racial inequality.

3. The symbolic-interaction paradigm is a framework for building theory that sees society as the product of the everyday interactions of individuals.

    a. The structural-functional and the social-conflict paradigms share a macro-level orientation, meaning that they focus on broad social structures that shape society as a whole. In contrast, symbolic-interactionism has a micro-level orientation; it focuses on patterns of social interaction in specific settings.

    b. Key figures in the development of this paradigm include Max Weber, George Herbert Mead, Erving Goffman, George Homans and Peter Blau.

    c. Critical evaluation: Symbolic interactionism attempts to explain more clearly how individuals actually experience society. However, it has two weaknesses:

        1. Its micro orientation sometimes results in the error of ignoring the influence of larger social structures.

        2. By emphasizing what is unique, it risks overlooking the effects of culture, class, gender, and race.

4. Applying the Perspectives: The Sociology of Sports.

    a. The functions of sports. A structural-functional approach directs attention to the ways sports help society to operate.

    b. Sports and conflict. A social-conflict analysis points out that sports are closely linked to social inequality.

    c. Sports as interaction. The symbolic-interaction paradigm sees sports less as a system than as an ongoing process.

5. CONTROVERSY AND DEBATE BOX—Is Sociology Nothing More Than Stereotypes? In contrast to stereotypes, good sociology involves making generalizations, but with three important conditions.

    a. Sociologists do not indiscriminately apply any generalization to all individuals.

    b. Sociologists are careful that a generalization squares with available facts.

    c. Sociologists offer generalizations fair-mindedly, with an interest in getting at the truth.

Chapter Objectives

1) Define sociology and examine the components of the sociological perspective.

2) Explain the importance of a global perspective for sociology.

3) Examine how social marginality and social crisis encourage people to use the sociological perspective.

4) Identify and describe four benefits of using the sociological perspective.

5) Identify and discuss three social changes especially important to the development of sociology.

6) Identify and describe the three-stage historical development of sociology as a science.

7) Discuss the importance of theory in sociology.

8) Summarize the main assumptions of the three major theoretical paradigms in sociology.

Essay Topics

1) How are societies all over the world increasingly connected and what are the consequences of these links?

2) After reviewing your text's discussion of the social factors which influence a student's decision regarding which college to attend, identify some of the social factors which might help explain why you selected your major or intended career.

3) Describe an incident in which you were a new member of a group and in which your marginality made it easier for you to observe something about that group which was not evident to those who had been in it longer.

4) List the benefits of the sociological perspective. Provide specific examples of how applying the sociological perspective to your daily life benefits you.

5) What sociological insights can the three theoretical paradigms give us about the American educational system?

6) Why is positivistic or scientific sociology generally considered to be superior to the pre-scientific perspectives preceding it in Western thought?

7) How have sociologists helped shape public policy and law?

8) Identify what you regard as some of the manifest and latent functions of American high schools.

9) What image of society is held by the three major theoretical paradigms? What core questions does each paradigm ask? Which of the three paradigms strikes you as the most useful? Why?

10) Develop your understanding of the three sociological paradigms by speculating on some of the issues which each would consider in investigating the 2000 Presidential election, the abortion rights controversy, or rap music.

Integrative Supplement Guide

1. **Transparencies - Series V:**
- T-1 Share of 1995 High School Graduates Entering College the Following Fall
- T-2 Rate of Death By Suicide, By Race and Sex, for the United States
- T-3 Economic Development in Global Perspective
- T-4 Suicide Rates Across the United States

Supplemental Lecture Material
Sociology and the Other Social Sciences

Sociology is only one of a number of interrelated ways of attempting to understand and account for human behavior.

Most earlier attempts were humanistic; that is, they were not guided by the principles of scientific methodology. Because they are predicated on relatively rigorous procedures for the gathering and assessment of empirical information, the social sciences provide a more satisfactory way to understand the causes of human behavior than do humanistic approaches, although the value of insights obtained through nonscientific methods should never be underestimated. Often such insights provide the starting point for scientific explorations.

Sociology is only one of a family of related social sciences. The following discussion examines the character of these other disciplines and explores sociology's relationship with each of them.

Psychology shares with sociology (and cultural anthropology) a broadly-based interest in understanding a wide variety of human behavior; the disciplines differ from each other in that psychology is principally concerned with the behavior of individuals, while sociologists more commonly study group behavior and the extent to which group membership (including factors such as race, class, and gender) influences individual behavior.

Psychology has both academic and applied branches. Applied psychology is a therapeutic effort to help people understand their own behavior and cope with their problems. Academic psychology is closer to the mainstream of sociology, placing its central emphasis on understanding such phenomena as learning, thinking, personality formation and functioning, intelligence, memory, and motivation. Academic psychology grew out of biology and is still strongly oriented toward experimental research. Some academic psychologists conduct research into animal behavior and the physiology of the brain, which is sharply distinct from sociological work; others concern themselves with very much the same sort of questions as those that interest sociologists, although always with special emphasis on individual behavior. The two fields meet in the subdiscipline of social psychology, which is commonly taught in both psychology and sociology curricula and which focuses on how human personality and behavior are influenced by an individual's social environment.

Anthropology, like psychology, has some concerns it shares with sociology but also studies some very different subjects. The two main subfields are physical anthropology and cultural anthropology, although some attention is also devoted to archeology and linguistics. Physical anthropology uses natural science research methods to study such topics as the biological evolution of the human race and the differences between the races. Cultural anthropology studies many of the same topics as does sociology, but there are two main differences between the fields: (1) anthropology tends to study small, preliterate, traditional societies, whereas most sociologists concentrate on modern industrial societies; (2) anthropology generally studies cultures as a whole, while sociology commonly studies smaller systems (for example, groups or institutions) within complex societies. However, sociology and cultural anthropology are closer than the other social sciences. Furthermore, as the traditional societies that anthropologists have historically preferred to study have become increasingly scarce, more and more cultural anthropologists are studying such aspects of contemporary society as street gangs, immigrant life, and ethnic subcultures, which are indistinguishable from the subject matter usually studied by sociologists. Cultural anthropologists and sociologists use similar research methods, although anthropologists are more likely to develop elaborate descriptive ethnographies of the social scenes they observe by means of extended periods of participant observation, whereas sociologists more commonly collect narrower and more quantitative data using survey research methods.

Economics is a much more narrow and focused discipline than sociology, psychology, or anthropology, concerning itself with the production, distribution, and consumption of goods and services. Because economists restrict their attention to phenomena that can be precisely measured, such as interest rates, taxes, economic production rates, and unemployment, they have developed by far the most sophisticated statistical techniques for manipulating and presenting data of any of the social sciences. On the other hand, this precision may limit the ability of economists to deal effectively with the sorts of larger issues that many people find most interesting and important. Sociologists who study economic behavior, in contrast to economists, focus on the relationship between economics and other aspects of social reality—for example, on the way in which value orientations (such as support for the environmental movement) may affect consumption patterns, on the ways in which corporations are organized and changed, or on how human beings experience the world of work subjectively.

Political science, like economics, focuses on a relatively narrow segment of human social behavior, in this case the issues of power and authority. Traditionally, political science focused either on political philosophy or on relatively limited studies of the ways in which governments and political parties are organized and function. More recently, under the influence of the developing field of political sociology, political scientists have been increasingly interested in such topics as political socialization, the social forces influencing voting behavior, the structure of institutional and noninstitutional power in local communities, and the origin and development of movements of political protest, all of which are shared concerns with sociologists working in this area. The two disciplines use broadly similar research methods, with political scientists having played an especially important role in the development of opinion polling and related techniques of survey research.

Two additional disciplines deserve mention, though each is only marginally com-

patible with the basic definition of a social science.

History straddles the line between the humanities and the social sciences. Traditionally the field studied historical developments as unique events, not as examples of general categories or patterns. More recently, however, many historians have become more interested in the social forces that shape historical events and in developing theories of broad patterns of sociohistorical change; they also have begun using more quantitative and precise data. To the extent that these trends continue, history is moving in the direction of becoming a true social science.

Social work is comparable to applied psychology in that its central purpose is not to understand human behavior but rather to help people, groups, and communities cope more effectively with their personal and social problems. Of course, it is essential to understand the causes of these problems, and social workers rely heavily on sociological and psychological research and theory, but the fundamental thrust of the field is different from that of sociology and academic psychology because of its practical orientation.

Discussion Questions

1) What are the strengths and weaknesses of humanistic and scientific approaches to understanding human behavior? Does the fact that poetry or drama are not scientific mean that we have nothing to learn from them?

2) Which of the social sciences strikes you as closest to sociology? Most distinct? Why?

3) Sociologists and political scientists both study political behavior. Sociologists and economists both study economic behavior. Is this simply duplication of effort, or do soci-

ologists, with their characteristic perspectives, have the ability to develop insights that might not occur to their fellow social scientists?

4) Sociologists have in the past several decades developed and refined a specialization called applied sociology. Like applied psychology, it focuses on coping with problems rather than studying what causes those problems. In what ways can sociology contribute to the more effective resolution of social problems at the individual, group, and community levels? Should we promote development of this subdiscipline or would it be better left to the social workers?

Supplemental Lecture Material
Teen Suicide

As noted in the textbook, suicide is more prevalent among certain parts of the U.S. population. According to new figures compiled by the Federal Centers for Disease Control & Prevention (CDC), suicide rates are rising steady for teenagers while holding steady in all other age groups. Between 1980 and 1995, the suicide rate rose 120 percent among those 10-to-14-year olds; for 15 to 19-year-olds it rose almost 30 percent. In part this may be attributed to the increasing availability of firearms, but in addition, claims Lanny Berman (the executive director of the American Association of Suicidology, "there are more depressed kids". While the actual number of suicides remains quite small among teenagers, a 1993 study of 16,000 high school students conducted by the CDC found that 1 in 12 said he or she had attempted suicide the previous year.

Suicide among black teenagers, once quite rare, has increased dramatically over the last two decades. The rise may well be related to the strain some black families feel in making the transition to middle class life (according to a 1998 study conducted by the CDC). A 1995 study of high school students across the country found that black students were as likely as whites to try suicide. Suicide is now the third leading cause of death for black 15 to 24-year olds (the leading cause being homicide, followed by accidents.)

According to a Time Magazine article (July 22, 1996), among teachers and counselors who deal with teens on a daily basis, such words as "crisis" and "overwhelming" come up repeatedly in discussions. Dr. David C. Clark of the Rush Medical College in Chicago and other experts believe that youth suicide is frequently triggered by a variety of factors that include clinical depression, substance abuse, a pattern of antisocial behavior, traumatic family disruptions, stress from school, and peer pressure. In the case of black youth suicide, several experts contend that the move to middle-class life might be accompanied by a splintering of community and family support networks, a weakening of bonds to religion, and the pressure of trying to compete in historically white-dominated professions and social circles. (Dr. Tonji Durant, the author of a CDC study of this subject, acknowledges that more research on the impact of economic status on suicide victims is needed to better understand patterns. But a 1995 study at Columbia University of teenage suicides in the New York metropolitan region found that unlike white and Hispanic teenagers, black teenagers who committed suicide tended to come from higher socioeconomic backgrounds than other blacks in the general population.)

The way teens choose to commit suicide is also relevant. "Access to lethal means – firearms and prescription drugs, plays a role", says Alex Crosby, an epidemiologist at the CDC's Division of Violence Prevention.

In the face of such bad news, grass-roots efforts are under way to prevent suicide among children. Most important for such efforts to succeed is a new awareness and willingness on the part of parents who have lost a child through suicide to speak publicly about their loss, a subject often fraught with guilt. Groups such as the Suicide Prevention Advocacy Network (SPAN) are petitioning Congress and state legislatures to treat suicide as a national problem as well as develop programs to prevent it. In the meantime, local programs are tackling the issue, particularly within schools, by trying to identify at-risk teenagers before it is too late. But while working in small ways is a beginning, it may not be enough.

According to David Brent, chief of child psychiatry at the Western Psychiatric Institute and Clinic in Pittsburgh, "there's been a mismatch between resources and where the need is….Crop-dusting where you give a little bit to everyone, may not be the best use of resources." Whatever needs to change to lower the youth suicide rate, will probably have to happen on a larger national and societal scale through new, more targeted approaches. While crises are hitting teenagers right and left, not only are schools burned out trying to identify at-risk teenagers before it is too late – so are the crises teams.

In summary, the textbook states that in 1994 suicide rates for white people were almost twice as high as those for African-Americans. The reason for this, according to Durkheim's theory, would be that white people enjoy greater wealth and autonomy while African-Americans experience tighter social ties and fewer social choices. This article, however, presents a trend that appears to go counter to Durkheim: suicide among young African-American males is

rising far more quickly than it is among young whites.

Sources

Pam Belluck. "Black Youth's Suicide Rate Now on the Rise." New York Times (March 20, 1998).

Elizabeth Gleick. "Suicide's Shadow". Time (July 22, 1996) 40-42.

Marks, Alexandra. "Prevention Push: Rise in Teen Suicides Spurs New Solutions" The Christian Science Monitor (March 5, 1997 – 1, 8-9).

Discussion Questions

1) Applying Durkheim's theory of social integration, why do you think the suicide rate might have risen so dramatically particularly among African-American teenagers?

2) What factors contributed to the suicides of "trenchcoat mafia" members at Columbine H.S. in Colorado in 1999?

3) Easy access to firearms seems to play a role in increased teen suicide. Discuss the manifest functions and the latent functions of "the right to bear arms." Where do you stand on this issue? Support your opinions.

4) What does a sociological perspective add to the understanding of teen suicide? What practical ideas might applied sociology offer?

5) **Activity:** Pretend you are part of a grassroots organization determined to prevent teen suicide. Devise a step-by-step action plan. What would you do to attack this

problem? How would you carry out various steps? How would you get funding?

Supplemental Lecture Material
The Liberation Sociology Tradition

Joe Feagin (University of Florida), in a 1997 plenary presentation, noted that there is a long liberation – sociology tradition in the discipline, which stretches back to Jane Addams and W.E.B. DuBois in the late 19th century. He describes liberation sociology as "sociology from the bottom up." From this perspective the point of sociology is to enhance the lives of ordinary people, to bring changes in social systems of discrimination and oppression.

A major 20th century figure to accent this progressive tradition was Robert S. Lynd, with a focus on class oppression. He hypothesized that "Private capitalism does not know how to operate and probably cannot be made to operate, to assure the amount of general welfare to which the present stage of our technological skills and intelligence entitle us; and other ways of managing our economy therefore, need to be explored." Thus, the question that social science appears to face is "What kind of culture would be that culture which would use its full array of knowledge and productive resources to maximize the quantity, quality, and useful variety of daily living for the maises of American people?"

Another major figure of the progressive tradition in sociology is the African American sociologist, Oliver C. Cox, who accented the importance of sociological research and passion in favor of change, particularly against racism. (See Oliver C. Cox: Caste, Class & Race [1948]).

The best known figure in 20th century progressive tradition is C. Wright Mills,

who accented the importance of sociologists listening to those who are insurgent (See C.Wright Mills: the Sociological Imagination [1959]). Alfred M. Lee (Sociology for Whom? [1978]) continued the criticism of mainstream sociology for its failure to deal with class and other oppressions.

In the late 1960s and early 1970s several feminist sociologists began to re-emphasize the maleness of traditional sociology and the need to incorporate a feminist perspective on gendered oppression in sociology. Jesse Bernard stated "without equivocation that sociology was a male science of society and that practically all sociology to date has been a sociology of the male world (Dale Spender: Man Made Language [1980]).

Source

The Southwestern Sociological Association's Newsletter, Vol. 23: No. 2 – Spring 1997: 4 & 5.

Discussion Questions

1) Oliver C. Cox wrote that "Clearly, the social scientist should be accurate and objective but not neutral; he should be passionately partisan in favor of the welfare of the people and against the interests of the few when they seem to submerge that welfare." What's your opinion of this position?

2) Explain how liberation sociology is related to the social conflict paradigm (cited in Chapter 1 of the text).

3) Explain the parallels that exist between contemporary liberation sociology and today's feminist sociology.

Supplemental Lecture Material
The Social Conflict Paradigm and the Sociology of Sport

As noted in the textbook, each of the three major paradigms may be applied to a wide variety of topics. The conflict perspective has been especially popular among sports sociologists. In fact, Harry Edwards, who published the first major text in this area in 1973 while a member of the faculty at San Jose State University, is a strong adherent of the conflict perspective.

More recently, Richard Lapchick, the director since 1984 of Northeastern University's Center for the Study of Sport in Society, has emerged as a second well-known conflict theory oriented sports sociologist. Unlike Edwards, Lapchick is white and was heavily involved as a civil rights supporter and anti-apartheid activist in his youth; he has repeatedly received death threats and has also been physically attacked by opponents of his struggle for racial justice.

The Center began with an operating budget of $125,000 which has now grown to over a million dollars a year. Lapchick and his twenty-one person staff have collected a massive amount of data documenting the persistent discrimination against minorities and women in sports. Some examples: In 1990–1991, although over 75 percent of the players in the NBA were black, only 22 percent of head coaches were African Americans. In that same year, just 3.6 percent of NFL head coaches and 7.7 percent of major league baseball managers were black. Only 16 percent of all women's intercollegiate athletic programs are administered by women.

In a tradition established by Marx, conflict-oriented sociologists have commonly felt obliged to go beyond merely documenting the existence of injustice. They actually work to overcome it. Harry Edwards at-tempted to organize a boycott by African-American athletes of the 1968 Mexico City Summer Olympics as a protest over the lack of black coaches on the U.S. team and related issues. Although the boycott failed, Edwards was instrumental in encouraging sprinters Tommie Smith and John Carlos to publicize their political beliefs by bowing their heads and giving black power salutes during the awards ceremony for the 200 meter dash.

Like Edwards, Lapchick is also an activist. His center has spent over twelve million dollars in tuition assistance for students who have used up their athletic eligibility. The organization also sponsors outreach programs such as TEAMWORK, which encourages professional athletes to speak to schoolchildren about the realities of high-level sports. A favored theme: stay in school and get your degree, because while 44 percent of black professional athletes believe that they will make it in the pros, in actuality, only 3 percent actually do so.

The following quiz, based on 1993 data, may help students to become aware of the extent to which minorities and women continue to experience discrimination in the world of sports:

1) What percentage of high school varsity athletes are black?
    a. 12.5% b. 25.5% c. 39.5% d. 53.5%

2) Twenty-nine percent of all high school varsity athletes are white females. How many are black females?
    a. 4% b. 10% c. 25% d. 34%

3) Twenty-seven percent of white, male high-school nonathletes participate in extracurricular activities. What percent of black male high school athletes participate in nonathletic extracurricular activities?
    a. 11% b. 20% c. 31% d. 47%

4) What percentage of athletic scholarships go to black athletes?
   a.10% b. 25% c. 35% d. 55%

5) What percentage of athletic scholarships go to women?
   a. 25% b. 35% c. 45% d. 50%

6) What percentage of players on Division I men's basketball teams are black?
   a. 31% b. 56% c. 71% d. 81%

7) What percentage of players on Division I women's basketball teams are black?
   a. 22% b. 33% c. 44% d. 55%

8) Statistics show that a black high school student has the best chance of making it in which of the following professions?
   a. Medical doctor
   b. Professional football player
   c. Professional basketball player
   d. Judge

9) What percentage of players on Division 1A football teams are blacks?
   a. 24% b. 37% c. 51% d. 69%

10) Minority high-school student-athletes do not do as well on achievement tests as their nonathletic peers.
   a. True b. False c. No difference

11) There are 265 Division I college baseball programs. How many have black managers?
   a. 0 b. 5 c. 10 d.15

12) In 1972, more than 90 percent of women's intercollegiate athletic programs were administered by women. What percentage of women's programs have female administrators today?
   a. 16% b. 68% c. 47% d. 35%

13) There are 29 black generals in the U.S. military. How many black head coaches are there in the National Football League?
   a. 0 b. 1 c. 2 d. 4

14) In major-league baseball, the third-base coach is the coordinator on the field. How many of the 26 pro teams have black third-base coaches?
   a. 0 b.2 c. 4 d. 6

Answers
1-a. 2-a. 3-d. 4-a. 5-b. 6-b. 7-b. 8-a, d.
9-b. 10-b. 11-a. 12-a. 13-b. 14-a.

Source
Bruton, Mike. "Trying to Make the Playing Field Fairer." Center for the Study of Sport in Society.

Discussion Questions
1) Do you think it is appropriate for sociologists like Edwards and Lapchick to become involved in reform efforts or would they be wiser to concentrate merely on studying society? Develop arguments supporting each position.

2) Why do you think many people find Lapchick's contention that African Americans are widely discriminated against in sports hard to accept?

Chapter 2

Sociological Investigation

I. The Basics of Sociological Investigation.
 A. Sociological investigation begins with two key requirements:
   1. Look at the world using the sociological perspective.
   2. Be curious and ask questions.
 B. Sociology is a type of **science**, a logical system that bases knowledge on direct, systematic observation. Scientific knowledge is based on **empirical evidence,** information we can verify with our senses.
 C. Scientific evidence sometimes contradicts common sense explanations of social behavior.

II. Science: Basic Elements and Limitations.
 A. Concepts, variables and measurement.
   1. **Concepts** are mental constructs that represent some part of the world, inevitably in a simplified form
   2. **Variables** are concepts whose value changes from case to case.
   3. **Measurement** is the process of determining the value of a variable in a specific case.
    a. Statistical measures are frequently used to describe populations as a whole.
    b. This requires that researchers operationalize variables, which means specifying exactly what one is to measure in assigning a value to a variable.
    4. APPLYING SOCIOLOGY BOX—Three Useful (and Simple) Statistical Measures.
    a. The **mode** is the value that occurs most often in a series of numbers
    b. The **mean** refers to the arithmetic average of a series of numbers.
    c. The **median** is the value that occurs midway in a series of numbers arranged from lowest to highest.
 B. For a measurement to be useful, it must be reliable and valid.
   1. Reliability refers to consistency in measurement.
   2. Validity means precision in measuring exactly what one intends to measure.
 C. Relationships among Variables.
   1. **Cause and effect** is a relationship in which change in one variable causes change in another.
    a. The **independent variable** is the variable that causes the change.
    b. The **dependent variable** is the variable that changes.
   2. Cause and effect relationships allow us to predict how one pattern of behavior will produce another.

   3. Correlation exists when two (or more) variables change together.

       a. **Spurious correlation** means an apparent, although false, association between two (or more) variables caused by some other variable.

       b. Spurious correlations can be discovered through scientific **control**, the ability to neutralize the effect of one variable in order to assess relationships among other variables.

D. Sociologists strive for **objectivity**, a state of personal neutrality in conducting research, whenever possible following Max Weber's model of value-free research.

    1. One way to limit distortion caused by personal values is through **replication**, repetition of research by others in order to assess its accuracy.

E. Limitations of scientific sociology.

    1. Human behavior is too complex to allow sociologists to predict precisely any individual's actions.

    2. Because humans respond to their surroundings, the mere presence of a researcher may affect the behavior being studied.

    3. Social patterns change; what is true in one time or place may not hold true in another.

    4. Because sociologists are part of the world they study, being value-free when conducting social research is difficult.

F. A Second Framework: Interpretive Sociology.

    1. Max Weber, who pioneered this framework, argued that the focus of sociology is interpretation. Interpretive sociology is the study of society that focuses on the meanings people attach to their social world.

    2. The interpretive sociologist's job is not just to observe what people do but to share in their world of meaning and come to appreciate why they act as they do.

G. A Third Framework: Critical Sociology.

    1. Karl Marx, who founded critical sociology, rejected the idea that society exists as a "natural" system with a fixed order. Critical sociology is the study of society that focuses on the need for social change.

    2. The point is not merely to study the world as it is but to change it.

H. Research can be contaminated by gender bias in five ways:

    1. **Androcentricity**, or approaching an issue from the male perspective.

    2. **Overgeneralizing** or using data drawn from studying only one sex to support conclusions about human behavior in general.

    3. **Gender blindness** or not considering the variable of gender at all.

    4. Double standards.

    5. **Interference** because a subject reacts to the sex of the researcher.

I. The American Sociological Association has established formal guidelines for conducting research.

J. SOCIAL DIVERSITY BOX—Conducting Research with Hispanics. Gerardo and Barbara Marin have identified five areas of concern in conducting research with Hispanics:

    1. Be careful with terms.

    2. Realize that cultural values may differ.

    3. Realize that family dynamics may vary.

4. Be aware that attitudes toward time and efficiency may vary.

5. Realize that attitudes toward personal space may vary.

III. The Methods of Sociological Research.

A **research method** is a systematic plan for conducting research. Four commonly used research methods are:

A. An **experiment** is a research method for investigating cause and effect under highly controlled conditions. Experimental research is explanatory, meaning that it asks not just what happens but why. Typically, researchers conduct experiments to test **hypotheses**, unverified statements of a relationship between variables. Most experiments are conducted in laboratories and employ experimental and control groups.

   1. The **Hawthorne effect** is a change in a subject's behavior caused by the awareness of being studied.

   2. The Stanford County Prison study was an experiment conducted by Philip Zimbardo that supported the notion that the character of prison itself, and not the personalities of prisoners and guards, causes prison violence.

B. A **survey** is a research method in which subjects respond to a series of statements or questions in a questionnaire or an interview. Survey research is usually descriptive rather than explanatory.

   1. Surveys are directed at **populations**, the people who are the focus of research. Usually we study a **sample**, a part of a population that represents the whole. Random sampling is commonly used to be sure that the sample is actually representative of the entire population.

   2. Surveys may involve **questionnaires**, a series of written questions a researcher presents to subjects. Questionnaires may be closed-ended or open-ended. Most surveys are self-administered and must be carefully pretested.

   3. Surveys may also take the form of **interviews**, a series of questions administered in person by a researcher to respondents.

   4. APPLYING SOCIOLOGY BOX—Survey Questions: A Word or Two Makes All the Difference. How researchers word questions affects how the public responds.

   5. Lois Benjamin used interviews and snowball sampling to study one hundred elite African Americans. Benjamin concluded that, despite the improving social standing of African Americans, black people in the United States still experience racial hostility.

   6. APPLYING SOCIOLOGY BOX—Reading Tables: An Important Skill. A table provides a lot of information in a small amount of space, so learning to read tables can increase your reading efficiency.

C. **Participant observation** is a method by which researchers systematically observe people while joining in their routine activities. Participant observation research is descriptive and often exploratory. It is normally **qualitative research,** inquiry based on subjective impressions.

   1. William Whyte utilized this approach to study social life in a poor neighborhood in Boston. His research, published in the book *Street Corner Society,* illustrates the value of using a key informant in field research.

D. **Secondary analysis** is a research method in which a researcher utilizes data collected by others.
>   1. SEEING OURSELVES—National Map 2–1: Affluent Minorities Across the United States.
>   2. E. Digby Baltzell's *Puritan Boston and Quaker Philadelphia* explored reasons for the prominence of New Englanders in national life. This study exemplifies a researcher's power to analyze the past using historical sources.

E. The interplay of theory and method.
>   1. **Inductive logical thought** is reasoning that builds specific observations into general theory.
>   2. **Deductive logical thought** is reasoning that transforms general ideas into specific hypotheses suitable for scientific testing.
>   3. Most sociological research uses both types of logical thought.

F. CONTROVERSY AND DEBATE BOX—Can People Lie with Statistics? The best way not to fall prey to statistical manipulation is to understand how people can mislead with statistics:
>   1. People select their data.
>   2. People interpret their data.
>   3. People use graphs to "spin" the truth.

IV. Putting it all together: Ten steps in sociological investigation:
A. What is your topic?
B. What have others already learned?
C. What, exactly, are your questions?
D. What will you need to carry out research?
E. Are there ethical concerns?
F. What method will you use?
G. How will you record the data?
H. What do the data tell you?
I. What are your conclusions?
J. How can you share what you've learned?

Chapter Objectives

1) Name the two requirements of sociological investigation.

2) Discuss the advantages of the scientific approach to knowing and examine how scientific evidence challenges our common sense.

3) Define concepts, variables, and measurement.

4) Distinguish between the concepts of reliability and validity.

5) Distinguish between independent and dependent variables.

6) Understand the distinction between a cause-and-effect relationship and a correlational relationship.

7) Examine the ideal of objectivity in sociological research and discuss ways that researchers can be as objective as possible.

8) Identify limitations of scientific sociology.

9) Summarize the three methodical approaches in sociology: scientific, interpretive, and critical.

10) Identify five ways in which gender-based issues may distort sociological research.

11) List ethical guidelines to follow in sociological research.

12) Summarize the four major methods by which sociologists conduct research and discuss the strengths and weaknesses of each method.

13) Understand the basic logic of experimental research.

14 Outline 10 steps in the process of carrying out sociological investigation.

Essay Topics

1) What are the advantages of choosing a scientific approach to understanding social reality? What are the disadvantages, if any?

2) The text discusses how sociologists operationalize the concept of social class. How would you operationalize such important concepts as intelligence, aggressiveness, masculinity or level of commitment to religion?

3) In what ways does interpretive sociology differ from scientific sociology?

4) What is the link between the three methodological approaches to sociology and the three theoretical paradigms?

5) Suppose you are a sociologist studying the rioting in Los Angeles following the failure of a jury to convict police officers who were videotaped beating motorist Rodney King. Construct two arguments, one proposing that you ought to be as objective as possible in your work and the other suggesting that, while striving for accuracy, you should take a stand against any injustices which your research may uncover. Which position do you find more convincing? Why?

6) What are ways that gender can shape sociological research?

7) What steps can researchers take to reduce the bias which results from the Hawthorne effect?

8) Do you think Zimbardo's Stanford County Prison experiment was ethical, or should he have been prevented from conducting this study? Defend your position.

9) Explain how you would develop a representative sample of students on your campus in order to conduct some survey research.

10) What are the advantages and disadvantages of both open-ended and closed-ended questions in survey research?

11) Develop several criticisms of the research methods employed in Lois Benjamin's study of elite African Americans.

12) What are three steps in the ideal experiment?

Integrative Supplement Guide

1. Transparencies - Series V:

Supplemental Lecture Material
Academic Freedom and "Political Correctness"

James S. Coleman, a highly distinguished scholar and recent president of the American Sociological Association, recently published an intensely controversial article arguing that what conservatives derisively call the "political correctness" movement poses a real threat to academic freedom.

Traditionally, university administrators have been viewed as the principal enemies of academic freedom, but Coleman sees a new and more serious threat resulting from collegial pressure. He writes, "The greatest enemy of academic freedom is the norms that exist about what kinds of questions may be raised in research (and in teaching as well) and what kinds of questions may not be raised.... The taboos that a sociologist is most likely to encounter are those concerning questions of differences between genders or differences among races which might be genetic in origin" (p. 28).

Such taboos are primarily designed to prevent attacks on what Coleman terms "the policies of conspicuous benevolence." "There are certain policies, certain public activities, that have the property that they stem from benevolent intentions toward others less fortunate or in some way oppressed — policies intended to aid the poor, or to aid blacks or Hispanics or women. Any research that would

hinder these policies is subject to much disapproval and attack" (p. 34).

For example, Coleman's widely-reported research into educational opportunity among the races discovered, among other things, that "....teachers' scores on vocabulary tests were related to the verbal achievements of students...." (p. 30). It is widely known that African-American teachers, "....themselves products of segregated school systems...(are) on the whole less well prepared, less qualified, with lower verbal skills, than their white counterparts" (pp. 30-31).

These observations lead to the disturbing conclusion that African-American students "....would do less well, on average, under black teachers than under white teachers. But the role-modeling or cultural-difference hypotheses implicit in much current theorizing would lead to the opposite conjecture, that they would be doing better, on average, under black teachers. If the first conjecture were right, it would have some disturbing implications. One would be that a major source of inequality of educational opportunity for black students was the fact that they were being taught by black teachers. Another, directly relevant to the policy issue, would be that both black and white students would have greater educational opportunity if they were not taught by these teachers. This potential implication was the cause of our not asking the question that followed naturally from our research" (p. 31). And this, according to Coleman, is the real problem: pressure for "political correctness" muzzles the impulse to ask the crucial questions. Researchers who are afraid to challenge the policies of conspicuous benevolence for fear of censure by their colleagues will be unable to investigate possible negative latent consequences of these policies, with the end result being failure to achieve the very goals promoted by their supporters.

There are several ways out of this dilemma. Coleman suggests an alteration in the hierarchy of values held within the academic community: "If, in the hierarchy of values held by the academic community of which one is a part, the value of freedom of inquiry is higher than the value of equality (the value that gives rise to conspicuous benevolence), then such constraints, such self-suppression of research into inconvenient questions, will no longer be effective" (p. 34).

Source
Coleman, James S. "A Quiet Threat to Academic Freedom." *National Review* XLII, 2 (March 18, 1991): 28-34.

Discussion Questions
1) What are some other examples of research topics that might challenge what Coleman calls policies of conspicuous benevolence?

2) How would sociologists who disagreed with Coleman defend their position?

Supplemental Lecture Material
The False God of Numbers

A recent New York Times article discussed the use--and misuse--of statistics in politics. An example of how numbers can be used to lead to oversimplified conclusions is President Clinton's recent declaration that welfare reform has been a success since in 1997, 1.4 million people dropped off the welfare rolls nationwide. Yet, is welfare reform the only possible cause of such a decrease?

One problem is that the numbers do not necessarily prove that those who left welfare actually went to work. Some of the former welfare recipients might simply have slipped away into even deeper poverty and despondency. Also, how much of the drop can be attributed to a booming economy and very low unemployment rather than reforms? In other words, the statistics used show a correlation, not necessarily cause and effect.

New air quality standards must be enacted because they will prevent precisely 15,000 deaths a year from respiration ailments. Sounds simple, doesn't it? Yet the problem is a thorny one. One might ask whether all those respiratory deaths are due only to air pollution. And what about the cost of new standards to industry? How will these affect the economy in the long run?

Here are a few other examples begging alternate explanations or further exploration:

U.S. quality of life is diminishing since, according to a 1996 study, the average one-way commute now takes 40 seconds longer than it did in 1986.

High divorce rates attribute to the breakdown of the family and poorer conditions for children.

Because corporations seek to save money by laying off full-time employees, the number of people working part-time or on a contract basis has increased.

All in all, these questions are complex and multi-dimensional. It is not likely that one answer alone is sufficient. Yet politicians and the media often make it sound simple and straightforward.

Source
"Keeping Score: Big Social Changes Revive the False God of Numbers." *The New York Times* (August 17, 1997):1 and 4.

Discussion Questions
1) What various elements of science are these statements violating?

2) Why would politicians be tempted to simplify statistics? How should social scientists handle statistics differently? In what way does their responsibility to society differ from that of politicians?

3) Name several alternative conclusions that might be drawn from the numbers quoted above.

4) **Activity:** Look through several newspapers for the statistics quoted there. Analyze them using scientific standards. Keep in mind such issues as the difference between cause and effect and correlation, sample size and population, and the way the study was conducted. Also consider interpretations of the data.

Supplemental Lecture Material
The Day America Told the Truth

Public opinion polls have become increasingly common in recent decades. A 1991 best-selling book entitled *The Day America Told the Truth* is packed with examples of the tantalizing bits of information that can be uncovered using this research procedure. The authors, James Patterson and Peter Kim, both executives at the J. Walter Thompson advertising agency, found, among other things:

- "New Englanders lead the country in cheating on their spouses, spying on their neighbors, and giving to charity."

- "Ninety-five percent of Americans believe in capital punishment; one in three would volunteer to pull the switch for the electric chair."

- "Twenty-two percent of males and seven percent of females say they had lost their virginity by the age of thirteen."

- "The profession Americans trust most is that of firefighter."

- "Fifteen percent of adult Americans would rather watch television than have sex."

- "One-third of surveyed married men and women confess to having had at least one affair."

- "One in seven people reports being sexually abused in childhood."

- "Sixty percent, six hundred percent more than official estimates, say they have been victims of a major crime."

- "Twenty percent of the women in the survey report having been raped by their dates."

- "More than seventy percent say they did not have even one hero."

The survey was given to "....a random sample of 2000 people, quizzed in 50 different locations over the period of a week. A shorter, mail-in version was sent to 3500 people." Respondents were guaranteed total anonymity and repeatedly urged to be completely honest.

The findings reported in *The Day America Told the Truth* are fascinating and could provide the impetus for more theoretically based research efforts by academic sociologists. These findings also suggest that the common suspicion that people answering questionnaires often fail to report unconventional attitudes and odd behavior may not be true — one of Patterson and Kim's respondents even admitted that he "...made out with two girls and a dog while immersed in hot wax and Jell-O."

Source
Gelman, David. "The Moral Minority." *Newsweek* (May 6, 1991): 63.

Discussion Questions

1) Are you always completely honest when you answer questionnaires?

2) How can researchers increase the chances that their respondents will not withhold or distort information?

Supplemental Lecture Material
ôThe Proper Study, A Poemö
By W. S. Slater

Seated before her window Mrs Jones
Described the passers-by in ringing tones.
"Look," she would say, "the girl at Number
   Three
Has brought her latest boy-friend home to tea;
And, see, the woman at the upstairs flat,
Has bought herself another summer hat!"
Her daughter Daphne, filled with deep disgust,
Expostulated, "Mother, really, must
You pry upon the neighbours? Don't you
   know
Gossip is idle, empty-minded, low?"
And Mrs Jones would murmer, "Fancy, dear!
There's Mr Thompson going for his beer!"
Daphne, an earnest girl of twenty-three,
Read Sociology for her degree
And every Saturday she would repair,
Armed with her tutor's latest questionnaire,
To knock on doors, demanding, "Are you
   wed?
Have you a child? A car? A double bed?"
Poor Mrs Jones would remonstrate each week,
"'Daphne, I wonder how you have the cheek.
And then to call me nosey!" Daphne sighed.
"Oh, will you never understand?" she cried.
"Mere curiosity is one thing, Mother:
Social Analysis is quite another."

Discussion Questions

1) What are the similarities between Mrs. Jones's "mere curiosity" and her daughter's "social analysis"?

2) In what ways do these two activities differ?

3) How important are these differences?

Supplemental Lecture Material
Separating the Wheat and the Chaff: Spurious Correlations

Researchers commonly encounter behaviors that seem to be related to one another in some way. In the case of the number of miles a car is driven and its gas consumption, there is an obvious and genuine connection. But simply because two behaviors share a significant statistical correlation does not always prove that there is a real relationship between the two variables.

With complex systems, it may be difficult to determine if a statistical correlation is genuine or completely coincidental and spurious. While the continental drift of the West Coast of North America may be highly correlated with the growth of the federal deficit in recent decades, it is unlikely that there is a meaningful connection between the two. Apparently, there is also a strong negative correlation between the number of PhDs and the number of mules in a state. As one commentator remarked, "Are the PhDs created when mules die?" Similarly, a positive correlation exists between ice cream sales and deaths by drowning. The same researcher humorously asked if "people buy more ice cream when they hear of a drowning?" Even when a connection exists, it may be trivial or misleading. In the end, correlation is worthless without interpretation, and that interpretation should be as well-grounded as possible. Consider the following examples:

- My favorite spurious correlation is between shoe size and the ability to solve mathematical equations (or any other task requiring schooling). The students usually express a lot of puzzlement over that one, until you point out that children's feet tend to grow as they go through school. (Wuensch, p. 3)

- One . . . [example of a spurious connection] is the strong positive correlation between places of worship in a locale and the number of bars in the same vicinity. The explanation is obvious: Religion drives people to drink. (Beins, p. 3)

In most research problems, however, the spurious nature of the correlation may not be immediately clear, requiring additional information and careful interpretation to establish the real nature of the connection between the variables. Indeed, important issues may be riding on correctly evaluating and understanding the correlation.

[A] story I sometimes use is based on a *Nova* television show from a few years back. Chinese medical researchers had found a correlation between incidence of human esophageal cancer and the incidence of tumors in chickens. Were the chickens the source of the human cancers? Were the humans giving the chickens their tumors? What they eventually found was that regional preferences for a fermented cabbage dish and minerals in the soil in which the cabbage was grown gave both the humans, who ate the cabbage, and the chickens, who ate the scraps, their tumors. (Street, p. 3)

Discussion Questions

1) What steps can individual researchers adopt to prevent spurious correlations? What can the community of researchers do?

2) What spurious correlations have you come across in your own thinking?

3) Can you think of spurious correlations that have had important effects upon history?

Source
Staff. 1993. "Examples of Spuriousness," in *Teaching Methods.* Fall (2).

Census 2000

The 2000 census provided an example of some of the issues that must be addressed when designing a survey, particularly one that could accurately measure a diversified population that included many subgroups spread over a widespread geographic area. The challenge that faced the U.S. Census Bureau was to reach every resident of the United States, regardless of citizenship or residency status, criminal history, or age, and putting them in the right place.

Response rate is a key factor in the success of any survey and particularly a census. In 1970, 78 percent of households on the Census Bureau's address list returned their forms voluntarily. By 1990, that rate had dropped to 65 percent (far worse than the Census Bureau's initial 70 percent estimate). It's hard to exaggerate the importance of the mail response rate to the success of the census. Cost estimates for the entire undertaking hinge largely on the number of households the Bureau projects will mail back their forms. Census enumerators must visit all households that do not respond voluntarily during the 'non-response follow-up' phase of the count, this fieldwork accounts for the largest portion of census costs. If mail response fails to meet expectations, the Census Bureau may run short of workers and money during the most difficult phase of the census. Conversely, a higher mailback rate not only reduces the field workload, it saves millions of dollars that can be redirected to the hardest-to-count neighborhoods.

Beginning in March, 2000, census forms were mailed to 96 million addresses and another 24 million forms were hand delivered in remote areas and on Indian reservations.

Complacency is often the Census Bureau's worst enemy. To combat this, the Bureau partnered with more than 20,000 national, state, and local organizations across the country.

The 2000 census redesign included:
1) simpler and clearer questionnaires;
2) new partnerships with local officials in an effort to improve the accuracy and completeness of the count;
3) new computer technology for linking questionnaires to weed out duplicate census questionnaires;
4) supplementing mailed questionnaires by placing them in public places (e.g., post offices) for mail return. (This was intended to reduce the undercount of traditionally hard to enumerate groups);
5) $100 million dollars spent on paid advertising to encourage public participation in the 2000 census; and
6) the opportunity for respondents to check more than one race group, unlike previous censuses when people of multiple racial backgrounds needed to check "other" and then write in a response. (This allowed the 2000 census to collect direct information on the

specific backgrounds for people of multiple racial ancestry).

Goals established by the Census Bureau for the 2000 census were to reduce costs and improve accuracy, and to reduce the persistent differential undercounts of minorities and the poor. For all the Bureau's efforts, only time will tell if they have been successful in achieving these goals.

Sources

The Population Reference Bureau – "The 2000 Census Challenge." February 1999.

American Sociological Association "Footnotes – "Census 2000: Counting on a Civic Movement." January, 2000.

Discussion Questions

1)   In addition to respondent apathy, what are some other factors that might contribute to a non-response to a census?

2)   What factors may contribute to distortions in the response of persons contacted by U.S. Census Buireau personnel during follow-up interviews?

3)   What changes have occurred in American society that make census questions on race and ethnicity a controversial topic?

4)   Discuss the potential for manipulation of statistical methods so that census counts might favor one political party over another.

Chapter 3

Culture

I. What Is Culture?
Culture refers to the beliefs, values, behavior and material objects that, together, form a people's way of life.

A. Culture has two basic components: **nonmaterial culture,** or the intangible creations of human society, and **material culture,** the tangible products of human society. Together, these two components describe a people's way of life. Culture also plays an important role in shaping the human personality.

1. GLOBAL SOCIOLOGY BOX—Confronting the Yanomamö: The Experience of Culture Shock.

B. Only humans depend on culture rather than instincts to ensure the survival of their kind.

C. Culture is very recent and was a long time in the making.

D. The concept of culture (a shared way of life) must be distinguished from those of nation (a political entity) or society (the organized interaction of people in a nation or within some other boundary.) Many modern societies are multicultural meaning that their people follow various ways of life that blend and sometimes clash.

II. The Components of Culture.
All cultures have five common components: symbols, language, values and beliefs, norms, and material culture and technology.

A. **Symbols** are defined as anything that carries a particular meaning recognized by people who share culture. The meaning of the same symbols varies from society to society, within a single society, and over time.

B. **Language** is a system of symbols that allows people to communicate with one another.

1. Language is the key to **cultural transmission**, the process by which one generation passes culture to the next. Through most of human history, cultural transmission has been accomplished through oral tradition.

2. WINDOW ON THE WORLD—Global Map 3–1: Language in Global Perspective. Chinese is the native tongue of one-fifth of the world's people. English has become the second preferred language in most of the world. Spanish is the preferred second language of the United States.

3. Only humans can create complex systems of symbols, but some other animals have the ability to use symbols in communicating.

4. The **Sapir-Whorf hypothesis** holds that people perceive the world through the cultural lens of language.

   C. **Values** are culturally defined standards by which people judge desirability, goodness and beauty, and which serve as broad guidelines for social living. Values are broad principles that underlie **beliefs**, specific statements that people hold to be true.

     1. Robin Williams identifies ten key values of U.S. culture:

       a. Equal opportunity

       b. Achievement and success

       c. Material comfort

       d. Activity and work

       e. Practicality and efficiency

       f. Progress

       g. Science

       h. Democracy and free enterprise

       i. Freedom

       j. Racism and group superiority

     2. Values within one society are frequently inconsistent and even opposed to one another.

     3. CRITICAL THINKING BOX—Don't Blame Me! The New "Culture of Victimization." Americans may be becoming increasingly unwilling to accept personal responsibility for their failings and misfortunes.

  D. **Norms** are rules and expectations by which a society guides the behavior of its members. They may be either proscriptive or prescriptive.

     1. There are two special types of norms that were identified by William Graham Sumner:

       a. **Mores** are norms that are widely observed and have great moral significance.

       b. **Folkways** are norms for routine, casual interaction.

     2. Sanctions are a central mechanism of **social control,** various means by which members of society encourage conformity to norms.

  E. Sociologists distinguish between **ideal culture,** social patterns mandated by cultural values and norms, and **real culture**, actual social patterns that only approximate cultural expectations.

  F. **Material culture** reflects a society's values and a society's **technology,** the knowledge that people apply to the task of living in their surroundings.

  G. Many rich nations have entered a postindustrial phase based on computers and new information economy.

  H. CRITICAL THINKING BOX—Virtual Culture: Is It Good For Us? Today's children are bombarded with virtual culture, images that spring from the minds of contemporary culture-makers and that reach them via a screen. Some of these cultural icons embody values that shape our way of life. But few of them have any historical reality and almost all have come into being to make money.

III. Cultural Diversity: Many Ways of Life in One World.

The United States is the most multicultural of all industrial countries. By contrast, Japan is the most monocultural of all industrial nations.

    A. **High culture** refers to cultural patterns that distinguish a society's elite; in contrast, **popular culture** designates cultural patterns that are widespread among a society's population. High culture is not inherently superior to popular culture.

        1. SEEING OURSELVES—National Map 3–1: What'll You Have? Popular Beverages Across the United States. What people consume is one mark of their status as a "highbrow" or "lowbrow."

    B. **Subcultures** are cultural patterns that distinguish some segment of a society's population. They involve not only difference but also hierarchy.

    C. **Multiculturalism** is an educational program recognizing the cultural diversity of the United States and promoting the equality of all cultural traditions.

        1. Multiculturalism stands in opposition to **Eurocentrism**, the dominance of European (especially English) cultural patterns.

            a. SEEING OURSELVES—National Map 3–2: Language Diversity across the United States. The 1990 U.S. Census reports that 14 percent of people over the age of five speak a language other than English in their home.

        2. Supporters of multiculturalism argue that it helps us come to terms with our diverse present and strengthens the academic achievement of African-American children. Some call for **Afrocentrism**, the dominance of African cultural patterns in people's lives.

        3. Opponents of multiculturalism argue that it encourages divisiveness rather than unity.

    D. **Counterculture** refers to cultural patterns that strongly oppose those widely accepted within a society.

    E. Cultural change.

        1. As cultures change, they strive to maintain **cultural integration**, the close relationship among various elements of a cultural system.

        2. William Ogburn's concept of **cultural lag** refers to the fact that cultural elements change at different rates, which may disrupt a cultural system.

        3. Three phenomena promote cultural change:

            a. Invention, the process of creating new cultural elements.

            b. Discovery, recognizing and understanding an idea not fully understood before.

            c. Diffusion, the spread of cultural traits from one cultural system to another.

    F. Ethnocentrism and cultural relativity.

        1. **Ethnocentrism** is the practice of judging another culture by the standards of one's own culture.

        2. Sociologists tend to discourage this practice, instead they advocate **cultural relativism,** the practice of judging a culture by its own standards.

    G. Some evidence suggests that a global culture may be emerging.

        1. Three key factors are promoting this trend:

            a. Global economy: the flow of goods.

            b. Global communications: the flow of information.

            c. Global migration: the flow of people.
        2. Three limitations with the global culture thesis:
            a. Global culture is much more advanced in some parts of the world than in others.
            b. Many people cannot afford to participate in the material aspects of a global culture.
            c. Different people attribute different meanings to various aspects of the global culture.

IV. Theoretical Analysis of Culture.

    A. The structural-functional paradigm depicts culture as a complex strategy for meeting human needs.
        1. **Cultural universals** are traits that are found in every known culture.
        2. Critical evaluation.
            a. The strength of the structural-functional analysis is showing how culture operates to meet human needs.
            b. The weakness of the structural-functional paradigm is that it ignores cultural diversity and downplays the importance of change.
    B. The social-conflict paradigm suggests that many cultural traits function to the advantage of some and the disadvantage of others.
        1. Critical evaluation.
            a. The social-conflict analysis recognizes that many elements of a culture maintain inequality and promote the dominance of one group over others.
            b. It understates the ways that cultural patterns integrate members of society.
    C. **Sociobiology** is a theoretical paradigm that explores ways in which human biology affects we create culture. Sociobiology has its roots in the theory of evolution proposed by Charles Darwin
        1. Critical evaluation.
            a. Sociobiology may promote racism and sexism.
            b. Research support for this paradigm is limited.

V. Culture and Human Freedom

    A. Culture as constraint. Humans cannot live without culture, but the capacity for culture does have some drawbacks.
    B. Culture as freedom. Culture forces us to choose as we make and remake a world for ourselves.
    C. CONTROVERSY AND DEBATE BOX—What Are the "Culture Wars?" Today's culture wars are this nation's latest round of **cultural conflict**, political differences often expressed with hostility, based on disagreement over cultural values.

Chapter Objectives

1) Provide the sociological definitions of culture, nonmaterial and material culture, and culture shock.

2) Explain how culture replaces instinct in human beings.

3) Identify the major components of all cultures.

4) Understand the role of language in the transmission of culture.

5) Understand the implications of the Sapir-Whorf hypothesis regarding cross-cultural communication.

6) List Robin Williams's ten central American values.

7) Distinguish between mores and folkways.

8) Distinguish between real and ideal culture.

9) Discuss the role of material culture and technology in our society.

10) Distinguish between high culture and popular culture.

11) Examine the diversity of subcultures and countercultures found in complex modern societies.

12) Summarize the contemporary debate over multiculturalism.

13) Discuss the concepts of cultural integration and cultural lag.

14) Identify and discuss three causes of cultural change.

15) Compare and contrast ethnocentrism and cultural relativism.

16) Discuss three factors influencing the emergence of a global culture and three limitations to the global culture thesis.

17) Summarize the three theoretical analyses of culture: structural-functional, social-conflict, and sociobiological.

18) Identify how culture both constrains and enhances human freedom.

Essay Topics

1) Do you think you can learn more about a people by studying their material or their nonmaterial culture? Why?

2) Why is culture a more effective strategy for survival than reliance on instinct?

3) What are some examples of symbols that different groups of people interpret differently?

4) What are key values of U.S. culture? Which of these do you embrace? Reject?

5) Provide examples of mores and folkways that you learned when growing up.

6) How are core American values other than achievement and success reflected in childhood games?

7) How has the virtual culture impacted you?

8) What are the primary means by which society attempts to exert social control over its members?

9) Is a technologically more advanced society necessarily a superior one?

10) Do you agree with the text's claim that high culture is not necessarily superior to popular culture? Why do many people assume that this is the case?

11) Do you think that teenagers constitute a distinct American subculture? Why?

12) Is cultural relativism always good? Under what circumstances do you feel that it is appropriate to condemn the practices of a culture other than your own?

Integrative Supplement Guide

1. Transparencies - Series V:
- T-10   Language in Global Perspective - Chinese
- T-11   Language in Global Perspective - English
- T-12   Language in Global Perspective – Spanish
- T-13   Car Ownership in Global Perspective
- T-14   Recorded Immigration to the United States, by Region of Birth, 1880-1890 and 1986-1996
- T-15   High Culture and Popular Culture Across the United States
- T-16   Language Diversity Across the United States
- T-17   Attitudes Among Students Entering U.S. Colleges, 1968-1996

Supplemental Lecture Material
Culture in a Nutshell

In 1990, the David M. Kennedy Center for International Studies at Brigham Young University published a so-called *Culturgram for the '90s.* This document, intended to further the understanding of other people, uses 22 pa-

rameters to describe a culture. Here is what it says about U.S. citizens in 14 of those parameters.

CUSTOMS AND COURTESIES
Greetings
In the United States, we are generally informal, introduce ourselves readily to others, and expect to be called by our first names whether at home or at work.

Visiting
Here, too, we are mostly informal, though we do expect guests to arrive at a specified time because the meal is often served at first. Gifts are not expected when visiting. The primary goal of the host is to have guests feel comfortable, "to sit where they like, and to do as they please."

Eating
Although in this melting pot there are some cultural variations, generally, the fork is used in the right hand for eating. The knife is used only for cutting or spreading, then put back down beside the plate. Some foods such as pizza or tacos are eaten with the hands. It is customary to leave a 15 percent tip in restaurants.

Gestures
We are comfortable only if there is considerable space between people conversing, i.e. at least two feet. A touch on the arm or shoulder during conversation, however, is common. Eye contact is important if the speaker is to be perceived as sincere. We sit casually, crossing our legs or putting them up.

THE PEOPLE
General Attitudes
Generally, outspokenness and frankness are valued, and few topics of conversation are taboo, although very personal questions are avoided by those who are not close friends. Although we might "criticize the government, most of us are very patriotic and believe the United States is one of the greatest countries

in the world. We strongly value our freedom and independence, both as a nation and as individuals."

Personal Appearance

Appearance and cleanliness are important to us. Style of dressing is a matter of personal choice in the United States, ranging from the casual to formal for certain occasions. Clothing is often used to make a statement.

Population

The United States is a mix of ethnic groups. Caucasians represent 85 percent. African Americans 12 percent, and the remaining 3 percent encompass Native Americans, people of Hispanic origins, and others. "One of the fastest growing populations is that of Asian descent."

Language

English is the predominant language, although there is also a sizable Spanish-speaking minority. American English is different from the Queen's English, using its own pronunciation, idioms, and slang.

Religion

Nearly two-thirds of U.S. citizens has some religious affiliation. Freedom of worship and tolerance of the religious preferences of others are ideals. "About 20 percent of the population is Roman Catholic, while over 30 percent belong to a variety of Protestant or other Christian Churches. Over 30 percent belongs to no church."

LIFESTYLE

The Family

While the family is still important as a social institution, it has changed in the recent past. Single-parent families or blended families are common. The family also no longer stays put, but moves frequently for education or job opportunities.

Dating and Marriage

"Dating is a social pastime in the United States." Premarital sex is common, and many people choose to live together before getting married. The average age for marriage is in the mid- to late-twenties.

Diet

Although fast food restaurants remain popular, eating habits have changed with health concerns. The variety of ethnic foods available is great, and many people are willing to experiment with other cuisines. We "consume large amounts of candy, ice cream, and other sweets."

Business

Common business hours are between around 8:00 a.m. and 6:00 p.m., although retail establishments often stay open until 9:00 p.m. or even twenty-four hours. A forty-hour work week is the norm, but many of us work longer.

Recreation

We love team sports, playing them, watching our children play them, or watching them on television. We also enjoy working out by cycling, jogging, racquetball etc. "Leisure activities include watching television, eating out, picnics, attending music concerts, and traveling."

Source

"Culturgram for the '90s." David M. Kennedy Center for International Studies, Brigham Young University.

Discussion Questions

1) Do you agree with the characterization of U.S. citizens used above? What other details would you add to each of the categories?

2) **Activity.** If you have a different cultural background, use that knowledge to fill in the categories above for that culture. If not, interview a person from a different culture to do so.

Supplemental Lecture Material
The Ecologically Noble Savage

As Europeans began to come into regular contact with the indigenous inhabitants of the New World in the sixteenth and seventeenth centuries, a number of stereotyped images of native peoples emerged. Along with the "bloodthirsty Indian," one of the most popular of these stereotypes was the myth of the "noble savage," which held that the "Indians" were innocent childlike beings living peacefully in harmony with nature and each other.

This view has recently enjoyed a renaissance among supporters of the ecological movement, who often assume that the world's preindustrial cultures maintained a state of balance with the natural environment. Consider the following example of this view: "In the world today there are two systems, two different, irreconcilable 'ways of life.' The Indian world — collective, communal, human, respectful of nature, and wise — and the Western world — greedy, destructive, individualist, and enemy of nature." (from a report to the International NGO Conference on Indigenous Peoples and the Land, 1981).

Recent analysis has revealed that this image of the ecologically correct savage is highly romanticized. In reality, most preindustrial cultures were perfectly willing to exploit the natural environment for their own purposes. For example, "paleobiologists, archaeologists and botanists are coming to believe that most tropical forests had been severely altered by human activities before European contact. Evidence of vast fires in the northern Amazonian forests and of the apparently anthropogenic origins of large areas of forest in Eastern Amazonia suggests that before 1500, humans had tremendously affected the virgin forest.... These people behaved as humans do now: they did whatever they had to feed themselves and their families" (p. 46). If the ecological damage done by these cultures was generally less than that resulting from the activities of modern-day industrial societies, it is only because preindustrial cultures affected the environment in situations of low population size and density, abundant land, and limited involvement with a market economy.

If the myth of the ecologically noble savage helps us to restrain some of our more environmentally damaging technologies, then it at least serves a useful purpose. At the same time, we must not allow our understanding of other cultures to be distorted through the lenses of our own wishful thinking.

Source
Redford, Kent H. "The Ecologically Noble Savage." *Cultural Survival Quarterly* Vol. 15, No. 1 (1991): 46–48.

Discussion Questions
1) What harmful consequences might result from naive acceptance of the myth of the ecologically noble savage?

2) Why do you think this view has been popular among many members of modern, technologically sophisticated cultures?

Supplemental Lecture Material
One Hundred Percent American

Many observers have felt that Americans have a tendency to be somewhat more ethnocentric than the citizens of most Western European nations. Certainly American tourists abroad who seem to be convinced that the "natives" will understand their English if they just speak slowly and loudly enough and who make a beeline for a Parisian McDonald's are familiar enough figures. However, as the following widely reprinted, tongue-in-cheek essay by anthropologist Ralph Linton makes abundantly clear, American culture, like that of all industrial societies, has in fact borrowed heavily from the very cultures upon which the "ugly American" looks with condescension.

One Hundred Percent American

There can be no question about the average American's Americanism or his desire to preserve this precious heritage at all costs. Nevertheless, some insidious foreign ideas have already wormed their way into his civilization without his realizing what was going on. Thus dawn finds the unsuspecting patriot garbed in pajamas, a garment of East Indian origin; and lying in a bed built on a pattern which originated in either Persia or Asia Minor. He is muffled to the ears in un-American materials: cotton, first domesticated in India; linen, domesticated in the Near East; wool from an animal native to Asia Minor; or silk whose uses were first discovered by the Chinese. All these substances have been transformed into cloth by methods invented in southwestern Asia.

On awakening he glances at the clock, a medieval European invention, uses one potent Latin word in abbreviated form, rises in haste, and goes to the bathroom. Here, if he stops to think about it, he must feel himself in the presence of a great American institution: he will have heard stories of both the quality and frequency of foreign plumbing and will know that in no other country does the average man perform his ablutions in the midst of such splendor. But the insidious foreign influence was invented by the ancient Egyptians, the use of glazed tiles for porcelain in China, and the art of enameling on metal by Mediterranean artisans of the Bronze Age. Even his bathtub and toilet are but slightly modified copies of Roman originals. The only purely American contribution to the ensemble is the steam radiator, against which our patriot briefly and unintentionally places his posterior....

Returning to the bedroom, the unconscious victim of un-American practices removes his clothes from a chair, invented in the Near East, and proceeds to dress. He puts on close-fitting tailored garments whose form derives from the skin clothing of the ancient nomads of the Asiatic steppes and fastens them with buttons whose prototypes appeared in Europe at the close of the Stone Age. This costume is appropriate enough for outdoor exercise in a cold climate, but is quite unsuited to American summers, steam-heated houses, and Pullmans. Nevertheless, foreign ideas and habits hold the unfortunate man in thrall even when common sense tells him that the authentically American costume of G-string and moccasins would be far more comfortable. He puts on his feet stiff coverings made from hide prepared by a process invented in ancient Egypt and cut to a pattern which can be traced back to ancient Greece, and makes sure they are properly polished, also a Greek idea. Lastly, he ties about his neck a strip of bright-colored cloth, which is a vestigial survival of the shoulder shawls worn by the seventeenth-century Croats. He gives himself a final appraisal in the mirror, an old Mediterranean invention, and goes downstairs to breakfast....

Breakfast over, he places upon his head a molded piece of felt, invented by the nomads of Eastern Asia, and, if it looks like rain, puts on outer shoes of rubber, discovered by the ancient Mexicans, and takes an umbrella, invented in India. He then sprints for his train—the train, not the sprinting, being an English invention. At the station he pauses for a moment to buy a newspaper, paying for it with coins invented in ancient Lydia. Once on board he settles back to inhale the fumes of a cigarette invented in Mexico, or a cigar invented in Brazil. Meanwhile, he reads the news of the day, imprinted in characters invented by the ancient Semites by a process invented in Germany upon a material invented in China. As he scans the latest editorial pointing out the dire results on our institutions of accepting foreign ideas, he will not fail to thank a Hebrew God in an Indo-European language that he is a one hundred percent (decimal system invented by the Greeks) American (from Americus Vespucci, Italian geographer).

Source

Linton, Ralph. "One Hundred Percent American." *American Mercury,* Vol. 15, No. 1.

Discussion Questions

1) Do you believe that Americans may be somewhat more ethnocentric than people in the other Western industrial nations? If so, why might this be the case? If not, why is this widely believed?

2) In what ways does a degree of ethnocentrism contribute to the positive functioning of American culture? How much is too much? What problems can result from excessive ethnocentrism?

Supplemental Lecture Material
Morals in the United States

The text points out that "Whether due to the ethnic mix of U.S. society or changes in our way of life, value inconsistency leads to awkward balancing acts in how we view the world and that "...the U.S. population may be losing a sense that it holds any key values at all" (according to a NORC [1996] survey). In his 1998 book, *One Nation, After All*, Alan Wolfe examined what middle-class Americans really think about God, country, family, racism, welfare, immigration, homosexuality, work, the "Right," the "Left", and each other. He contends that middle-class Americans share a greater respect for diversity than one might think. This Boston College sociologist rejects the "culture war" theory of America.

In Wolfe's opinion the "culture war" theory is the creation of right-wing intellectuals who projected their own "petty squabbles" onto society as a whole – and got the Republican Party to buy the idea. He contends that the news media are "profoundly out of touch", and perhaps even incapable of grasping the full complexity of what and how Americans think.

Wolfe used in-depth interviewing as a data-gathering device in the research for his book that is based on what he calls the Middle Class Morality Project. The research was financed in part by the Russel Sage Foundation and was designed to illuminate what people actually think about a wide variety of subjects. The people Wolfe and his colleagues talked to were more sympathetic to the poor, to civil rights, to women's rights, to religious diversity, and to many other things than commentators have traditionally allowed. Even moral relativists (who had firm views of right and wrong) believed that no one person's religious beliefs were morally binding on everyone.

Wolf writes that "Conservative Christians are often more willing to acknowledge the degree to which America has changed since the battles over 70s and 80s fundamentalism than are those adherents to the American Civil Liberties Union who act as if religious intolerance, rather than nonjudgementalism, is still the dominant tone of the country's religiosity."

Homosexuality is a somewhat different story, but no less complex. Three times as many people condemned homosexual behavior, as were willing to offer positive acceptance. Even so, the respondents distinguished between homosexual acts and the people who practice them. Nearly three out of four respondents said that homosexuals should be tolerated and allowed to do as they wish in their personal lives.

For the most part, according to Wolfe, Americans practice a kind of "capacious individualism", trying to be faithful to their own values while, to the largest possible extent, respectful and nonjudgmental of others values. He concludes that American people "...are seeking a middle way, molding traditional moral presumptions to fit difficult modern realities."

Source

Brent Staples. "Common Ground" *The New York Times* (March 8, 1998). Editorial section, p. 6.

Alan Wolfe. *One Nation, After All.* (New York: Viking Press, 1998).

Discussion Questions

1) How do your experiences discussing people's feelings about diversity compare to Wolfe's findings?

2) What are some factors that impact on the validity of in-depth interviews as a source of research data?

Supplemental Lecture Material
Speaking of Language: The Development of Human Communication

Linguistics, the academic study of human language, has undergone a series of profound shifts in recent decades. Until the late 1950s, most linguists believed that humans as a species developed language from a blank slate in infancy. The behavioristic principles of seeking pleasure and avoiding pain provided the theoretical basis to these views of language development. Most linguists rejected the notion that any type of internal, biological mechanism was hardwired into the brains of infants, steering them inevitably in any par-

ticular developmental path. And because there was no fundamental basis to human language in the brain, linguists rarely tried to compare widely divergent languages — such as English and any of the indigenous languages of the Amazonian basin — as they viewed these languages as essentially lacking in any meaningful connections to a particularly "human" structure.

Noam Chomsky, a Massachusetts Institute of Technology linguist, fundamentally changed many of these basic tenets of linguistics. According to Kathryn Hirsch-Pasek, a psychologist at Temple University, "Up until the late 1950s, linguists had always focused their efforts on describing the differences between languages and dialects. What Noam Chomsky did was point out that beneath the differences, languages were amazingly similar." With extensive cross-cultural studies of the structures or "universal grammar" underlying all languages, Chomsky had found striking evidence of the importance of instinctive behavior to language in humans. Children don't so much "learn" language as they developmentally "grow" into language, much like the refinement of spatial skills or the changes leading to sexual maturity.

And because language is so deeply hardwired into humans, we are born with a grammar that is sophisticated enough to handle complex language. In fact, the actual "learning" that children pursue with language is often the set of exceptions to this basic grammar. As linguist Judy Kegl points out, English-speaking children must learn the often confusing set of rules for plural words, such as "feet" instead of "foots." Children often resist these exceptions, trying to make the language more consistent.

There are numerous important implications from these findings, especially to the millions of Americans who still hold views of language that derive from behaviorism-based linguistics. It is common, for instance, for

Americans to believe that language is the most important "invention" of humans, but language itself is not so much an invention as a highly flexible but genetically programmed and instinctual behavior.

Furthermore, many consider slang or the languages of technologically primitive cultures to be less expressive, evolved, or powerful than languages such as English or Russian. But because all languages share the same basic structure, no language is more primitive or less expressive of human feeling than another. And slang itself — perhaps to the disdain of numerous English teachers — cannot erode or "corrupt" a language or the quality of thinking of its speakers. English is certainly not in decline because so many speakers incorporate lower-status "street" words and phrases into their vocabulary.

Perhaps the most controversial set of implications drawn from Chomsky's research concern the instinctive nature of language. If language — one of the most important bases for human culture — is an instinctive behavior that is genetically controlled, then perhaps many other types of human behavior are also preprogrammed. Behaviorism assumed that consciousness and culture can always override and control instinct, but Chomsky has led linguists to think otherwise. And many researchers and thinkers are suggesting that such characteristics as criminal behavior and intelligence may also be hardwired. Certainly a great deal more research will have to be explored to see how far the implications of language development can be extended.

Source
Bowden, Mark. "Speaking of Language, Linguists Have Big News." *Philadelphia Inquirer* (February 13, 1995): D1–D5.

Discussion Questions

1) Do you agree with the contention that the slang or street language of Harlem or the Bronx is as expressive as Shakespeare's English? Why or why not?

2) How might our view of intelligence change if research provides convincing evidence that an IQ may be heriditary and genetically determined? What social policy changes might this view lead to?

3) What other human behaviors are based on instinct?

Supplemental Lecture Material
The Shape of the World

Before you read on, take a blank sheet of paper and, to the best of your ability, draw a map of the world. Once you are done, keep it by your side and see whether some of the conclusions that follow are also true of your drawing.

As a whole, we trust in fact and figures. Even more, we trust in maps. Who wouldn't? We use them to drive, to orient ourselves in the world, so they have to be correct, right? Wrong.

Until recently, cartographers used the so-called Mercator projections, a badly skewed method of translating a spherical globe onto a piece of paper. As a result, because the closer a landmass is to the pole, the larger is appears, Greenland looks huge, Europe is very large, and Africa smaller than it should be. So maybe that's the reason why in a study conducted by Thomas F. Saarinen most students (80%), no matter what nations they belonged to, drew very similar maps, with Europe in the center, the Americas on the left and Asia on the right. Problem solved...but wait a minute, something is still wrong with the picture. Given this style of map, North America and Asia should also be larger than life. Not so, Saarinen discovered. Only Europe's size was exaggerated.

Saarinen posits that this distortion reflects a world-wide cultural bias. Overall, we tend to know a lot about Europe—its history, culture—but little about Africa. As a result, Africa shrinks in importance in our minds and also in our mental maps of the world.

But are there practical consequences to this misunderstanding? Possibly, says geographer Reginald G. Golledge at the University of California, Santa Barbara. "What I would suggest is that your view of the world is going to influence things like who your closest trading partners are."

Once again, as the textbook illustrates in other areas, our values and beliefs color how we see the world, in this case in a very concrete way.

Source

Monastersky, Richard. "The Warped World of Mental Maps." *Science News*, Vol. 142 (October 3, 1992):142 and 223.

Discussion Questions

1) Did your map reflect the biases discussed above? Would you agree with the reasons given for the distortion? Can you think of others?

2) In what ways are language and cartography similar in their role in transmitting culture? What are the solutions to correcting the flaws of our mental maps?

3) Aside from choosing trading partners, can you think of other consequences of a map exaggerating Europe's size and diminishing Africa's? Are there parallels of such disparity in other cultural arenas?

Chapter 4

Society

I. Society.
Society refers to people who interact in a defined territory and share culture. This chapter explores four important theoretical views explaining the nature of human societies.

II. Gerhard Lenski and Jean Lenski: Society and Technology.
Gerhard and Jean Lenski focus on **sociocultural evolution,** the changes that occur as a society acquires new technology. This perspective identifies five types of societies.

    A. **Hunting and gathering societies** use simple tools to hunt animals and gather vegetation. Until about twelve thousand years ago, all humans were hunter-gatherers. At this level of sociocultural evolution, food production is relatively inefficient, groups are small, scattered and usually nomadic. Society is built on kinship, and specialization is minimal, centered chiefly around age and gender. These societies are quite egalitarian and rarely wage war.

    B. **Horticultural and pastoral societies** employ a technology based on using hand tools to raise crops. In very fertile and also in arid regions, **pastoralism**, technology that supports the domestication of animals, develops instead of horticulture. In either case, these strategies encourage much larger societies to emerge. Material surpluses develop, allowing some people to become full-time specialists in crafts, trade or religion. Expanding productive technology creates social inequality.

    C. **Agrarian societies** are based on **agriculture,** the technology of large-scale cultivation using plows harnessed to animals or more powerful sources of energy. These societies initiated civilization as they invented irrigation, the wheel, writing, numbers, and metallurgy. Agrarian societies can build up enormous food surpluses and grow to an unprecedented size. Occupational specialization increases, money emerges, and social life becomes more individualistic and impersonal. Inequality becomes much more extreme. Religion underlies the expanding power of the state.

        1. SOCIAL DIVERSITY BOX—Technology and the Changing Status of Women. Women's status declines sharply in agrarian societies.

    D. **Industrial societies** are based on **industrialism,** the production of goods using advanced sources of energy to drive large machinery. At this stage, societies begin to change quickly. The growth of factories erodes many traditional values, beliefs, and customs. Prosperity and health improve dramatically. Occupational specialization and cultural diversity increase. The family loses much of its importance and appears in many different forms. In the early stages of industrialization, social inequality increases. Later on, while poverty continues to be a serious problem, most people's standard of living rises. Demands for political participation also escalate.

    E. **Postindustrial societies**, based on technology that supports an information-based economy. In this phase, industrial production declines while occupations that process information using computers expand. The emergence of postindustrialism dramatically changes a society's occupational structure.

    F. The limits of technology. While expanding technology can help to solve many existing social problems, it creates new problems even as it remedies old ones.

III. Karl Marx: Society and Conflict.

Karl Marx's analysis stresses **social conflict,** the struggle between segments of society over valued resources.

    A. Society and Production.

        1. Marx divided society into profit-oriented **capitalists**, people who own factories and other productive enterprises, and the **proletarians**, people who provide labor necessary to operate factories and other productive enterprises. Marx believed that conflict between these two classes was inevitable in a system of capitalist production. This conflict could end only when people changed capitalism itself.

        2. All societies are composed of **social institutions**, defined as the major spheres of social life, or societal subsystems, organized to meet human needs.

        3. He considered the economy the infrastructure on which all other social, i.e., institutions, the superstructure, were based. The institutions of modern societies, he argued, tend to reinforce capitalist domination.

        4. Marx's approach is based on materialism, which asserts that the production of material goods shapes all aspects of society.

        5. According to Marx, most people in modern societies do not pay much attention to social conflict, because they are trapped in **false consciousness,** explanations of social problems that blame the shortcomings of individuals rather than the flaws of society.

    B. Conflict and History. Marx argued that early hunting and gathering societies were based on highly egalitarian primitive communism, and that society became less equal as it moved toward modern industrial capitalism dominated by the bourgeoisie class (capitalists).

    C. Capitalism and Class Conflict. Industrial capitalism contains two major social classes—the ruling class and the oppressed—reflecting the two basic positions in the productive system. Marx viewed **class conflict,** antagonism between entire classes over the distribution of wealth and power in society, as inevitable.

        1. In order for conflict to occur, the proletariat must achieve class consciousness, workers' recognition of their unity as a class in opposition to capitalists and, ultimately, to capitalism itself. Then workers must organize themselves and rise in revolution. Internally divided by their competitive search for profits, the capitalists would be unable to unify to effectively resist their revolution.

    D. Capitalism and Alienation. Marx also condemned capitalism for promoting alienation, the experience of isolation resulting from powerlessness.

       1. Marx argued that industrial capitalism alienated workers in four ways:
          a. Alienation from the act of working.
          b. Alienation from the products of work.
          c. Alienation from other workers.
          d. Alienation from human potential.
       2. SOCIOLOGY OF EVERYDAY LIFE BOX—Alienation and Industrial Capitalism.
   E. Revolution. Marx was certain that eventually a socialist revolution would overthrow the capitalist system.

IV. Max Weber: The Rationalization of Society.

In contrast to Marx's pessimistic view, Weber's work reflects the idealist perspective that human ideas shape society. To make comparisons, he used **ideal types,** abstract statements of the essential characteristics of any social phenomenon.

   A. Two World Views: Tradition and Rationality. Weber wrote that members of preindustrial societies embrace **tradition**, sentiments and beliefs passed from generation to generation, while industrial societies are characterized by **rationality**, deliberate, matter-of-fact calculation of the most efficient means to accomplish a particular task.
       1. The Industrial Revolution and the rise of capitalism both reflect the **rationalization of society,** the historical change from tradition to rationality as the dominant mode of human thought.
       2. WINDOW ON THE WORLD—Global Map 4–1: High Technology in Global Perspective. While countries with traditional cultures either cannot afford, ignore, or sometimes resist technological innovation, nations with highly rationalized ways of life quickly embrace such change.
   B. Is Capitalism Rational? Weber considered industrial capitalism the essence of rationality; since capitalists pursue profit in whatever ways they can. Marx, however, believed capitalism was irrational because it failed to meet the basic needs of most of the people.
   C. Weber's great thesis: Protestantism and Capitalism. Weber traced the roots of modern rationality to Calvinist Protestantism, which preached predestination and the notion that success in one's calling testified to one's place among the saved. Weber's analysis demonstrates the ability of ideas to shape society.
   D. Rational social organization. Weber identified seven characteristics of rational social organizations:
       1. Distinctive social institutions.
       2. Large-scale organizations.
       3. Specialized tasks.
       4. Personal discipline.
       5. Awareness of time.
       6. Technical competence.
       7. Impersonality.
   E. The growth of rational bureaucracy was a key element in the origin of modern society.
   F. Weber feared that the rationalization of society carried with it a tendency toward dehumanization or alienation. He was pessimistic about society's ability to escape this trend.

V. Emile Durkheim: Society and Function.

For Emile Durkheim, a **social fact** is a pattern that is rooted in society rather than in the experience of individuals. Society is an elaborate, collective organism, far more than the sum of its parts. It shapes individuals' behavior, thought and feeling.

    A. The function of a social fact extends beyond its effect on individuals and helps society itself to function as a complex system.

    B. People build personalities by internalizing social facts.

    C. Durkheim warned of **anomie**, a societal condition in which individuals receive little moral guidance.

    D. The **division of labor,** or specialized economic activity, has increased throughout human history.

        1. Traditional societies are characterized by a strong collective conscience or **mechanical solidarity,** social bonds, based on shared moral sentiments, that unite members of preindustrial societies.

        2. In modern societies, mechanical solidarity declines and is partially replaced by **organic solidarity,** social bonds, based on specialization, that unite members of industrial societies. This shift is accompanied by a decline in the level of trust between members of the society.

    E. APPLYING SOCIOLOGY BOX—The Information Revolution: What Would Durkheim (and Others) have Thought?

VI. Critical Evaluation: Four Visions of Society.

    A. What holds societies together?

    B. How have societies changed?

    C. Why do societies change?

    D. CONTROVERSY AND DEBATE BOX—Is Our Society Getting Better or Worse? What societies gain through technological advances may be offset, to some extent, by the loss of human community.

Chapter Objectives

1) Define society.

2) Explain how the Lenskis use technological development as a criterion for classifying societies at different levels of evolutionary development and identify five types of societies according to their technology.

3) Summarize how technology shapes societies at different stages of sociological evolution.

4) Explain the central role of social conflict in Marx's theory.

5) Outline Karl Marx's model of society.

6) Explain Marx's analysis of conflict throughout history.

7) Cite Marx's ways in which capitalism alienates workers.

8) Explain Weber's notion of ideal types.

9) Examine how Weber used the concept of the rationalization of society as a means of understanding and interpreting historical change.

10) Identify seven characteristics of a rational social organization.

11) Define Durkheim's concepts of structure by function and personality.

12) Explain how, according to Durkheim, an expansion in a society's division of labor promotes a shift from mechanical to organic solidarity.

13) Identify major similarities and differences among the analyses of society developed by the Lenskis, Marx, Weber, and Durkheim.

Essay Topics

1) Provide an example of each type of society outlined by the Lenskis. Which would you most like to live in? Why?

2) To what extent does contemporary U.S. society still reflect the industrial model and in what ways are we now fully postindustrial?

3) Identify several modern examples of false consciousness. What are some of the consequences of widespread false consciousness in a society?

4) Have you or your friends or family worked in jobs which were alienating? How accurately does Marx describe the characteristics of these jobs?

5) According to Marx, how does capitalism alienate workers? How did Marx feel that workers could overcome their alienation?

6) What ideas from Marx remain relevant to contemporary society and what ideas must be discarded in the wake of the collapse of the Soviet Union and the Marxist societies of Eastern Europe?

7) What vision of society do you hold? Do you think societies are getting better or worse? Defend your position.

8) What are the characteristics of a rational social organization? Do you think that the changes that have resulted from the widespread rationalization of society have improved people's lives or made them worse?

9) How can modern societies reduce the level of anomie? Can this be done without limiting people's individual freedom?

10) What have we gained and what have we lost as our society has moved from mechanical to organic solidarity?

Integrative Supplement Guide

1. **ABC Videos:**
- If the Economy Is So Good, Why Do We Feel So Bad? (*Nightline*, 10/2/95)

2. **Transparencies - Series IV:**
- T-18   The Increasing Number of Technological Innovations
- T-19   Karl Marx's Model of Society
- T-20   High Technology in Global Perspective

Supplemental Lecture Material
The Postindustrial Workplace

The challenges that workers must negotiate in a postindustrial society are well documented. On the other hand this new work world raises new challenges for supervisors. It is harder today to insist that all employers be at their posts at a specified time and stay there for a specified length of time. Requests for exceptions, conditions, and special schedules are growing.

Diane Crispell, Executive Editor of American Demographics, offers five rules for managers to keep in mind when addressing workplace issues. The shift from time-based to task-based performance is occurring fastest in industries that rely most on online communication. Crispell points out that this is because workers who use computers "can switch from work to play seamlessly – playing games, chatting on bulletin boards, and checking the weather forecast before heading out on vacation". In an environment conducive to even mild levels of "time theft", supervisors are well advised to measure performance in terms of quality and productivity, not in the number of hours worked or when work is performed. In some areas of the labor force, performance will always depend on showing up on time and putting in a solid shift (e.g., manufacturers, retailers, and construction workers). But in financial services, government, and a variety of other "information industries", many workers are already measuring up to quality and productivity standards instead of punching a clock, and the number is certain to grow.

Crispell also contends that workers appearances don't always count – for "behind-the-scenes workers," the quality of work matters much more than the cut of the clothes, how people wear their hair, or whether workers have wrinkles or gray hair. Even for frontline workers whose appearance does count, employers need to be flexible about the "uniform" they impose, "lest they encounter resistance from individually-minded workers."

Today, the line between individual and organizational responsibility has become blurred. Employers now expect employers to accommodate their personal lives. To a large extent, baby boomers and younger workers bring their personal lives to work out of necessity. When both father and mother are employed, or when a single adult is raising children, work schedules can be upset at any moment. (According to the Census Bureau, four in ten preschool children live with two parents who work, and 18 percent live with a single parent who works.) Offering child-care assistance is an effective way to keep valued workers on the job more often and keep them focused on their work. Ignoring the issue is certain to bring about increased work absence, increased turnover and stressed-out workers worrying about children who are home alone.

Another emerging workplace issue is an increasing number of middle-aged baby boomers who find themselves responsible for an aging parent. While not as great a problem as the child-care dilemma, it's one that is destined to grow. (According to American Demographic's projections, the number of households headed by someone aged 75 will increase 32 percent between 1995 and 2010.) Coordinating business travel with family concerns is one way, according to Crispell, that employers may ease the angst associated with work-related travel. An employer who can combine a business trip with a visit to an elderly parent or sibling will be eager to make repeated trips to the area, and will probably be content to stay there for a longer period of time.

A major challenge in today's workplace is employers helping employees balance their work and personal lives, but they also have to balance the needs of workers and customers with those of the organization. Crispell suggests that "Perhaps the overriding rule should be to minimize the rules."

Source

Diane Crispell. "How to Manage A Chaotic Workplace." American Demographics (June, 1996): 50-52.

Discussion Questions

1) Is it reasonable to expect employers to accommodate employee personal life needs? Why or why not?

2) How do race/ethnicity, social class, and gender impact on issues that employees must address in conjunction with work-place responsibilities?

3) What are some issues that persons who have their office in their home must negotiate? What are the pros and the cons of such an arrangement?

Supplemental Lecture Material
Marx's Concept of Alienation versus Durkheim's Concept of Anomie

Both Marx and Durkheim, as was suggested in Chapter 1, were fundamentally guided in their choice of topics to study by their desire to understand and try to solve the problems that arose as the societies in which they lived moved from a preindustrial to an industrial state. For Marx, one of the most serious of these problems was what he termed alienation; for Durkheim, the more critical problem was anomie. While both of these important concepts call forth images of profound human discontent, and while both are often seen as increasingly prevalent in modern society, they are fundamentally distinct and in certain ways antagonistic. An examination of these two notions may help us to better understand the underlying differences between the visions of society developed by these two seminal sociological thinkers.

Marx's notion of alienation reflects a perception that people in modern society are becoming increasingly unable to control the social forces that shape their lives. For Marx,

it is an essential part of human existence that we collectively create the social world in which we live. Governments, economic systems, educational institutions, and even religions are the products of human activity and consciousness. We created them and, in principle, we can change them. But over time, and especially as societies become more complex (and more capitalistic), people begin to lose track of the fact that they have created the society in which they live. Social institutions begin to be perceived as oppressive. Instead of something we shape and create, they come to be seen as, in effect, coercive external realities to which we must conform. Ultimately, we come to feel powerless to influence the circumstances of our own lives. Marx felt that this progressive process of alienation results from the capitalist mode of economic production, but it could equally well be argued that it is inherent in any sufficiently large-scale, economically advanced modern society.

Marx saw modern man as alienated in many dimensions of life. For instance, in the world of work, the assembly line serves as an excellent example of objectified alienation. Humans created it, yet the individual worker standing on the line feels totally powerless, unable to alter the character of the task he or she is compelled to perform or even the pace at which the work must be done. Furthermore, workers lose a sense of how their contribution to the overall effort promotes the final end of the manufacturing process — they feel not only powerless but also that their work is meaningless. Beyond that, Marx notes that highly alienated workers also lose a sense of commonality with their fellow workers. They feel not only controlled, but also isolated. Ultimately, highly alienated workers come to lose the sense that they can control any aspect of their lives, whether at work or at home, and become highly self-estranged. Such people are profoundly discontent, prone to alcohol and drug abuse, mental illness, violence, and the support of extreme social and political movements, in addition to experiencing other pathologies.

What occurs in the workplace is echoed in other dimensions of life. For example, people who are politically alienated feel powerless to affect important decisions made by elected leaders. The government they elect comes to be seen as "they," not "we." People no longer perceive any value in participating in politics, and they no longer derive a sense of shared identity with others through joint political activity.

Note that, for Marx, alienation ultimately results from a societal situation in which there are too many rules, rules the individual feels are being imposed upon him or her, despite the fact that ultimately all of these rules are the products of human social activity.

Durkheim also sees a strongly negative quality creeping into life in modern industrial societies, but he diagnoses the situation quite differently. For him, the problem stems from the destruction of the close ties that bonded the individual to family, church, and community in the traditional, preindustrial village. In such a society, high in mechanical solidarity, individuals knew exactly what was expected of them. There was little or no normative ambiguity. But with the advent of the urban and industrial revolutions — the same changes Marx saw as leading to alienation — Durkheim saw the new urban industrial worker as subject to a breakdown of the moral consensus that was characteristic of the village community. Thrust into industrial cities in jarring juxtaposition to dozens of different subcultures, members of the developing modern societies of Western Europe and America began to lose their moral compasses. With the decline of the absolute and inflexible norms found in traditional society, modern man was cast adrift on a relativistic ocean where right and wrong were

no longer easily defined. Durkheim called this condition of society anomie, from the Latin *a* (without) *nomos* (order). In a state of anomie, often defined as normlessness, people in modern society drift from one definition of proper behavior to the next, never sure they are acting as they ought to. The result of this endemic moral rootlessness, according to Durkheim, is social pathology much like that envisioned by Marx as the consequence of alienation: drug abuse, family dissolution, high rates of crime and mental illness, high suicide rates, and so forth.

But while alienation and anomie may both be endemic to industrial societies and may lead to similar behavioral problems, they are fundamentally different concepts. An alienated individual is one who is exposed to too many rules, to too strict a set of constraints. Far from being in a state of drift, the alienated individual is oversteered, overguided, dominated, and ultimately crushed by the very society that he and others like him established. In contrast, the anomic individual is in a state of moral free-fall, desperately anxious for structure or constraint but unable to find enough moral guidance to be able to know how to live his or her life. The problem is that society is too weak, not too strong. People who are alienated know exactly what is expected of them, but find the yoke of these expectations crushing. People with anomie yearn for the guiding hand of society but find only a chaotic freedom that fails entirely to liberate. For Marx, the problem is the powerlessness of the individual to shape or even resist the coercion of society; for Durkheim, modern people desperately wish for society to be more, not less, coercive. Ultimately, Marx's vision is of people striving to free themselves from the fetters of excessive regulation, while Durkheim suggests that people cannot live happy or productive lives unless properly guided by the invisible hand of society.

Discussion Questions

1)   Which vision — Marx's or Durkheim's — strikes you as a more accurate explanation for the numerous social pathologies that characterize modern industrial and post-industrial societies?

2)   How can we attempt to remedy the problem of alienation? How can we try to reduce anomie? Is it possible to achieve a balance between too much and too little normative constraint, so that people can be neither alienated nor anomic?

Supplemental Lecture Material
The People that Time Forgot

Deep in the rain forest of Irian Jaya, a province of Indonesia in the western half of New Guinea, live a people whose contact with the modern world has been virtually nonexistent. That is about to end, however. Vast forests are becoming a natural resource targeted for cutting. Once they are gone, so will the Korowai, whose existence depends on those trees.

As a matter of fact, the forest itself is where they live, in huts constructed of branches and bark, high up in the trees, and accessible only by notched climbing poles. For clothing, they use leaves, palm fronds and rattan. The forest also provides game for hunting.

The Korowai live as perhaps our ancestors might have lived. Each clan is ruled by a war chief. Alliances are formed through trade or arranged marriages involving a bride price.

Calling themselves Lords of the Garden, the Korowai combine hunting and gathering techniques with horticulture and some pastoralism. They raise pigs, cultivate gardens of many types of banana and sweet potatoes, and tend sago fields where the women work during the day. The sago is food, and as are beetle larvae, a delicacy. The Korowai chop down palms with stone axes, then bore holes in the trunks. Scarab beetles lay eggs in those holes. When the grubs hatch, they are pulled out of the holes and baked, wrapped in banana leaves.

One aspect of Korowai life is the never-ending clan warfare generally fought over women or pigs, and often part of a chain of old offenses to be revenged. Battles always take place during the day since spirits at night are hostile. Special arrows designed for killing humans are used. "A yard of weathered bamboo is lashed with vine to a handspan of bone with six sharp barbs carved on each side. This ensures the arrowhead will cause terrible damage when removed from the victim." Unless the dead are carried away by their own clan, they are then eaten. So are men or women who transgress against clan members by stealing pigs or committing adultery.

Cannibalism, however is not the major killer of the Korowai. Accidents, disease, and war take the greatest toll, and life expectancy is only 35. So poor are the chances for infants, that children do not even receive names until they are about 18 months old.

Yet though their way of life may be precarious, the Korowai value it deeply, as is revealed by the ceremonial overtones of the grub feast. "The grub feast binds us closer, makes us strong. Always remember you are a Korowai.... Never abandon our way of life."

Yet soon, as has been prophesied, the *lale* — the white-skinned ghost demons —will come and take away the Korowais' trees, their land. It will be the end of the Korowai world. Just as the prophecy foretold. . . .

Source

Raffaele, Paul. "The People That Time Forgot." *Reader's Digest*, Vol. 149 No. 892 (August, 1996):101-107.

Discussion Questions

1) Using Gerhard and Jean Lenski's categories, characterize Korowai society, discussing various social institutions typical for such a society. Should efforts be undertaken to save their way of life, or is their disappearance acceptable as a function of sociocultural evolution?

2) In your opinion, if the Korowai are ultimately deprived of the rain forest, what should be done for them? Is there a way to save them? Can they survive in the modern world?

3) **Activity:** Either read an ethnograpy or check out a video to watch on a society with rudimentary technology, then write a sketch of that society using the Lenskis' insights.

Chapter 5

Socialization

I. Social Experience: The Key to Our Humanity.
   A. **Socialization** is the lifelong social experience by which individuals develop their human potential and learn culture.
   B. Social experience is also the foundation for the **personality**, a person's fairly consistent patterns of thinking, feeling and acting.
   C. In the 19th century there was an intense debate regarding the relative importance of **nature** (biology) and **nurture** (socialization) in the shaping of human behavior. Modern sociologists view nurture as much more important than nature in shaping human behavior.
   D. Research on the effects of social isolation has demonstrated the importance of socialization. All the evidence points to the crucial role in social development in forming personality. This research includes:
      1. Harry and Margaret Harlow's experimental work with rhesus monkeys.
      2. Studies of isolated children such as Anna, Isabelle, and Genie.

II. Understanding Socialization.
   A. Sigmund Freud: The elements of personality:
      1. The personality is shaped by two opposed forces: **eros**, the life instinct, and **thanatos**, the death instinct.
      2. The personality includes three basic components:
         a. The **id**, the human being's basic drives.
         b. The **ego**, a person's conscious efforts to balance innate pleasure-seeking drives with the demands of society.
         c. The **superego**, the operation of culture within the individual.
      3. Critical evaluation.
         a. Freud's notion that we internalize norms and his idea that childhood experiences have lasting importance in the socialization process remain critical.
         b. Some of his work has been criticized as reflecting a sexist bias.
   B. Jean Piaget: Cognitive development.
      1. Piaget identified four stages of cognitive development:
         a. The **sensorimotor stage,** the level of human development in which individuals experience the world only through sensory contact.
         b. The **preoperational stage,** the level of human development in which individuals first use language and other symbols.
         c. The **concrete operational stage,** the level of development at which individuals first perceive causal connections in their surroundings.
         d. The **formal operational stage,** the level of human development at which individuals think abstractly and critically.

2. Critical evaluation.
   a. Piaget showed that human beings' ability to shape their social world unfolds gradually as the result of both biological maturation and social experience.
   b. His theory may not apply to people in a society.
C. Lawrence Kohlberg: Moral development.
   1. Kohlberg suggests that the moral development of children passes through the **preconventional**, conventional, and postconventional stages.
   2. Critical evaluation.
      a. Kohlberg's model presents moral development in distinct stages.
      b. However, his theory is based on research using exclusively male subjects.
D. Carol Gilligan: Bringing in gender.
   1. Gilligan found that boys' moral development reflects a justice model which stresses formal rules, whereas girls put more emphasis on caring and responsibility and less on the rules.
   2. Critical evaluation.
      a. Gilligan's work enhances our understanding of gender issues.
      b. However, she does not adequately address the issue of the origin of the gender-based differences that she has identified.
   3. CRITICAL THINKING BOX—The Importance of Gender in Research. Carol Gilligan has shown how gender guides social behavior.
E. George Herbert Mead: The social self.
   1. The **self** is a dimension of personality composed of an individual's self-awareness and self-image.
      a. It emerges from social experience.
      b. This social experience is based on the exchange of symbols.
      c. Understanding someone's intentions requires imagining the situation from that person's point of view, a process called taking the role of the other.
   2. Mead's associate, Charles Horton Cooley, developed the notion of the **looking-glass self,** the idea that self-image is based on how others respond to us.
   3. The self has a dual nature:
      a. The "I" is the self as subject.
      b. The "me" is the self as object.
   4. The self develops through several stages:
      a. Imitation.
      b. Play, in which children take the roles of significant others.
      c. Games, in which they take the roles of several other people at the same time.
      d. Acquisition of the **generalized other,** defined as widespread cultural norms and values we use as references in evaluating ourselves.
   5. Critical evaluation.
      a. Mead showed that symbolic interaction is the foundation of both self and society.
      b. He may be criticized for ignoring the role of biology in the development of the self.

F. Erik H. Erikson: Eight Stages of Development
  1. Erik Erikson viewed development as occurring throughout life by facing 8 challenges:
    a. Stage 1 — Infancy: the challenge of trust (versus mistrust).
    b. Stage 2 — Toddlerhood: the challenge of autonomy (versus doubt and shame).
    c. Stage 3 — Preschool: the challenge of initiative (versus guilt).
    d. Stage 4 — Preadolescence: the challenge of industriousness (versus inferiority).
    e. Stage 5 — Adolescence: the challenge of gaining identity (versus confusion).
    f. Stage 6 —Young adulthood: the challenge of intimacy (versus isolation).
    g. Stage 7 — Middle adulthood: the challenge of making a difference (versus self-absorption).
    h. Stage 8 — Old age: the challenge of integrity (versus despair).
  2. Critical Evaluation.
    a. Erikson's thoery views personality formation as a lifelong process.
    b. Not everyone confronts these challenges in the exact order; nor is it clear that failure to meet the challenge of one stage means that a person is doomed to fail later on. And his theory may not apply to all peoples in all times.

III. Agents of Socialization
A. The family is crucial. Socialization within the family varies markedly by social class.
B. Schooling introduces students to being evaluated according to universal standards.
  1. The hidden curriculum passes on important cultural values, mostly implicitly.
C. **Peer groups** are also important, whose members have interests, social position and age in common.
  1. **Anticipatory socialization,** the process of social learning directed toward gaining a desired position, commonly occurs among peers.
D. The **mass media,** impersonal communications directed at a vast audience, also shape socialization. Television has become especially important in this regard.
  1. SEEING OURSELVES BOX—National Map 5–1: Television Viewing and Newspaper Reading Across the United States.
  2. SOCIAL DIVERSITY BOX—How Should the Media Portray Minorities? The mass media has become more sensitive in recent years to the possibility that they might offend people by making use of ethnic stereotypes.

IV. Socialization and the Life Course.
A. Childhood became an increasingly separate phase of life with industrialization; it is currently becoming shorter.
  1. WINDOW ON THE WORLD—Global Map 5–1: Child Labor in Global Perspective. Industrialization prolongs childhood and discourages children from work.
B. Adolescence is often a period of social and emotional turmoil reflecting cultural inconsistency. It is a time of social contradictions when people are no longer children but not yet adults. Like all phases of the life course, it varies with class position.

C. Adulthood is divided into several stages:
   1. Early adulthood involves working toward goals set earlier in life.
   2. Middle adulthood is characterized by greater reflectiveness.
D. Old age begins in the mid-sixties. The U.S. is currently experiencing an increase in the elderly population.
E. Elisabeth Kübler-Ross identifies five stages in coming to accept death: denial, anger, negotiation, resignation and acceptance. Today fear and anxiety about death are common, but greater acceptance is likely in the future.
F. The Life Course: An Overview:
   1. Although linked to the biological process of aging, essential characteristics of each stage of the life course are socially constructed.
   2. Each stage presents characteristic problems and transitions that involve learning something new and, in many cases, unlearning what has become familiar.
   3. General patterns relating to age are always modified by social variables such as race and gender.
   4. People's life experiences vary depending on when they were born. A cohort is a category of people with a common characteristic, usually their age.

V. Resocialization: Total Institutions.
A. Total institutions are settings in which people are isolated from the rest of society and manipulated by an administrative staff.
B. Their purpose is resocialization: radically altering an inmate's personality through deliberate control of the environment.
C. This is a two-stage process:
   1. The staff breaks down the new inmate's existing identity.
   2. The staff tries to build a new self.
D. CONTROVERSY AND DEBATE BOX—Are We Free Within Society?

Chapter Objectives

1) Define socialization.

2) Examine nature versus nurture debate and state how most contemporary sociologists would resolve it.

3) Summarize reserach findings on the effects of extreme social isolation on children.

4) Outline Freud's model of personality development.

5) Identify and describe Piaget's four stages of cognitive development.

6) Identify and describe Kohlberg's three stages of childhood moral development.

7) Examine moral development as researched by Gilligan.

8) Define Mead's theory of the social self and outline the development of the self.

9) Identify and describe Erikson's eight stages of development.

10) Examine the role of the family, the school, peer groups, and the mass media in the socialization process.

11) Discuss how socialization varies at different stages along the life course.

12) Describe the two-stage process of re–socialization that occurs in total institutions.

Essay Topics

1) Identify and describe Erikson's stages of development as each applies to your own personality formation. How did success at one stage prepare you for meeting the next challenge?

2) Do you think that Americans today, in comparison with their parents and grandparents, put more or less emphasis on the importance of "nature" in shaping human beings? How would you explain this?

3) How does one's preference for a nature or nurture explanation of human behavior influence the type of social policy that one favors to reduce such problems as crime, poverty, or violence?

4) How much confidence do you feel we can have in generalizing the results of Harlow's monkey studies and the cases of Anna, Isabelle and Genie to the human population in general? Discuss.

5) Do you think Mead believed that a person who could not use symbols could ever become fully human? Discuss.

6) How much impact do you feel that recent changes in the American family system have had on this institution's ability to effectively socialize children?

7) As you moved through your childhood and adolescence, how did the relative importance of your family, school, peers and the mass media as agents of socialization change? How would you account for these changes?

8) Critics often charge that television's portrayal of violent and sexual themes powerfully affects its viewers, especially children. How much of a role do you think TV plays in the socialization process? Does it affect everyone to the same extent? Defend your positions.

9) What cultural inconsistencies lead to adolescent turmoil? What can parents, teachers, and other agents of socialization do to help adolescents develop?

10) What can be done to reduce our society's anti-elderly bias?

Integrative Supplement Guide

1. **Transparencies - Series V:**
- T-21 Building on Social Experience
- T-22 Television Ownership in Global Perspective
- T-23 Television Viewing Across the United States
- T-24 Newspaper Reading Across the United States
- T-25 Child Labor in Global Perspective

Supplemental Lecture Material
Social Class and Childrearing in Taiwan

A substantial body of research has grown up in support of Melvin Kohn's thesis that middle-class parents in the United States tend to emphasize self-direction in child socialization, whereas working-class parents are more likely to stress obedience to external authority. Kohn also found that middle-class families frequently shun physical punishment in favor of reasoning, isolation, and appeals to guilt. The reverse pattern is more characteristic of the working class.

Li-Chen Ma and Kevin Smith recently conducted interviews with a stratified random sample of 1210 Taiwanese parents in order to see whether Kohn's conclusions can be generalized to this industrializing non-Western society.

They found little support for the hypothesis that middle-class Taiwanese parents differed from working-class parents in putting more emphasis on moral autonomy. Parents from both classes stressed filial duty and obedience. Ma and Smith suggest that this finding may reflect the lingering importance in all classes of Confucian ethics which mandate conformity to the social order. They also note that rapid social change in Taiwan — especially the strong emphasis on mass education — may have blurred whatever differences once existed between the classes.

On the other hand, the researchers did find some support for the second part of Kohn's thesis, concerning the types of discipline favored by parents from different classes. Middle-class Taiwanese fathers used isolation and with-holding allowances more frequently, whereas working-class fathers preferred spanking and other types of physical chastisement. The working class also was found to be more likely to scold and threaten their children and somewhat less likely to inquire into the reasons behind their misbehavior. Furthermore, working-class parents tended to reward approved behavior with money or gifts whereas the middle-class preferred to praise their offspring verbally.

Finally, the study found all of these variations to be more pronounced for fathers than for mothers. The researchers explained this pattern by reference to the continuing power of Confucianism, which requires mothers to adopt a secondary and supportive role in all decisions regarding child socialization.

Source
Ma, Li-Chen, and Kevin Smith. "Social Class, Parental Values and Child-Rearing Practices in Taiwan." *Sociological Spectrum* Vol. 10 (1990):577–589.

Discussion Question
1) If there are students in the class who were raised in foreign cultures, do their experiences support Kohn's generalizations regarding class and childrearing?

Supplemental Lecture Material
The Cycle of Generations

William Strauss and Neil Howe recently published a provocative and controversial book entitled *Generations*, in which they argue that U.S. social history can be understood as a regular progression of four distinct types of generational cohorts (defined in the text), shaped by shared early experiences: "how they were raised as children, what public events they witnessed in adolescence, and what social mission elders gave them as they came of age" (p. 26).

There have been eighteen generations, each roughly 20 to 25 years in length, born in the U.S. since the 1620s. Seven remain alive today, two remnant generations that have mostly died out and five major cohorts:

The **G.I. Generation** was born between 1901 and 1924. Strauss and Howe characterize this cohort as an example of the civic type, which grows up as a protected generation after a period of spiritual awakening (in this case, the fundamentalist and populist ferment of the 1890s). A civic generation "comes of age by overcoming a secular crisis, unites into an heroic and achieving cadre of rising adults, builds institutions as powerful mid-lifers, and later finds itself attacked as elders during the next great awakening" (p. 31). The G.I. Generation "are 20th century America's confident, rational problem-solvers, the ones who have always known how to get big things done. They were America's original Boy Scouts and Girl Scouts, victorious soldiers, and the builders of rockets, suburbs, and highways. No generation. . . can match their 30-year hold on the White House. Today's G.I.'s are busy 'senior citizens' and 'mature consumers,' possessed of boundless civic optimism and a sense of public entitlement, of having earned late-life rewards through early-life heroism" (p. 26).

The **Silent Generation,** born between 1925 and 1942, is an adaptive cohort, as are all generations born following a civic generation. Members of adaptive cohorts "grow up as suffocated children of crisis, come of age as adult-emulating conformists, produce the indecisive mediators of the next awakening, and age into sensitive and other-directed elders." More specifically, the Silent Generation "arrived too late for World War II combat and too early to feel the heat of the Vietnam draft. They were the unobtrusive children of depression and war, the conformist 'Lonely Crowd,' and the youngest-marrying generation in America's history. They were volunteers for Kennedy's Peace Corps and divorced parents of multi-child households. Now they are the litigators, arbitrators, and technocrats of a society they have helped make more complex. They give freely to charity, are inclined to see both sides of every issue, and believe in fair process more than final results" (p. 26).

Following the Silent Generation is the famous **Baby Boom,** born between 1943 and 1960 and characterized as an idealist cohort. Following on the heels of an adaptive generation, idealists "grow up as indulged youths after a crisis, come of age inspiring an awakening, fragment into narcissistic rising adults, cultivate principle as midlife moralizers, and emerge as visionary elders who ... guide the next crisis" (p. 30). The Boomers "were heirs to a national triumph, born into an era of optimism and hubris. They went on to become the inquisitive students of Sputnik-era grammar schools, flower-child hippies and draft resisters, Jesus freaks and New Age bran-eaters, yuppie singles and (most recently) the leaders of ecological, educational, and drug-prohibition crusades. Boomers are marked by a weak instinct for social discipline combined with a desire to infuse new values into the institutions they are inheriting. In all spheres of life, they display a bent toward inner absorption, perfectionism, and individual self-esteem " (pp. 26-27).

The **Thirteenth Generation,** born between 1961 and 1981, exemplifies the reactive pattern. Like all cohorts following an idealist generation, they "grew up as under-protected and criticized youths during an awakening [and] came of age as alienated risk-takers" (p. 31). If the pattern holds, they will "burn out young before mellowing into mid-life pragmatists and family-oriented conservatives, and age into caustic but undemanding elders" (p. 31). "They were the babies of the 1960s and 1970s, the throwaway children of divorce and poverty, the latchkey kids in experimental classrooms without walls. As college students they have been criticized as dumb. . . . They are the most Republican-leaning youths of the 20th century" (p. 27). Their worldview is characterized by a "blunt, even cynical realism" (p. 27).

The **Millennial Generation** consists of today's children. Strauss and Howe see this cohort's circumstances as similar to those that shaped the civic style of the G.I. Generation.

At the heart of this whole progression is a series of " 'secular crises' (threats to national survival and a reordering of public life), and 'spiritual awakenings' (social and religious upheavals and a reordering of private life)" (p. 30). Each crisis occurs roughly eighty or ninety years after the last — most recently, the Civil War and the twin challenges of the Great Depression and World War II. Almost precisely halfway between crises, an era of spiritual awakening seems to arise, the most recent being the counterculture of the 1960s and 1970s. It is this regular progression of crises and awakenings that gives birth to the cycle of civic-adaptive-idealist-reactive cohorts identified by Strauss and Howe.

The authors point out marked similarities between the present and the years just before World War I, the last time when the sequence of styles among the four youngest cohorts was identical to that of our era. Then as now, "individualism (was) flourishing, confidence in institutions (was) declining, and secular problems (were) deferred. . . . Then as now, frustration was mounting over a supposed loss of community, civility and sense of national direction. Then as now, the nation's leaders engaged in a diplomatic dither over how to design an interdependent and legalistic new world order while new armies massed and old hatreds festered. Then as now, feminism was gaining serious political power, moralistic attacks were growing against substance abuse, and family life was seen as precious but threatened" (p. 32). Similar patterns can be observed in the 1650s, 1750s, and 1840s. In each of these eras, "powerful and worldly civics [were] passing from the scene, sensitive and pro-

cess-oriented adaptives entering elderhood, moralizing idealists [were] entering midlife, survivalist reactives [were] coming of age, and a protected new generation of civics [were] just being born" (p. 32).

The real test of this theory is its ability to predict the future. Strauss and Howe note that in the next thirty years, if the pattern holds, the sense of drift and pessimism will intensify, then a crisis will emerge, compelling Americans to unite in the face of perceived public peril (p. 32).

More concretely, "The G.I.'s will remain a politically favored generation deep into their old age. Younger generations will admire and start to miss their old civic virtues of community, citizenship and material progress... The Silent Generation will become a new breed of elder. They will be other-directed, sympathetic to the needs of the disadvantaged, and prone to take the risks and seek the adventures that many will feel have eluded them early in life. . .The extended family will enjoy a renaissance. In public life, Silent elders will press for compromise solutions. They will deplore the erosion they will see in civil rights, due process, and other social kindnesses they spent a lifetime trying to implant. . . Boomers will assume control of national politics with the same perfectionism and moral zeal that they are currently bringing to family and community life. . .They will become contentious moral regulators. They will see a high purpose in what they do. . .Upon reaching old age. . .they will see themselves. . . as wise visionaries willing to accept private austerity in return for public authority, and they will summon the nation toward unyielding principle. The 13ers have so far lived a luckless life-cycle, as America's most economically disadvantaged generation. The hard luck will age with them. When bad news hits, 13ers will sink further into the alienation and pragmatism that has already attracted so much criticism...After burning out young, many a 13er will retreat into — and strengthen — family life. . . . Finally. . . today's cute Millennial tots could become the next great cadre of civil doers and builders. Like the child G.I.'s of 75 years ago, they will grow up basking in adult praise for their intelligence, obedience and optimism" (p. 32).

Source

Straus, William, and Neil Howe. "The Cycle of Generations." *American Demographics*, Vol. 13, No. 4 (April, 1991):24-33 and 52.

Discussion Questions

1) What do you think were some of the principal events that shaped your generation in its youth? Do you feel that Strauss and Howe's theory does a good job of describing your generational cohort?

2) Can this theory help us to understand the different political styles of the G.I. Generation (including John Kennedy, Jimmy Carter, Ronald Reagan, George Bush, and Robert Dole) and the Baby Boom (including Dan Quayle, Bill Clinton, Albert Gore, and Jack Kemp)?

Supplemental Lecture Material
Socialization of Children (Ages 6-14)

From May through June, 1999, New York-based pollsters Penn, Schoen, and Berland Associates conducted a poll among 1,172 children, ages 6 to 14, in 25 U.S. cities. The poll was conducted for Nickelodeon, the children's TV channel, and *Time*. They found that the much lamented decline of family values, the anarchic influence of such television shows as "South Park", and the collapse of parental authority and discipline have been greatly exaggerated. Asked whom they admire most, 79% said it was Mom and Dad; and additional 195 named their grandparents. Religion continues to be an important agent of socialization in the lives of this generation as 95% of the respondents said they believed in God, nearly half claimed to attend religious services every week, and 8 out of 10 said they pray.

Jean Bailey, the coordinator of child and adolescent mental health services at Lutheran Medical Center in Brooklyn, N.Y., says that "Parents remain the most significant people in children's lives, until age 14 or 15". Personal values about religion, sex and obeying authority are all shaped primarily by parents right up to the teenage years, when things suddenly shift.

Peer pressure increases dramatically during the middle school years. Kids in the 9-14 age group noted the importance of "fitting in" at school. Those age 9 to 11 defined "fitting-in" as being a good friend, being good at sports, and being funny or popular. But kids in the 12 to 14 age group have different criteria. Clothes come first, then "being popular" and third, good looks. Psychologist Anthony Wolfe notes that "This is a bit sad but it also shows parents what they're up against if they're trying to draw the line on certain clothes." The emphasis on having the "right stuff" to wear may also help explain why low-income kids in the poll worry most about fitting in.

The early teen years are when parents fall off the pedestal. While 57% of 9 to 11-year-olds say they want to be like their parents, only 26% of 12 to 14-year-olds do. "This is 1005 normal, virtually inevitable moment when kids develop an allergy to their parents" says Wolfe. "They don't want to breathe the same way their parents do."

Still, 60% of the respondents ages 12 to 14 say, as most kids do, that they would like to spend more time with their parents.

The problem is finding the time which is at a premium in the increasing number of two-earner households and those headed by single parents. One indication of how families have changed is the fact that only 41% of those sampled said they spend an equal amount of time with both parents. Dr. Leon Hoffman, who co-directs the Parent-Child Center at the New York Psychoanalytic Society, believes this to be one of our most significant cultural changes. He has found a "very dramatic difference in the involvement of the father – in everything from care-taking to general decision making around kids lives." (This change has been slower to reach black children. 76% of black kids surveyed said they spend more time with their mothers than with their fathers.)

While technology and computers clearly have transformed American society in many ways, it is still the family, peers, religion and the media that dominate the socialization process for kids.

Source

Claudia Wallis. "The Kids Are Alright". Time (July 5, 1999): 56-58.

Discussion Questions

1) How much of a role does education play in the socialization of children today?

2) What impact do race/ethnicity, gender, and social class have on childhood and early adolescent socialization?

Supplemental Lecture Material
Cohorts or Generations: Characterizing Age-Related Groups

Sociologists have long struggled with two related problems: how to accurately describe similarities between groups of people born within a few years of each other, and how to compare one age group to another. The most common approach may be dividing a population into "generations," which are marked by relatively arbitrary birth-year ranges. Typically, a generation spans the time from the birth of members of a group until the period when that group begins to reproduce. Twenty-year spans are fairly common for generation divisions. Sexual mores, political attitudes, musical tastes, marital patterns, religiosity, and the inclination to save have all been said to distinguish given generations from one another.

Consider the age group called Generation X. Sometimes referred to as the Baby Bust, the Lost Generation, or the Youth Generation, members of this group were born between the mid-1960s and mid-1970s and are now concentrated in their twenties. Numerous studies and commentators have claimed that members of this group tend to be economically insecure, difficult to motivate, traumatized by and resentful of AIDS, and lovers of things grunge and retro.

These characteristics are often contrasted with the other four older generations in the United States that still have substantial populations: the Baby Boomers, who were born between 1946 and 1964; the Silent Generation, born between 1933 and 1945; and the Depression Generation, born before 1932.

Social analysts in politics, the business community, and on campuses have been arguing for some time over the meaningfulness and utility of these generational distinctions. Are there real, important differences in interests, culture, and behavior between groups of individuals born between a given set of years?

Some sociologists argue that most "generational" differences are simply a reflection of changes in the life cycle. For instance, the number of Generation Xers in nursing homes is quite small compared to the Depression Generation. Clearly, as Generation Xers grow older and enter different stages of their lives, they will become more interested in and then enter nursing homes.

Some changes, however, do not reflect differences in the life cycle. Boomers and Generation Xers are unlikely to start listening to Lawrence Welk as they age; musical tastes tend to be stable over the lifetimes of individuals, so when the boomers reach those nursing homes, they'll keep listening to the Beatles and the Rolling Stones.

But many issues are less clear than either of the above examples. Researchers have noted for some forty years that coffee consumption tends to rise until age sixty, when it levels or declines only slightly. In contrast, soft drink consumption has tended to fall off with increasing age. Are these trends simply age-related, as with nursing homes, or will the Baby Boomers and Generation Xers change this long-standing trend because these generations drink coffee and soft drinks differently? The question is not completely academic since the boomers make up such a substantial part of the population and are followed by much smaller age-groups. If consumption patterns do change, then the coffee and soft drink markets could radically differ in ten or twenty years.

Understanding such market changes may be important for strategic business planning, but more pressing social issues than soft drink consumption are also involved, such as the rate of savings and the ensuing demand on the Social Security system, the size and kinds of families in the future, and lifestyle trends like smoking rates that affect the use of the health-care system. Obviously, having a grasp of age-related differences has important applications. But how meaningful are differences between age groups?

There seem to be two common reactions to this question. The first is that differences

between generations, while they exist, are usually exaggerated. A *Reader's Digest* poll, for instance, suggests that the so-called generation gap is often insignificant and in some cases nonexistent. One poll "compared fundamental beliefs and values across four generations. The results . . . show that even though young people buy different CDs and clothes, they do *not* buy into a set of values different from their elders." The four generations the poll identified — Xers (18 to 30), Boomers (31 to 48), Silents (49 to 62), and Depression Era (63 and over) — tended to answer the poll questions in similar ways. In the words of *Reader's Digest*,

• Americans young and old still believe this is a land where hard work will be rewarded and dreams can be realized.

• Americans young and old oppose limiting individual opportunity to enforce equality of income.

• Americans young and old increasingly fear the threat of big government.

• Americans young and old believe in God, pray often, and continue the religious heritage that has always marked this nation. (p. 50)

Unfortunately, *Reader's Digest* did not thoroughly explore their respondents' interpretation of such general statements as "Do you truly believe in the words of the Declaration of Independence — that all people are created equal and 'endowed by their Creator with certain inalienable Rights?'" And agreement with these statements does not necessarily mask profound disagreement with actions professedly based on those statements. In essence, *Reader's Digest* was claiming that its poll showed that few important distinctions existed between generations.

The second common reaction to the use of generations assumes another stand, arguing that the concept of cohorts is more powerfully descriptive. *American Demographics* defines a birth cohort as "a group of people born during a given time period who share the same historic environment and many of the same life experiences, including tastes and preferences." Shared formative events help define the experience and world view of age-mates, and these "cohort effects do not change with one's age or stage of life." The Kennedy assassinations, the Great Depression, World War II, Watergate, the O. J. Simpson murder trial, and Rodney King's beating and the subsequent riots in Los Angeles have all been cited as examples of cohort-forming events.

A cohort interpretation might suggest that soft drink consumption will not level off because Boomers and Generation Xers have proven to be more "cola-intensive" than other cohorts. As *American Demographics* put it, "When President Clinton turns fifty, he will still love McDonald's." And Boomers and Generation Xers will become even more important in the consumer market as members of the Silent and Depression Generations die off.

While cohorts may be a more sophisticated tool than generations, it is important to remember that the use and makeup of cohorts are in wide dispute. How defining is a particular event or period? How many people does it define? How long do those effects last? While people may "resemble the times more than their fathers," as an Arab proverb states, clarifying the differences and similarities between age groups will continue to be a matter of hot dispute.

Sources
Ladd, Everett C. "Exposing the Myth of the Generation Gap." *Reader's Digest.* (January 1995).

Meredith, Geoffrey, and Charles Schewe. "The Power of Cohorts." *American Demographics* (December 1994).

Zill, Nicholas, and John Robinson. "The Generation X Difference." *American Demographics* (April 1995).

Discussion Questions
1) Do generations or cohorts seem more accurately descriptive? Are there advantages to one perspective over the other?

2) Do the qualities often used to describe your generation seem accurate? How widely applicable are such generalizations?

Chapter 6

Social Interaction in Everyday Life

I. Social interaction is the process by which people act and react in relation to others.

II. Social structure guides human behavior rather than rigidly determining it.

III. Status is a social position that an individual occupies.
    A. A **status set** consists of all the statuses a person holds at a given time.
    B. Ascribed and achieved statuses.
        1. An **ascribed status** is a social position that someone receives at birth or involuntarily assumes later in life.
        2. An **achieved status** is a social position that someone assumes voluntarily and that reflects personal ability and effort.
    C. A **master status** is a status that has special importance for social identity, often shaping a person's entire life.
        1. SOCIAL DIVERSITY BOX—Physical Disability as Master Status.

IV. A **role** consists of behavior expected of someone who holds a particular status.
    A. **Role set** refers to a number of roles attached to a single status.
    B. Role conflict and role strain.
        1. **Role conflict** refers to conflict among roles corresponding to two or more different statuses. It can be reduced by "compartmentalizing" our lives.
        2. **Role strain** refers to incompatibility among roles corresponding to a single status.
    C. **Role exit** is the process by which people disengage from important social roles.

V. The **social construction of reality** is the process by which individuals creatively shape reality through social interaction.
    A. What people commonly call "street smarts" really amounts to constructing reality.
    B. The **Thomas Theorem** states that situations we define as real become real in their consequences.
        1. APPLYING SOCIOLOGY BOX—The "Spin" Game: Choosing Our Words Carefully.
    C. **Ethnomethodology** is a subfield of sociology developed by Harold Garfinkel which studies the way people make sense of their everyday lives.
    D. People in different cultures experience reality very differently.
        1. SEEING OURSELVES BOX—National Map 6–1: Baseball Fans Across the United States: Do We All Feel the Same?

VI. Dramaturgical analysis, developed by Erving Goffman, consists of the definition of social interaction in terms of theatrical performance.
  - A. The **presentation of self,** the effort of an individual to create specific impressions in the minds of others, is a central focus of dramaturgy.
  - B. An individual's performances include dress, props, and manner.
    1. Performances have back and front regions.
  - C. **Nonverbal communication** consists of communication using body movements, gestures and facial expressions rather than speech. Most of it is culture-specific. Close attention to nonverbal communication is often an effective way of telling whether or not someone is telling the truth.
  - D. Gender affects personal performance in areas such as:
    1. Demeanor.
    2. Use of **personal space** — the surrounding area over which an individual makes some claim to privacy.
    3. Staring, smiling and touching.
  - E. GLOBAL SOCIOLOGY BOX—The Sociology of Emotions: Do People Everywhere Feel the Same?Emotions in Global Perspective. People the world over experience the same basic emotions, but what triggers a particular emotion, how and where a person expresses it, and how people cope with it all vary with culture.
  - F. Performances usually idealize our intentions.
  - G. APPLYING SOCIOLOGY BOX—Hide Those Lyin' Eyes: Can You Do It? To know if someone is deceiving you, pay attention to four elements of performance: words, voice, body language, and facial expression.
  - H. Embarrassment and tact are additional important dramaturgical concepts.

VII. Interaction in Everyday Life: Two Applications.
  - A. Language: the gender issue. Language defines men and women differently in several ways:
    1. The control function of language.
    2. The value function of language.
    3. The attention function of language.
    4. SOCIOLOGY AND EVERYDAY LIFE BOX—Gender and Language: "You Just Don't Understand!"
  - B. Humor: Playing with reality.
    1. The foundation of humor: contrasting incongruous realities.
    2. The dynamics of humor: "getting it." To "get" humor, the audience must understand the two realities involved well enough to appreciate their difference.
    3. The topics of humor. For everyone, humor deals with topics that lend themselves to double meanings or controversy.
    4. The functions of humor. Humor provides a way to express an opinion without being serious; and humor relieves tension in incomfortable situations.
    5. Humor and conflict. Humor is often a sign of real conflict in situations where one or both parties choose not to bring the conflict out into the open.
    6. SOCIOLOGY AND EVERYDAY LIFE BOX—Double Take: Real Headlines that Make People Laugh.

Chapter Objectives

1) Define social interaction and identify its components.

2) Distinguish between ascribed and achieved status and describe master status.

3) Distinguish between role set, role strain, and role conflict.

4) Discuss the extent to which reality is socially constructed.

5) Explain the Thomas Theorem.

6) State the ~ ⎓ ⎓ ɔʈ methodological research.

7) Outline the characteristics of Goffman's dramaturgical analysis.

8) Discuss the importance of nonverbal communication in human social interaction.

9) Examine ways in which gender influences personal performances, including use of language.

10) Examine the character of humor.

Essay Topics

1) What are the principal statuses which you are presently occupying? Which are ascribed and which achieved? Are any of them important enough to constitute a master status?

2) Apply what you learned in this chapter to explore the character of humor.

3) Identify situations in your life in which you have experienced role strain and role conflict. How did you reduce these situations?

4) Suppose you want to study the social contradictions that adolescents experience and the consequences of such contradictions in their development. How would you study this question using ethnomethodology?

5) Recount some instances in which you have realized after interacting with someone from a different culture (or subculture) that that person's socially constructed perception of reality was quite different from yours. How did this difference influence the ongoing ⁻ᵗᵗᵉᵣⁿ of interaction?

6) Develop ⎓ ᵈramaturgical analysis of an interaction you have recently experienced, demonstrating your familiarity with terms such as presentation of self, performance, front and back region, ⁻ˡization, embarrassment, and tact.

7) Have you been in a situation in which someone's nonverbal messages clashed with their words? Which type of communication more accurately reflected that person's intentions?

8) Describe a recent incident in which your interaction with someone of the opposite gender clearly reflected some of the differences in demeanor, use of space, staring, smiling and physical contact discussed in the chapter.

9) Can you recall a situation in which you engaged in active idealization? Describe it. Were you successful in convincing your audience to accept the idealized image that you were projecting?

10) Many people in contemporary society downplay the significance of language in shaping relations between the genders. How would you respond to such a position?

Integrative Supplement Guide

1. **ABC Videos:**
*   Baseball, Black and White (*Nightline*, 9/26/94)

2. **Transparencies - Series V:**
*   T-26 Status Set and Role Set
*   T-27 Baseball Fans Across the United States
*   T-28 Happiness: A Global Survey

Supplemental Lecture Material
Race as a Master Status

In the United States, being a member of a minority race is frequently so important in shaping the way that others (especially whites) react to an individual that race membership becomes a master status. Many biographies of African Americans feature poignant remembrances of the subjects' dawning realization of the significance of their racial identity. Here are examples from the lives of two well-known leaders of the civil rights movement, James Farmer and Martin Luther King, Jr. Farmer writes:

A small boy holding onto his mother's finger as they trudge along an unpaved red dirt road on a hot mid-summer day. The mother shops at the town square and they trudge homeward, the child still clinging to her finger. She removes a clean handkerchief from her purse and pats her son's face and then her own. The boy looks up at his mother and says, "Mommy, I want to get a Coke."

"You can't get a Coke here, Junior," the mother replies. "Wait till we get home. There's lots of Coke in the icebox."

"But, mommy," says the boy, "I don't want to wait. I want my Coke now. I have a nickel; daddy gave it to me yesterday."

"Junior, I told you you can't get a Coke now. There's lots of Coke in the icebox at home."

"Why can't I get a Coke now, when I have a nickel?"

"You just can't."

The child sees another boy enter a drugstore across the street. "Look, mommy," exclaims Junior, "I bet that boy's going to get a Coke. Come on, let's go see."

He pulls his mother by the finger across the street, and they look through the screen doors, closed to keep out the flies. Sure enough, the other kid is perched on a stool at the counter sipping a soft drink through a straw.

"See that, mommy," said the small boy. "We can get a Coke here. He got one. Let's go get ours."

"Son, I told you to wait till we get home. We can't get a Coke in there."

"Then why could he?"

"He's white."

"He's white? And me?" inquires the boy.

"You're colored."

As King recalled it fifteen years later, his early childhood years were spent in "a very congenial home situation," a family "where love was central and where lovely relationships were ever present." Only one incident, he later said, marred those early childhood years. That came at age six, just after he had begun his actual first grade education at Yonge Street Elementary. For several years one of his close playmates had been a white child whose father owned a small grocery near the King home. After they began attending separate schools, they saw much less of each other. As King later described it:

> This was not my desire but his. The climax came when he told me one day that his father had demanded that he would play with me no more. I never will forget what a great shock this was to me. I immediately asked my parents about the motive behind such a statement. We were at the dinner table when the situation was discussed, and here, for the first time, I was made aware of the existence of a race problem. I had never been conscious of it before.

Another distressing occurrence took place two years later, when King and his high school teacher, Miss Sarah Bradley, traveled to a South Georgia town for an oratorical contest sponsored by the black Elks. M. L. did well, delivering his speech on "The Negro and the Constitution" without either manuscript or notes, but on their way back a white bus driver insisted that the two surrender their seats to newly boarding white riders. M. L. resisted at first, but his teacher finally encouraged him to get up, and the young man had to stand for several hours as the bus made its way to Atlanta. "It was," King recalled twenty years later, "the angriest I have ever been in my life."

That was the most traumatic encounter with segregation that young King suffered. He had seen his father refuse to accept second-class service in stores, tell white policemen that a forty-year-old black minister should be addressed as "Reverend," not "boy," and himself had been called "nigger" by a hostile white in a downtown store. Looking back on these experiences a decade later, King recalled that he had never fully gotten over the shock of his initial discovery of racial prejudice as a six-year-old. "From that moment on," he remembered, "I was determined to hate every white person. As I grew older and older, this feeling continued to grow," even though "my parents would always tell me that I should not hate the white man, but that it was my duty, as a Christian, to love him."

Sources

Farmer, James. *Lay Bare the Heart.* New York: New American Library, 1985, p. 31.

Garrow, David J. *Bearing the Cross: Martin Luther King, Jr., and the Southern Christian Leadership Conference.* New York: Random House, 1986, pp. 33–35.

Discussion Questions

1) The incidents recounted in these excerpts took place in the South before the civil rights era. Do you think that race is less of a master status today than it was at that time?

2) What are some other common statuses which can have a similarly great effect on how an individual is treated by others?

Supplemental Lecture Material
Humor as Social Bond

As you have already learned from the textbook, humor has many important functions in social life, including working as a safety valve to allow the exploration of the status quo, or promoting bonding in those who "get" the joke. The latter function can, in fact be taken a step further by applying Durkheim's notions of social integration or differentiation. Humor is one way a group can include or exclude people, integrate or differentiate them. Often this dynamic is fueled by status inequality in a setting where all involved try to deal with this inequality in various ways, humor being one of them.

A good example of this is a recent observational study in a clinic housed in a Division of General Internal Medicine at a major university medical center, where physicians, medical students fulfilling their residency requirements, the clinic's Nurse Coordinator, and, of course, patients interact. Obviously, physicians enjoy the highest status, with the residents next in the status hierarchy, the Nurse Coordinator next. Since residents have to work between 70-80 hours a week during their three year stint and are often exhausted, scheduling is an issue of prime importance to them.

Here is one exchange between an attending physician and residents, who are worried about having to be on call more often:

> The Attending laughs and asks somewhat lightheartedly if they ever imagined that things might actually get better. . . . Why do you *always* imagine the worst, he asks while jokingly suggesting at the same time that he somewhat agrees with their projection. One of the interns responds by joking that they do that because their projections are supported by *huge* reams of data. Everyone laughs.

Here humor is used to further integration in various ways. First of all, the residents bond since they all share the same concern, and the physician also addresses them as one group, saying "why do you. . ." The residents' reply using the medical metaphor of "hard data" also makes them members of the medical establishment, thereby bonding them with the physcian.

The residents themselves bond by joking with each other about workloads or the patients, most of whom were nonwhite (80%) and of disproportionately lower income and education. One resident, for example, called his patients the "Two Hundred Club" because they all weighed over 200 pounds. Patients with psychiatric histories are referred to as "schizos." While this helps residents and physicians to bond, patients are cast as outsiders, the butt of jokes.

The researchers explained it this way: "The combination of humor and viewing patients as 'other,' along with the time pressure of heavy workloads, contribute to the residents' tendency to embrace ready-made societal labels when referring to patients. . . Such humor often reflects, we believe, a feeling of frustration, or perhaps thwarted idealism."

When in direct contact with patients, however, both physicians and residents treat them with respect. Humor is often used to make the patient feel more at ease. "Just after we enter the room, she jokingly tells the patient, after he responds rather slowly to one of her questions, 'That's OK. I'm having the same kind of day you are' — meaning tiring, and exhausting. Everyone laughs."

This instance blurs status lines and integrates the patient. On the other hand, patients occasionally ward off embarrassing or personal questions from residents or physicians by giving their answers jokingly.

The Nurse Coordinator serves as a liaison between patients and various medical staff. Though her position holds lower social prestige, she has the final say over scheduling the residents, and thereby holds tremendous power, which perhaps explains why humor between the nurse and residents or attending physicians flows both ways. The nurse makes fun of their ability or commitment to medical care while the residents joke about her power and call her the "boss," possibly indicating a certain uneasiness about power relations in the clinic. On the other hand, nurses also bond with residents by mentoring them through humor.

The researchers conclude: "We suggest that humor functions as an organizational, emotional thermostat of sorts. Persons are continually responding to situations in terms of their ease or dis-ease with power and status, two critical dimensions of the organization's emotional climate."

Source
Yoels, William C. and Jeffrey Michael Clair, "Laughter in the Clinic: Humor as Social Organization. *Symbolic Interaction*, Vol. 18 No. 1: 39-58.

Discussion Questions
1) Use what you have learned about roles to analyze the interactions of the various groups above. What are the role sets? Is there role conflict or strain?

2) As you have seen above, as part of bonding, physicians and residents occasionally denigrate patients. Do you agree with the researchers' conclusions regarding that issue? Why or why not?

3) **Activity:** Find a setting where you might observe the use of humor, ideally where people of differing statuses have to deal with each other, such as a party or club, or a sports event. Write your analysis of the functions of humor in that setting.

Supplemental Lecture Material
Living to Laugh: The Evolution of African-American Humor

According to Mel Watkins, a historian of African-American humor, the long-term oppression of blacks led to the formation of a highly developed approach to humor. African-American humor, like that of other alienated groups such as Jews and the Irish, has a keen sense of irony, of the differences between the declared and actual values of our social system.

Sometimes this humor has been primarily ignorant of race in its content, as with contemporary comedian Bill Cosby. At other times, the humor has been driven by a sense of race, as with Richard Pryor.

Moms Mabley, another racially aware comedian, often focused on the tension her northern black audience felt with southern culture: "They shipped me some neckbones with a whole lot of meat on it. Not like the neckbones you get up here. When they say neckbones, they mean neck *bones*. . . . nothin' on 'em but bones"; or "Now they want me to go to New Orleans. . . . It'll be Old Orleans 'fore I get down there. The Greyhound ain't goin' take me down there and the bloodhounds run me back, I'll tell you that."

Why did African Americans develop a separate form of humor from white Americans? For a long time humor was one of the few ways most blacks could point out the hypocrisy and pain of their lives, the lack of justice and depth of pain, without creating despair or inciting retaliation. As Lawrence Levine says, "Black Americans have used humor not to escape from reality but to escape from unreality: the unreality of slavery, segregation, discrimination, brutality, and shattered hopes in a land founded on the 'inalienable rights' of 'life, liberty, and the pursuit of happiness.' If ever a paradox called for wit, this one did."

But African-American humor has faced two conflicting roles: presenting a black audience with genuine and meaningful entertainment, and avoiding the co-opting of that humor by whites and thereby perpetuating negative stereotypes. Often, a particular comedian or comedy team began as the former and ended as the latter before disappearing from public view.

One of the earliest mass media examples of this phenomenon is the career of film comedian Lincoln Perry, whose stage name was Stepin Fetchit. Perry began working in carnivals for black audiences in a role with a "shuffling, apparently inept and inarticulate character [with traits that] had clearly defined folk roots" according to Watkins. The nonchalance and ineptitude Perry displayed could be found in many traditional black stock characters. Perry remembered that "The first fifteen minutes of my act is getting to the middle of the stage." But the role of Fetchit lost a sense of humanity on the mainstream stage, and as Watkins states, "He came through as a pathetic, cartoonlike figure who . . . invited ridicule." Fetchit was removed from the screen after World War II by blacks who were tired of his contribution to negative stereotypes.

Richard Pryor may have been the first black American comic who accurately pulled genuine African-American humor into the mainstream. Watkins writes that Pryor "completely unmasked the complex matrix of pride, self-mockery, blunt confrontation of reality, double-edged irony, satiric wit, assertive defiance, poetic obscenity, and verbal acuity that finally define the elusive identity that may be called African-American humor." For example, Pryor said in 1971 of Martin Luther King, Jr., that "I been to the mountaintop, too, and what did I see? Mo' white folks with guns." On another occasion, Pryor said, "I was a nigger for twenty-three years. I gave it up, no room for advancement."

His appeal to whites as well as blacks marked a turning point in American humor. While African-American humor retains distinctive qualities, mainstream tastes have moved closer to integration and appreciative coexistence.

Sources

Levine, Lawrence. "Laughing Matters: How Black Americans Have Used Humor as Strategy for Survival." *New York Times Book Review* (February 27, 1994) pp. 1, 27–28.

Mel Watkins, *Laughing, Lying, and Signifying: The Underground Tradition of African-American Humor That Transformed American Culture, From Slavery to Richard Pryor.* Simon & Schuster. New York: 1994.

Discussion Questions

1) Do you think the kinds of stereotypes portrayed in pre–World War II movies could succeed in a mainstream context today? If so, can you think of any recent examples?

2) Have changes in African-American humor been the result of differences in the civil rights status of African Americans? Why or why not? How might a researcher determine this?

Supplemental Lecture Material
Profiling American Musical Tastes

What patterns of musical preferences do Americans have? The National Endowment for the Arts commissioned a survey in 1992 to provide a glimpse into the musical tastes of Americans. The survey asked respondents how they felt about twenty different musical genres, including blues and rhythm and blues (which were lumped together), reggae, country and western, rock, rap, classical, opera, and easy listening music. The survey found numerous variations by age, gender, socioeconomic level, educational background, and race.

Generally speaking, the number of genres respondents liked increased with age, education, and socioeconomic level. The five most popular genres are (in order of preference) country and western, mood and easy listening, rock, blues and rhythm and blues, and hymns and gospel music, all of which are liked by 40 percent or more of

Americans. Country and western is the only genre that enjoyed by more than half of Americans (52 percent, or roughly 96 million adults). Country was also cited most frequently as the single "favorite" genre of most Americans at 21 percent. The other leading favorites fell considerably behind: rock at 14 percent, hymns and gospel and mood and easy listening at 9 percent each, classical at 6 percent, and jazz at 5 percent.

Country's lead is somewhat surprising since it places only second to rock in record sales, although country recording sales have almost tripled, growing from 7 percent of total sales in 1989 to 18 percent in 1993. Country listeners tend not to listen to other genres very frequently, and they have a more definable demographic profile than other types of music listeners. For instance, country listeners are more likely to have a lower educational background; 57 percent of the respondents with no more than a high school diploma enjoy country, compared to only 42 percent of college graduates. In fact, while as a rule musical tastes broaden with increased education, country is the exception as the number of country listeners decreases with education.

In spite of the rapidly increasing sales of country music, however, the number of listeners who like country has actually decreased by six points in the ten years since 1982. Country was the only genre to register a decrease in audience change. It seems most likely that the increased sales represents an increase in the willingness of country fans to buy more music.

Rock, the third-most widely popular music, is also the biggest-selling genre. While 70 percent of Americans aged eighteen to twenty-four in the survey said they liked rock, a mere 9 percent of those between sixty-five and seventy-four and only 7 percent of those seventy-five and older said they liked rock. Otis Dudley Duncan, a de-

mographer, called this difference a "cohort chasm," pointing to the relative stability of some musical tastes throughout adulthood. The older respondents preferred such genres as big band, country, and mood and easy listening music, genres that were more widely appreciated when these adults came of age before the birth of rock. They probably didn't like their children listening to this music, and their appreciation has probably not materially increased.

On the other hand, the number of adults who like rock has increased overall as the percentage of adults who grew up listening to rock has also grown. As time passes, rock lovers will probably dominate the American music scene.

African Americans do not listen to many of the white-dominated genres, including rock. Only 39 percent of blacks reported liking rock, compared to 50 percent of white listeners. At 19 percent, even fewer blacks like country (57 percent of whites). Other genres such as opera, folk, show tunes, classical, big band, and easy listening fared badly relative to white listeners. As a group, blacks clearly prefer blues and rhythm and blues (59 percent versus 38 percent) and jazz (54 percent versus 32 percent).

A few gender differences appeared as well, though these differences were not very substantial. The women surveyed tended to like music that is considered "gentler" and "more lyrical," with somewhat higher preferences for easy listening, show tunes, and opera. Men were more likely to prefer stereo-typically faster and louder genres and rated rock, blues and rhythm and blues, and jazz higher than women.

The survey clearly showed that most Americans enjoy listening to at least two genres of music. Interestingly, the attempts of marketers to try to "deliver" a specific audience appears to have narrowed what a particular venue will play. The "Ed Sullivan

Show" could broadcast rock singer Elvis Presley and classical violinist Isaac Stern, but such musical variety shows seem to be, for now, at an end. Likewise, most radio stations represent a single genre. Perhaps the result will be that Americans will be exposed to a smaller variety of musical genres.

Source

Zill, Nicholas, and John Robinson. "Name That Tune." *American Demographics.* (August 1994) pp. 22–27.

Discussion Questions

1) What kinds of music do you like? How is your taste different from your peers? your children? your parents? your grandparents?

2) Why might blacks enjoy rock less than whites when rock is based on black-originated musical forms?

3) What factors determine the musical tastes of Americans? How have these factors been present in your own life?

Supplemental Lecture Material
The Philosophy of Deception

The Clinton years in the White House will be remembered for many things, not the least of which is the issue of honesty. Clinton was nearly impeached…not for his sexual proclivities but over the question of "Did he lie (or tell someone else to)?" Substantial concern arose over the fear that if the President would lie about one thing, he would lie about another.

The issue of honesty really must be examined in a way that distinguishes between public and private life. Perjury, by its very nature is public, and the consequences can be tremendous. In a trial, a jury's as-sumption that a person who lies about one thing will lie about another is perfectly justified. Sex, with a few obvious exceptions, is part of our private life. And just about everyone is less than forthright about sex. Robert C. Solomon, a professor of philosophy at the University of Texas at Austin, notes that while lying about sex may have grave significance for people in an intimate relationship, it has nothing to do with one's public credibility. Indeed, when publicly asked a rudely in appropriate question about one's private life, it seems "not only natural but even obligatory to lie, finesse, or refuse to answer."

Solomon contends that "Not all untruths are malicious. Telling the truth can complicate or destroy social relationships." When honesty would be cruel, deception becomes not a vice, but a social virtue. In such cases systematic deception becomes an essential part of the order of the social world. In some ways, seeking the truth at all costs is an ethnocentric peculiarity that is, at least in part, a product of our strong sense of individualism, and what Solomon sees as a dangerously unsociable conception. He concludes "Deception and self deception are part and parcel of our engagements in the world, including, not least, the development and maintenance of our sense of ourselves." For public figures, lying is sometimes a way of protecting their private lives. A lie or an invitation to lie that is provoked by a breach of sacred personal boundaries is what Solomon calls "moral limbo" and in no violation of a public trust.

Source

Robert C. Solomon. "Is It Ever Right to Lie? The Philosophy of Deception". The Chronical of Higher Education (Feb. 27, 1998) p. 60.

Discussion Questions

1) Is a lie told in desperation any less wrong than a calculated, merely convenient lie? Why or why not?

2) Thomas Aquinas and Immanuel Kant both believed that lying is always wrong. What's your feeling about their Absolutist stand on lying?

Chapter 7

Groups and Organizations

I. A **social group** is defined as two or more people who identify and interact with one another.
  A. Primary and secondary groups.
     1. A **primary group** is a small social group whose members share personal and enduring relationships.
        a. People in primary groups share many activities, spend a great deal of time together, and feel they know one another well.
        b. Families are primary groups in that they are the first groups we experience in life and because they are of central importance in the socialization process.
        c. Members think of the group as an end in itself rather than as a means to other ends.
        d. Members view each other as unique and irreplaceable.
     2. **Secondary groups** are large and impersonal social groups devoted to some specific interest or activity.
        a. They involve weak emotional ties.
        b. They are commonly short-term.
        c. They are goal oriented.
        d. They are typically impersonal.
     3. SEEING OURSELVES BOX—National Map 7–1: The Quality of Relationships: Lawsuits Across the United States. In regions of the country where litigation is least common, people's social ties are typically more primary, and litigation is more common in regions where social ties tend to be secondary.
  B. Group leadership.
     1. **Instrumental leadership** emphasizes the completion of tasks; expressive leadership emphasizes collective well-being.
     2. There are three styles of decision making in groups:
        a. **Authoritarian leadership** focuses on instrumental concerns, takes personal charge of decision-making, and demands strict compliance from subordinates.
        b. **Democratic leadership** is more expressive and tries to include everyone in the decision-making process.
        c. **Laissez-faire leadership** allows the group to function more or less on its own.
  C. Group conformity.
     1. Asch's research into group conformity showed that many of us are willing to compromise our own judgment and to avoid being different, even from people we do not know.

2. Milgram's research into obedience suggests that people are likely to follow directions from not only "legitimate authority figures," even when it means inflicting harm on another person.

3. Janis' research into **groupthink,** the tendency of group members to conform by adopting a narrow view of some issue.

 D. A **reference group** is a social group that serves as a point of reference for people making evaluations or decisions.

  1. Stouffer's research on reference group dynamics showed that we do not make judgments about ourselves in isolation, nor do we compare ourselves with just anyone.

 E. An **ingroup** is a social group commanding a member's esteem and loyalty; an **outgroup** is a social group toward which one feels competition or opposition.

 F. Group size

  1. A **dyad** is Georg Simmel's term for a social group with two members.

   a. Social interaction in a dyad is typically intense.

   b. Dyads are typically less stable than larger groups.

  2. A **triad** is a social group with three members.

   a. Triads are more stable than dyads.

   b. Any two members can form a majority coalition.

 G. Social diversity influences intergroup contact in four ways:

  1. The larger a group, the more likely members will maintain relationships only with other group members.

  2. The more internally heterogeneous a group is, the more likely that its members will interact with outsiders.

  3. The greater the overall social parity within a setting, the more likely it is that people from diverse backgrounds will mingle and form ties.

  4. Physical space affects the chances of contacts among groups.

 H. A **network** is a web of social ties.

  1. GLOBAL SOCIOLOGY BOX—The Internet: A Global Network. From one vast network, a host of social groups are emerging.

  2. WINDOW ON THE WORLD—Global Map 7-1: Cyberspace: A Global Network. While 180 of 191 world nations are connected to the Internet, a majority of the world's people do not have access to this resource.

II. Formal organizations are large, secondary groups that are organized to achieve goals efficiently.

 A. There are three types of formal organizations:

  1. **Utilitarian organizations,** which people join in pursuit of material rewards.

  2. **Coercive organizations,** distinguished by involuntary membership.

  3. **Normative organizations** or voluntary associations, in which people pursue goals they consider morally worthwhile.

 B. **Bureaucracy** became common during the Industrial Revolution.

C. Bureaucracy is an organizational model rationally designed to perform tasks efficiently. Max Weber identified six key characteristics of bureaucracy:
>   1. Specialization.
>   2. Hierarchy of offices.
>   3. Rules and regulations.
>   4. Technical competence.
>   5. Impersonality.
>   6. Formal, written communications.

D. **Organizational environment** refers to a range of factors outside the organization that affects its operation, including:
   1. technology.
   2. economic and political trends.
   3. population patterns.
   4. other organizations.

E. The informal side of bureaucracy is that members of organizations try to personalize their procedures and surroundings.

F. Problems of bureaucracy.
>   1. Bureaucratic alienation.
>   2. Bureaucratic inefficiency and ritualism.
>   3. Bureaucratic inertia.
>   4. Robert Michels made the link between bureaucracy and **oligarchy**, the rule of the many by the few. The "iron law of oligarchy" refers to the pyramid shape of bureaucracy placing a few leaders in charge of organizational resources.

III. The Evolution of Formal Organizations.

A. Scientific management is the application of scientific principles to the operation of a business or other large organization.
   1. Scientific management involves three steps:
>   a. Managers observe the tasks performed by the workers.
>   b. Managers analyze their data to discover ways for workers to become more efficient.
>   c. Management provides guidance and incentives to workers to be more efficient.

B. During the 1960s, big businesses were inefficient and unfair in their hiring practices.
   1.   By the end of the twentieth century, white men in the United States held 61 percent of management jobs.
   2.   Women bring a "female advantage" to companies striving to be more flexible and democratic.

C. Differences between formal organizations in Japan and in the United States:
   1.   Hiring and advancement.
   2.   Lifetime security.
   3.   Holistic involvement.
   4.   Broad-based training.
   5.   Collective decision making.

D. GLOBAL SOCIOLOGY BOX—The Japanese Model: Will It Work in the United States? Competition from Asia and Europe is forcing U.S. companies to rethink how corporate organizations should operate in a global marketplace.
E. Ways in which today's organizations differ from those of a century ago:
    1.   Creative autonomoy.
    2.   Competitive work teams.
    3.   A flatter organization.
    4.   Greater flexibility.
F. The **"McDonaldization" of society.**
    1. Four principles of McDonaldization:
        a. Efficiency.
        b. Calculability.
        c. Uniformity and predictability.
        d. Control through automation.
    2. Rationality, although efficient, may be highly dehumanizing.

IV. The Future of Organizations: Opposing Trends
    A. "Intelligent organizations" have become more productive than ever.
    B. The postindustrial economy has created many highly skilled jobs, more routine service jobs, and offers few of the benefits that today's highly skilled workers enjoy.
    C. Organizational "flexibility" that gives better-off workers more autonomy carries the threat of "downsizing" for rank-and-file employees.

Chapter Objectives

1) Distingush between primary and secondary groups.

2) Distinguish between instrumental and expressive leadership and identify and describe leadership styles in terms of decision-making.

3) Summarize the research findings on group conformity, including the research of Asch, Milgram, and Janis.

4) Explain the functions of reference groups.

5) Distinguish between ingroups and outgroups.

6) Discuss how group dynamics change as group size changes.

7) Examine four ways in which social diversity influences intergroup contact.

8) Discuss the importance of networks in social interaction.

9) Identify and describe three types of formal organizations.

10) List Max Weber's six defining characteristics of buraucracy.

11) Recognize ways that informal interaction alters the behavior of real-life bureaucracies.

12) Discuss problems of bureaucracy, including bureaucratic alienation, bureaucratic inefficiency and ritualism, and bureaucratic inertia.

13) Outline the scientific management model.

14) Describe three challenges in the twentieth century that gradually led to the "flexible organization."

15) Identify and define four basic organizational principles of McDonaldization.

Essay Topics

1) Distinguish between primary groups and secondary groups. Provide examples of primary and secondary groups to which you have belonged.

2) Identify and describe three leadership styles. Provide examples of these styles in society.

3) The Asch and Milgram experiments discussed in this chapter were conducted on groups of subjects who had not met before the experimental session. Do you think that groups of people who already knew each other would demonstrate more or less conformity if put in these experimental situations? Discuss.

4) Do you think that the Milgram experiment was ethical? Why or why not?

5) What are some of the steps a group might take to reduce or eliminate groupthink?

6) What are some of the reference groups that are important to you? How did you choose them? What functions do they serve?

7) What are some examples of groupthink in American history? Have you ever found yourself seeking to conform in a group situation that resulted in a narrow view of some issue?

8) Which of Etzioni's three types of formal organizations is generally most efficient in pursuit of its goals? Which is least efficient? Why?

9) Although sociologists usually explain the pervasiveness of bureaucracies in contemporary society as a result of their efficiency, many people think of bureaucracy as synonymous with inefficiency. Why do you think this view is widely held? How much truth is there in it?

10) Select a bureaucracy with which you are familiar and analyze the extent to which it is accurately described by Weber's six-point ideal type model. How would you account for any variations you may have identified?

11) Suggest some ways in which bureaucracies might reduce the problems that result from tendencies toward bureaucratic waste and incompetence, ritualism, and inertia.

12) What do you regard as the principal positive and negative characteristics of the Japanese model of formal organizations? Explain.

Integrative Supplement Guide

1. **ABC Videos:**
- Changes in the Workplace (*World News Tonight/American Agenda*, 12/27/95)

2. **Transparencies - Series V:**
- T-29 Primary and Secondary Groups: A Summary

- T-30 The Quality of Relationships: Lawsuits Across the United States
- T-31 Cards Used in Asch's Experiment in Group Conformity
- T-32 Group Size and Relationships (two, three, and four people)
- T-33 Group Size and Relationships (five, six, and seven people)
- T-35 Membership in Cultural or Educational Organizations
- T-36 U.S. Managers by Race, Sex and Ethnicity, 1996
- T-37 Concerns About Privacy Across the United States
- T-38 Membership in Voluntary Associations with Bachelor's Degrees or Higher
- T-39 Membership in Voluntary Associations with Less than a Bachelor's Degree

---

Supplemental Lecture Material
A Nation of Joiners

Ever since de Toqueville described us as a nation of joiners, observers have commented on our strong and continuing inclination to participate in formal organizations of various sorts. Between 1975 and 1990, the number of membership groups in the U.S. jumped 77 percent, to a total of 23,000. Seven out of ten adults belong to at least one such association. Here are some of the most popular:

Group	Members (millions)
American Automobile Association	29.0
American Assoc. of Retired Persons	28.0
YMCA of the USA	14.0
National Geographic Society	10.5
National Right-to-Life Committee	7.0
National PTA	6.1
National Wildlife Federation	5.1
National Committee to Preserve Social Security and Medicare	5.0
4-H Program	4.8
Boy Scouts of America	4.8
Women's Intern. Bowling Congress	3.7
American Bowling Congress	3.3
American Farm Bureau Federation	3.3
Girl Scouts of the USA	3.1
National Rifle Association	3.0
American Legion	2.9
International Friendship League	2.8
Little League Baseball	2.5
National Alliance of Senior Citizens	2.2
Veterans of Foreign Wars	2.1

Source

"A Nation of Joiners." *U.S. News & World Report* (May 21, 1990):78.

Discussion Question

1) Why do you think that citizens of the U.S. are more likely to join voluntary associations than are most Europeans?

Supplementary Lecture Material
Computers and the Threat to Privacy

It's hardly news any longer: we live in the so-called Information Age. Information, virtually all of it stored in computer databases, is the lifeblood of the public and private bureaucracies that dominate postindustrial society. The quest for ever-greater levels of efficiency has led to a scramble to obtain more and more information about individual citizens and consumers.

Yet, while many people express concerns about the loss of their privacy, most of us are willing accomplices. Do you use a bank card at ATM machines? Do you shop by mail order or visit commercial websites? Do you browse websites on the Internet? If so, you are being tracked, and most of us realize it. Yet, we are unwilling to change our habits? Why? Because, perhaps when it comes right down to it, we value convenience over privacy.

Here are just a few examples of how by doing very simple, everyday things you inadvertently leave electronic footprints, and how those might be used by others:

- At work, you send an e-mail saying unflattering things about your boss. Your company (as do many corporations) routinely reviews e-mails, so your boss reads yours. You are dismissed. You file a suit, but lose. The prospective employer at the next job you apply for uses an Internet investigation service to check records and your lawsuit is discovered. What do you think your chances are of being employed by that firm?

- You have allergies and call an 800 number to check pollen count in your area. Your number is recorded by caller ID, and you are put on a list of allergy sufferers. The list is sold to a drug company. Next thing you know, you are sent a coupon for that company's allergy medication.

- You're eating out, and order a burger with fries. At the restaurant, your order is entered into a computer. You pay by credit card. The restaurant then checks your credit rating and sends you a discount offer for your next visit. Unfortunately, the restaurant goes bankrupt, and its list of burger and fries lovers goes on the information market.

Those are just a few examples, some innocuous sounding, some not. But what about direct abuses?

Here are a few examples:

- In 1995, "a convicted child rapist working as a technician in a Boston hospital riffled through 1,000 computerized records looking for potential victims (and was caught when the father of a nine-year-old girl used caller ID to trace

the call back to the hospital). (Quittner p. 31).

- "A banker on Maryland's state health commission pulled up a list of cancer patients, cross-checked it against the names of his bank's customers and revoked the loans of the matches." (Ibid).

- "Sara Lee bakeries planned to collaborate with Lovelace Health Systems, a subsidiary of Cigna, to match employee health records with work performance reports to find workers who might benefit from antidepressants." (Ibid).

Unusual? No. About a third or more of all FORTUNE 500 companies check health information before hiring someone.

But what if government started gathering information about you, how would you feel? As early as 1982, the federal government "possessed more than 3.5 billion files on individual Americans — an average of 15 per person. . ." (Lacayo, p. 39). The FBI is currently creating a database on the 25 million people who have ever been arrested, even if they were not convicted.

Government abuses are currently regulated by the Privacy Act of 1974, but many feel that this law needs to be updated to keep pace with technological innovation. Bills have been introduced "to apply the Freedom of Information Act to electronic files as well as paper," and hearings have been held "about the spreading use of Social Security numbers to link an individual's multiple files in far-flung computers" (Miller). Another bill would create a new federal data protection board. Others go even further. Harvard law professor Lawrence Tribe supports an amendment to the Constitution ensuring that the Bill of Rights will not be endangered by developing communication and computer technologies.

Critics who wonder whether such safeguards are really necessary need only look to the Orwellian steps now being taken by the Thai government. By 2006, information on "65 million Thais (will be stored) in a single, integrated computer network. . . . Each citizen over age 15 will be required to carry a card bearing a color photo. . . . (and) an identification number" (Elmer-Dewitt). With this number, the government will be able to obtain the citizen's fingerprints, height, home address, parents' and children's names, marital status, education, occupation, income, nationality, religion, and, potentially, criminal records.

Yet, at times, government is actually trying to help you out, as was the Social Security Administration when it created an Internet site "that supplied information about individuals' personal income and retirement benefits," (Pear p. A15) so that people might be able to project their benefits and take appropriate steps in creating additional savings for retirement. Anyone accessing the site had to provide a name, address, telephone number, Social Security number, and mother's maiden name. Since Social Security numbers and mother's maiden names are available in public databases, the site was considered not secure. "It was easy to imagine misuse of the service by ex-spouses, landlords, employers, co-workers, intrusive neighbors and credit agencies.

In spite of resistance to these pools of private information, the means of accessing some basic data about individuals seems to be growing easier. Through search engines on the Internet's World Wide Web such as Lycos and Yahoo, anyone with Internet access can enter an individual's name to look for his or her phone number, residential address, email address, and — in some cases — a map showing where in a city that person lives. Once that far, anyone can find out what that person does for a living, the names

and ages of a spouse and children, the kind of car that person drives, the value of the person's house and the taxes paid on it.

Given these concerns, experts are grappling for reasonable solutions. Perhaps a new government agency providing legal protection?

Kevin Kelly, executive editor of *Wired* magazine disagrees. According to Kelly, privacy also didn't exist in the traditional village or small town. The difference was that people knew about each other, creating a kind of symmetry of knowledge. That's what has changed. In other words, knowledge is the answer, an awareness of who watches you and where that knowledge might be going.

Sources
Bernstein, Nina. "On Frontier of Cyberspace, Data Is Money, and a Threat." *The New York Times* (June 12, 1997).

Elmer-Dewitt, Philip. "Peddling Big Brother." *Time* (June 24, 1991): 62.

Lacayo, Richard. "Nowhere to Hide." *Time* (November 11, 1991):34-40.

Pear, Robert. "Social Security Closes On-Line Site, Citing Risks to Privacy." *The New York Times* (April 10, 1997):A15.

Quittner, Joshua. "Invasion of Privacy." *Time,* Vol. 150 No. 8 (August 25, 1997):27-35.

Discussion Questions
1) What sorts of personal data should be kept private? Should data-gathering companies be allowed to sell information about your income? bill-paying history? medical history? product purchases? arrest history?

2) Should data-collection firms be required to ask permission from individuals before selling their names?

3) Is this an area in which government should play an active role, or will marketplace forces adequately protect the consumer? What do you think about Kelly's argument that knowledge is the answer?

Supplemental Lecture Material
Using Small Group Interaction to Break Racism's Hold

In late 1989 and 1990, a series of events, such as the killing of a black teenager by white youths in the Bensonhurst district of Brooklyn, the election of Klansman David Duke to the Louisiana state legislature, and the popularity of such openly bigoted performers as Andrew Dice Clay and Guns 'N' Roses, led to a widespread perception that racism was once again on the rise in America.

Social psychologists who have studied the phenomenon of racial prejudice believe that they have come up with an innovative way of combating this trend, one that makes use of the dynamics of small group interaction.

Prejudice is largely a result of people's natural tendency to use categories to simplify everyday life. "Essentially, the mind seeks to simplify the chaos of the world by fitting all perceptions into categories. Thus it fits different kinds of people into pigeonholes, just as it does with restaurants or television programs. . . . Too often people see the category and not the individual. Once these categories are formed, beliefs and assumptions that underlie them are confirmed at every possible opportunity, even at the cost of disregarding evidence to the contrary."

Researchers such as Dr. Robert Slavin of Johns Hopkins University have built on earlier small-group research by Gordon Allport and Muzafer Sherif in constructing interracial "learning teams" in junior high schools and high schools around the country. Like sports teams, these learning teams can knit people together through a shared purpose that can lead to friendship and undercut the categories that lead to stereotyped thinking.

These teams are typically composed of four or five members. "While members study together and are encouraged to teach each other, they are tested individually. But the team gets a score or other recognition of its work as a unit. Teams work together for about six weeks, and then students are reassigned to a new team to promote as many contacts as possible among students." The students are not told that one purpose of the groups is to reduce prejudice and stereotyping. The results have been encouraging, and similar strategies are being used "in Israel. . . to defuse tensions between Jewish students of Middle-Eastern and European descent, in Canada between Canadians and immigrants, and in California between Hispanic and non-Hispanic students." These techniques may be especially effective with grade-school children, whose biases have not yet had the time to harden.

Integrated learning groups are not enough by themselves, Dr. Slavin stresses. There must also be an overall social climate that stresses no tolerance for racist speech or behavior, and there must be a feeling amongst members of all groups that they will be treated fairly. But this is an excellent example of how small group dynamics can be used to secure a socially beneficial end, the reduction of racial prejudice.

Source

Goleman, Daniel. "Psychologists Find Ways to Break Racism's Hold." *New York Times* (Sept. 5, 1989):17 and 20.

Discussion Questions

1) Ask students to consider to what extent small group interactions at their college or university are segregated by race and/or ethnic group. Do members of a given group tend to room together in the dorms? to eat at the same tables in the union? to sit together in class? What are the consequences of such segregation?

2) How could the group dynamics principles discussed here be used to reduce prejudice on your campus?

3) Under what circumstances might intensive small group interaction actually promote prejudiced thinking? How can such a possibility be circumvented?

Supplemental Lecture Material
The Female Advantage

As the textbook notes, women are still underrepresented as managers of businesses, yet some people, such as Sally Helgesen see women as the business leaders of the future. Why? Because their style of management is more democratic and flexible, and therefore able to adjust more easily to the fast-changing, dynamic business environment, or thrive in an company where educated young professionals expect to be treated as individuals.

In a recent article summing up their book, *Megatrends for Women*, Patricia Aburdene and John Naisbitt describe women leaders as sharing these qualities:

- Encourage participation;
- Share power and information;

- Enhance other people's self-worth;
- And get others excited about their work. (Aburdene, p. 46)

While these qualities all sound "nice," the authors warn that this would be an oversimplification. "Caring about people and supporting them always must be balanced with objectivity. . . . Anyone who thinks 'supporting people' and being 'nice' alone cut it in the business world is in need of a serious reality check." (Ibid).

One thing that helps women, according to Judith Hall, a psychology professor at Northeastern University, is that women traditionally are better at interpreting body language and other non-verbal cues. They also are able to tolerate ambiguity and to juggle many things at once.

Men, however, who see job performance" as a series of transactions--rewards for services rendered or punishment for inadequate performance," (Ibid) might misinterpret women's management style. A female manager's willingness to empower employees by asking them for help, might, for example, look like ignorance, and as though she truly doesn't know what she is doing. Also, other employees might feel freer to criticize a woman, or to challenge her authority.

Source

Aburdene, Patricia and John Naisbitt. *Megatrends for Women.* New York: Villard Books, 1992.

Discussion Questions

1) Characterize women's management style according to the two leadership roles and three leadership styles discussed in the book. Do you agree with these conclusions? Do you think the female management style is indeed the style of the future? If so, how will men adjust?

2) The trend mentioned above, and that of humanizing organizations and bureaucracies seems to be at odds with the future McDonaldization of society. How do you think the future will look? Why?

3) **Activity:** Interview a woman manager and try to determine whether her management style does indeed reflect the characteristics as described above. If there are discrepancies, how do you explain them sociologically?

Chapter 8

Deviance

I. What Is Deviance?

A. **Deviance** is defined as the recognized violation of cultural norms. What deviant actions or attitudes have in common is some element of difference that causes us to regard another person as an "outsider."

B. Deviance calls forth **social control,** attempts by society to regulate people's thoughts and behavior.

  1. The **criminal justice system** is a formal response to an individual's alleged violations of law from police, courts and prison officials.

C. The biological context.

  1. Genetic research seeks possible links between biology and crime.

D. Personality factors.

  1. Reckless and Dinitz's containment theory suggests that strong moral standards and positive self-image can keep boys from becoming delinquent.

  2. Critical evaluation. Most crimes are committed by people who are psychologically normal.

E. The social foundations of deviance:

  1. Deviance varies according to cultural norms.

  2. People become deviant as others define them that way.

  3. Both rule-making and rule-breaking involve social power.

II. Structural-Functional Analysis.

A. Emile Durkheim: The functions of deviance:

  1. Deviance affirms cultural values and norms.

  2. Responding to deviance clarifies moral boundaries.

  3. Responding to deviance promotes social unity.

  4. Deviance encourages social change.

B. Merton's strain theory.

  1. The "strain" between our culture's emphasis on wealth and the limited opportunity to get rich gives rise, especially among the poor, to theft, the sale of drugs, or other street crime.

  2. Merton's four types of deviance (responses to failure):

    a. Innovation.

    b. Ritualism.

    c. Retreatism.

    d. Rebellion.

C. Deviant subcultures.
   1. Cloward and Ohlin extended Merton's theory, proposing that access to illegitimate opportunities for success is also problematic. As a result of this, three different types of delinquent subcultures may arise:
      a. Criminal subcultures.
      b. Conflict subcultures.
      c. Retreatist subcultures.
   2. Albert Cohen suggests that delinquency is most pronounced in lower-class youths because they have the least opportunity to achieve conventional success.
   3. Walter Miller characterizes deviant subcultures:
      a. Trouble.
      b. Toughness.
      c. Smartness.
      d. A need for excitement.
      e. A belief in fate.
      f. A desire for freedom.
D. Critical evaluation.
   1. Durkheim's work remains important, but communities do not always come together in reaction to crime.
   2. Merton's theory explains some types of crime better than others; and ignores the fact that not everyone seeks success in conventional terms of wealth.
   3. The general argument that deviance reflects the opportunity structure of society falls short in assuming that everyone shares the same cultural standards for judging right and wrong; focuses undue attention on the behavior of the poor; and falsely implies that everyone who breaks the rules will be defined as deviant.

III. Symbolic-Interaction Analysis.
   A. **Labeling theory** is the idea that deviance and conformity result, not so much from what people do, but from how others respond.
      1. Primary deviance refers to passing episodes of norm violation; and secondary deviance is when an individual repeatedly violates a norm and begins to take on a deviant identity.
      2. A **stigma** is a powerfully negative social label that radically changes a person's self-concept and social identity, operating as a master status.
         a. Stigmas are often attached in formal rituals called degradation ceremonies.
      3. Stigmas are deepened by retrospective labeling, the interpretation of someone's past consistent with present deviance. People may also engage in projective labeling.
      4. Labeling and mental illness: Thomas Szasz argues that "mentally ill" is a label we attach to people who are only different and concludes that we should abandon the concept of mental illness entirely.
      5. GLOBAL SOCIOLOGY BOX—Cockfighting: Cultural Ritual or Abuse of Animals?
   B. The **medicalization of deviance** is the transformation of moral and legal issues into a medical condition.

      1. SEEING OURSELVES—National Map 8-1: Where Psychiatrists Practice Across the United States.

      2. Whether deviance is defined morally or medically has three profound consequences.

            a. It affects who responds to deviance.

            b. It affects how people respond to deviance.

            c. It affects whether the deviant is regarded as being personally competent.

C. Edwin Sutherland's differential association theory suggests that all deviance is learned in groups.

D. Hirschi's control theory.

      1. Control theory states that social control depends on imagining the consequences of one's behavior.

      2. Hirschi asserts that conformity arises from four types of social controls:

            a. Attachment.

            b. Commitment.

            c. Involvement.

            d. Belief.

E. Critical evaluation.

      1. Labeling theory is most applicable to minor forms of deviance.

      2. The consequences of deviant labeling may vary.

      3. Not everyone resists deviant labeling.

IV. Social-Conflict Analysis.

A. Principles of deviance and power:

      1. The norms of any society generally reflect the interests of the rich and powerful.

      2. The powerful have the resources to resist deviant labeling.

      3. The laws may be inherently unfair.

B. Deviance and capitalism: Steven Spitzer suggests that deviant labels are chiefly applied to those who impede the operation of capitalism.

C. **White-collar crime** consists of crimes committed by persons of high social position in the course of their occupations.

      1. It is usually controlled by civil rather than criminal law.

      2. Most white-collar criminals are treated leniently.

D. **Corporate crime** refers to the illegal actions of a corporation or people acting on its behalf.

E. **Organized crime** is a business supplying illegal goods or services.

F. Critical evaluation.

      1. Social conflict analysis falsely assumes that laws benefit only the rich.

      2. It implies that crime arises only in societies that treat their members unequally.

V. Deviance and Social Diversity.

A. Gender is an important variable affecting deviant labeling and other aspects of deviant behavior.

B. **Hate crimes** are criminal acts carried out against a person or a person's property by an offender motivated by racial or other bias.

1. CRITICAL THINKING BOX—Hate Crimes: Do They Punish Actions or Attitudes?

VI. Crime.
A. Crime involves two components, the act itself and criminal intent or *mens rea.*
B. Types of crime:
   1. **Crimes against the person** involve direct violence or the threat of violence against others.
   2. **Crimes against property** involve theft of property belonging to others.
   3. **Victimless crimes** are violations of law in which there are no readily apparent victims.
C. Criminal statistics show crime rising between 1960 and 1990, but declining over the past decade.
   1. Victimization surveys may provide more accurate data.
D. The "street" criminal: A profile.
   1. Age. Official crime rates rise sharply during adolescence and peak in the late teens, falling thereafter.
   2. Gender. Men are arrested three times as often as women for property crimes. In the case of violent crimes, the disparity is even greater, with a six-to-one ratio.
   3. Social class. Street crime is more widespread among people of lower social position. Yet the link between class and crime is more complicated than it appears on the surface.
   4. Race and ethnicity. Both race and ethnicity are strongly correlated to crime rates, although the reasons are many and complex.
E. **Crime in Global Perspective:** The U.S. crime rate is high. Two factors which may help to explain this are:
   1. Our culture's emphasis on individual economic success.
   2. The extensive private ownership of guns.
   3. WINDOW ON THE WORLD—Global Map 8–1: Prostitution in Global Perspective. In general, prostitution is widespread in societies where women have low standing compared to men.

VII. The Criminal Justice System
A. Police.
   1. The police serve as the primary point of contact between the population and the criminal justice system.
   2. Police quickly size up a situation in terms of six factors:
      a. How serious is the alleged crime?
      b. What is the victim's preference?
      c. Is the suspect cooperative or not?
      d. Have they arrested the suspect before?
      e. Are bystanders present?
      f. What is the suspect's race?
B. Courts.

1. **Plea bargaining** is a legal negotiation in which the prosecution reduces a defendant's charge in exchange for a guilty plea.
C. Punishment. Four basic reasons to punish:
   1. **Retribution** is an act of moral vengeance by which society subjects an offender to suffering comparable to that caused by the offense.
   2. **Deterrence** is the attempt to discourage criminality through punishment.
      a. Specific deterrence demonstrates to the individual offender that crime does not pay.
      b. In general deterrence, the punishment of one person serves as an example to others.
   3. **Rehabilitation** involves reforming the offender to prevent subsequent offenses.
   4. **Societal protection** is rendering an offender incapable of further offenses temporarily through incarceration or permanently by execution.
   5. Critical evaluation:
      a. Punishment deters some crime, yet our society has a high rate of criminal recidivism.
      b. The death penalty has limited value as a general deterrent.
      c. Prisons do little to reshape attitudes or behavior in the long term.
      d. SEEING OURSELVES—National Map 8-2: Capital Punishment Across the United States. The United States is the only industrial nation in which the federal government imposes the death penalty. Yet the fifty states have broadly divergent capital punishment laws: half of the roughly 3,000 prisoners on death row are in five states.
   6. APPLYING SOCIOLOGY BOX—Violent Crime is Down—But Why?
      a. Change in policing.
      b. More prisons.
      c. A better economy.
      d. The declining drug trade.

Chapter Objectives

1) Define deviance.

2) Evaluate the general biological and psychological explanations of deviance and criminality.

3) Identify three social foundations of deviance.

4) List the functions of deviance identified by Emile Durkheim.

5) Explain Merton's strain theory of deviance and identify and describe four types of deviant responses.

6) Characterize deviant subcultures.

7) Outline the major dimensions of labeling theory, including the concepts of primary and secondary deviance, stigma, degradation ceremonies, and retrospective and progressive labeling.

8) Evaluate the consequences of the medicalization of deviance.

9) Summarize Edwin Sutherland's differential association theory.

10) Describe Hirschi's four types of social control.

11) Examine the social-conflict interpretation of deviance and criminality.

12) Define white-collar crime, corporate crime, and organized crime.

13) Discuss how gender is linked to deviance.

14) Discuss how racial and ethnic hostility movtivates hate crimes.

15) Identify and define three major types of crime.

16) Discuss limitations of official crime statistics.

17) Provide a profile of the "street" criminal.

18) Discuss reasons why the U.S. crime rate is unusually high in comparison with that of other postindustrial societies.

19) Identify and discuss the major components of the U.S. criminal justice system.

20) Name four justifications that have been advanced for punishment and how adequately each is being carried out by the contemporary U.S. criminal justice system.

Essay Topics

1) Sociologists stress that the definition of what is deviant varies from time to time and from place to place. Some people feel that our society is moving toward regarding cigarette smoking as deviant. Do you agree? If so, how is this being accomplished?

2) Clarify your understanding of Durkheim's four functions of deviance by considering how rock-n-roll in the 1950s and marijuana smoking today provide each of the functions.

3) Use Merton's strain theory to interpret the popularity of methamphetamines.

4) What social policies would be likely to be recommended by a sociologist who favored Merton's strain theory in order to reduce property crime by the poor?

5) Labeling theorists commonly regard people such as the mentally ill, the physically handicapped, or the severely obese as deviant; however, many students resist such an interpretation. Why? Take a position yourself and defend it.

6) Most of us have been labeled at least mildly deviant at some time in our lives. Recount your own experiences with deviant labeling, making reference to relevant terms such as primary and secondary deviance, stigma, and retrospective labeling.

7) From the standpoint of a deviant individual, is the medicalization of deviance likely to be seen as an entirely positive development or are there also some negative aspects of this shift in interpretative content?

8) What are the primary reasons the U.S. crime rate is very high in global context? What steps would you recommend to try to reduce this rate?

9) Which of the four justifications for punishment do you find most appropriate? Which would you reject? Why?

10) Americans have historically been more willing to accept biological and psychological explanations of criminality than sociological ones. Why do you think this has been the case?

Integrative Supplement Guide

1. ABC Videos:
- The Enemy Within - The Growing Rate of Police Suicide (*Prime Time Live,* 2/8/95)
- Who's Watching the Guards? (*20/20,* 3/11/94)
- The Attempt to Expand Police Powers (*Nightline,* 2/15/95)
- Three Strikes: Is It Working? (*Nightline,* 3/7/95)
  Dangerous Lessons-Violence in the Nation's Schools (*Prime Time Live,* 4/5/95)
  Police and Teens (*World News Tonight/AA*-12/12/95)
  Solutions: Public Housing Restrictions Curb Crime (*World News Tonight,* 9/12/96)
  Dealing with Juvenile Offenders (*World News Tonight,* 10/23/96)
  Young Criminals, Adult Punishment (*Nightline,* 6/18/96)
  Recipe for Violence (*Prime Time Live,* 6/24/98)
  Horrific Hate Crime in Texas Town (*This Week with Sam & Cokie,* 4/26/98)

2. Transparencies - Series V:
- T-40   Merton's Strain Theory of Deviance
- T-41   Where Psychiatrists Practice Across the United States
- T-42   Crime Rates in the United States, 1960-1996 – Violent Crimes
- T-43   Crime Rates in the United States, 1960-1996 – Property Crimes
- T-44   Criminal Offenses
- T-45   Number of Murders by Handguns, 1996
- T-46   Prostitution in Global Perspective
- T-47   Incarceration Rates, 1993
- T-48   Capital Punishment Across the United States
- T-49   Favor Death for a Convicted Murderer

Supplemental Lecture Material
An Epidemic of Cheating?

Several recent studies suggest that academic dishonesty may be on the upswing. In 1987, a national survey conducted by UCLA's Graduate School of Education found that 18 percent of a sample of college sophomores admitted to having cheated on their exams, and that 29 percent said they had copied someone else's homework, 36 percent had done both. More recently, Rutgers anthropology professor Michael Moffatt distributed questionnaires to 232 students and found that 33 percent had cheated on a fairly regular basis and an additional 45 percent admitted to having done so less frequently. Economics majors and members of fraternities or sororities were found to be especially prone to academic dishonesty. Popular methods included copying from another student's test paper, studying with the help of old exams, using "cheat sheets," plagiarizing term papers and even stealing tests in advance. Widely publicized scandals at several military academies reinforce the suspicion that cheating is rampant on some campuses.

Ironically, the Internet hasn't just made research easier, but also cheating as the availability of student papers either for sale or even free has exploded. When Anthony Krier, a reference librarian at Franklin Pierce College searched the net in January 1997, he found about 50 sites that offered term papers. Just six months later, he was able to find about twice as many on-line. Though Krier intended the list for professors worried about plagiarism among their students, he also received requests for the list from students apparently looking for more sites to find papers.

Not that buying papers is a new notion. Traditional term paper mills or the legendary dorm stash have existed for a long time. What is new, though, "is the number of places where papers are available, the ease with which they can be obtained and the often brazen ways that do-it-yourself Internet sites now flaunt the ability to cheat and plagiarize electronically." Some sites add disclaimers, but others openly invite students to use their material to cheat.

Students' reasons for cheating vary, from the time-honored preference for partying over studying to more recent pressures to succeed in an increasingly competitive environment. The fact that academic dishonesty seems to be especially common in large classes and at larger schools suggests that the impersonality of the multiversity may also be a contributing factor. For this reason, Moffatt suggests that smaller classes and more teacher-student contact, along with more frequent revision of tests and less reliance on multiple choice questions may be effective ways of reducing the prevalence of cheating.

Even when it comes to those infamous term papers, Bruce Leland, an English professor at Western Illinois University, doesn't think it is necessarily all doom and gloom. He maintains that the sites simply present a challenge to professors. He says ". . . teachers who tailored assignments to work done in class, monitored the students' progress — from outline to completion, rather than just seeing a finished work — and were alert to papers that were radical departures from a student's past work were unlikely to be fooled."

Sources

Applebome, Peter. "On Internet Sites, Term-Paper Files Become Hot Items." *The New York Times*, August 8, 1997, pp. 1 and 30.

Gordon, Larry. "Survey By a Rutgers Professor Shows Widespread Student Cheating," *Philadelphia Inquirer* (November 25, 1991).

Discussion Questions

1) Ask students how widespread they believe cheating to be on their campus. Do they think that this is becoming an increasingly serious problem? What steps might help to alleviate it?

2) Given the sociological definition of deviance, if well over half of the students at a college admit to academic dishonesty, can this practice still be regarded as fully deviant?

Supplemental Lecture Material
Women in Prison

Historically, sociologists have devoted very little attention to female criminal behavior, primarily because women have been, and continue to be, far less prone than men to commit crimes. However, there is evidence of a sharp upturn in female criminality in recent years. This trend has been reflected in all segments of the criminal justice system, including the prisons. Whereas for decades women had constituted a steady 4 to 6 percent of all prisoners, by 1989 they made up 8.7 percent of new admissions to correctional institutions.

Many of the problems that women experience in prison are a direct result of their smaller numbers. Most states have provided only one women's prison, which has meant that hardened criminals were likely to be mixed in with lesser offenders and that the variety and the educational, rehabilitative and vocational programs available to female inmates have generally been greatly inferior to those provided in men's prisons.

But the most serious problem for imprisoned women usually concerns their children. About 70 percent of female prisoners are mothers. When fathers are locked away, their children are usually looked after by their mothers, but when mothers are imprisoned, their children normally live with their grandparents or are placed in foster care. Separation from their children is usually intensely painful for these women; one, living apart from her 17-year-old daughter and 7-year-old son, said "I miss them to death. [Separation] was the worst of all my experiences in jail. Being locked up wasn't so bad. [Separation] almost destroyed me. My son is my heart."

Because, as previously noted, most states have only one prison for women, mothers are frequently confined hundreds of miles away from their children, making visiting difficult and expensive. Only one U.S. prison — Bedford Hills in New York — provides an onsite nursery. Under these circumstances, many mothers worry about being able to establish and maintain adequate bonds with their children.

Proposals to help these women center around the expansion of alternative sentencing. If female offenders could serve their sentences in the community, families would not be broken up and more advantage could be taken of rehabilitative services located outside prison walls.

Source
Fessler, Susan Raikovitz. "Behind Bars: Women's Needs Are Unmet." *Albany Times Union* (August 4, 1991).

Discussion Questions
1) Should serious female offenders be allowed to maintain regular contact with their children or should separation be considered part of their punishment?

2) Co-correctional institutions have been widely proposed as a partial solution to the special problems which women face in the penal system. Do you support such institutions, or should prisoners continue to be generally segregated by gender?

Supplemental Lecture Material
Youth Gangs on the Rise

Imagine two scenarios:
1. You live in an apartment in a big city. You look out the window one afternoon and see a group of teenage African-American boys hanging out at the corner. What is your first thought?
2. You're driving through a small Texas town and pull in to the local fast-food restaurant, passing a group of teenage white boys hanging out by a car. What is your first thought?

If the first scenario instantly made you think of a gang, think again. These days, rural areas and small towns are just about as likely to be the site of gang activity, according to the 1995 National Youth Gang Survey conducted by the National Youth Gang Center (NYGC).

The NYGC contacted over 4,000 law enforcement agencies throughout the country. Not only did they find that there were more than 660,000 youth gang members and more than 23,000 gangs active in those jurisdictions. Here are some of the survey's findings:

- All states have gangs, with — not surprisingly — the most gangs in the states with the highest populations. Therefore, the more than 58 percent of gang members can be found in California, Illinois and Texas.

- Few large cities were gang-free.
- Of the agencies that replied to the survey, 90 percent felt the problem would either stay the same or get worse.
- Over half (59 percent) of those law enforcement agencies reported gang activity had specially allocated personnel in response.
- Youth gangs are appearing in new places, particularly smaller and rural communities. "Ninety-four percent of police departments and 93 percent of sheriff's departments serving fewer than 10,000 persons reported that had '1-9 gangs.'" (p. 14) In fact, "half the respondents reporting youth gang problems in 1995 serve populations under 25,000."(p. 20)

Source
Bilchik, Shay (admin.), 1995 National Youth Gang Survey (August 1997)

Discussion Questions
1) Without considering whether they have committed crimes or not, in your opinion, should gang members be considered deviant? If so, use the structural-functional, and symbolic-interaction paradigms to explain why young men in particular might be drawn to gangs. What might be some of the negative results of labeling these young people as deviant?

2) What might explain the increase of gang problems in smaller or rural communities?

3) Why might gang members be more prone to commit crimes? What might be done to avert more young people joining gangs?

Supplemental Lecture Material
**Gun Control and Crime Control:
The Same Issue?**

Gun control easily ranks as one of the most persistent and divisive issues for Americans over the past few decades, particularly in regard to handguns and "assault" weapons. Both proponents and opponents of gun control look to rising crime rates for support for their positions.

America certainly seems to have a problem with using guns, especially handguns. Gun murders in the U.S. are far more common than they were 30 years ago, and more common than they are in any other Western industrial section. And the number of people killed in America with handguns appears to be increasing. Why do so many in the United States die from shootings? What role does our relative lack of gun control play in the high death rate? Why are we different from other Western industrialized countries?

Cultural reasons appear to play an important role. In the United States, the fear of crime often leads to the possession of weapons even when the fear of crime is not well founded. A 1998 Gallup poll found that 40 percent of Americans had a gun in their household, which is linked to Gallup's finding that some 90 percent of the respondents believed that the amount of crime in the United States has risen over the previous twelve months — in spite of FBI figures that show that the amount of crime has actually been decreasing in recent years. And while juvenile crime as a whole is down even more dramatically than adult crime, the number of youths murdered by firearms went up 153% from 1988 to 1995.

Like the citizens of a number of other countries, many Americans react to the level of shootings by demanding more gun control; some 70 percent of Americans favored stricter gun control in a 1993 *Time* poll. But Americans also seem to have little faith in gun control as an ultimate solution for reducing the number of shootings, especially when compared to the perception of crime. This attitude is perhaps best characterized by the National Rifle Association (NRA) slogan that "Guns don't kill people. People kill people."

Other countries appear to have more faith in police protection, the restriction of firearm sales, and the process of certifying and registering legal handgun users than Americans. More to the point, voters in these countries seem more prepared to connect the spread of firearms and the increase in the number of deaths from those firearms, whereas Americans do not see a contradiction between owning a weapon and being more likely to suffer from its use.

How will this attitude change? There is no clear direction from legislation. Some weak federal gun control laws have been passed, such as the so-called Brady Bill of 1993 that imposed a five-day waiting period and a limited background check. Later, a Clinton-backed law banned the manufacture and importation of assault weapons.

These relatively mild laws faced stiff opposition, particularly from the NRA. (The NRA's hard line stances, however, have contributed to a 20% drip in membership from 3.5 million in 1995 to 2.8 million in 1998.) Interestingly, gun sales reached record levels just before the passage of the bill, perhaps reflecting a perception that the Brady Bill would be more restrictive than it actually is. What may be even more telling is that the number of states allowing their citizens to readily obtain concealed handgun permits has taken a sharp upsurge, beginning a new stage in our experimental, contradictory, and dangerous relationship with handguns.

Sources

Herbert, Bob. "Deadly Data on Handguns." *New York Times* (March 2, 1994): E6.

Hornblower, Margot. "Have Gun, Will Travel." *Time* (July 6, 1998): 44-46.

Lacayo, Richard. "Still Under the Gun." *Time* (July 6, 1998).

Placayo, Richard, "Beyond the Bardy Bill." *Time* (December 20, 1993:28-31.

Van Biema, David. "License to Conceal." *Time* (March 27, 1995):26-29.

Discussion Questions

1) Recent data from Florida suggest that a rapid increase in the number of concealed handgun permits may not substantially increase the number of handgun deaths. Does this support the traditional position of the NRA or the views of gun-control proponents? Why or why not? What might explain the lack of change?

2) Do you or anyone in your household own a gun? For what purpose? If not, would you purchase one for your home if your safety felt threatened in your neighborhood? Why or why not?

Supplemental Lecture Material
Copycat Crime

Copycat crimes are certainly not a new phenomena. Tylenol bottles laced with poison on supermarket shelves (1982), syringes planted in pepsi cans (1993) and letters purposely containing deadly anthrax (1998) all occurred in years when a wave of similar crimes suddenly began appearing across the country. "Ever since the Columbine High School killings, the copycat syndrome has been working overtime" says Adam Cohen (*Time*, May 31, 1999). Within weeks of those shootings, hundreds of schools were hit with threats of Columbine-style threats at their own schools, and 20% said their schools had been evacuated because of a bomb threat.

Harvard psychologist William Pollack believes that the epidemic of imitation "starts with kids who are already close to the edge." Copycats model themselves on crimes (both real and fictional) that get a lot of attention. Sometimes copycats are just looking for pointers on how to commit a crime effectively (mode copying). But copycat criminals are often bored more by the sheer thrill of making headlines. "It becomes a power trip for the powerless, those who feel they have nothing to lose" says Cohen.

While some say less attention should be given to notorious crimes when they happen, others argue that what's needed is not less coverage but more information about how these cases turn out. That's part of the story few copycats have in mind while day-dreaming about their "moment in the sun."

Source

Cohen, Adam. "Criminals as Copycats." *Time* (May 31, 1999):38.

Discussion Questions

1) What's your feeling about keeping events like the Columbine shootings off the front page (as the Chicago Sun-Times did after the tragic shootings) or national television coverage?

2) What are some of the factors that create a sense of powerlessness among Americans today (thus making them more vulnerable to seeking a sense of power through copycat crime)?

3) What role does the Internet play in contributing to copycat crimes?

Chapter 9

Sexuality

I. Understanding Sexuality.
  A. **Sex** refers to the biological distinction between females and males.
  B. Sex and the body.
      1. **Primary sex characteristics** refer to the organs used for reproduction, namely, the genitals. **Secondary sex characteristics** are bodily differences, apart from the genitals, that distinguish biologically mature females and males.
      2. In rare cares, a hormone imbalance before birth produces a **hermaphrodite**, a human being with some combination of female and male genitalia.
      3. **Transsexuals** are people who feel they are one sex even though biologically they are the other.
  C. Like all dimensions of human behavior, sexuality is also very much a cultural issue.
      1. Almost any sexual practice shows considerable variation from one society to another.
      2. One cultural universal is the **incest taboo**, a norm forbidding sexual relations or marriage between certain relatives.

II. Sexual Attitudes in the United States.
  A. Alfred Kinsey set the stage for the **sexual revolution** by publishing a study of sexuality in the United States in 1948.
      1. The sexual revolution came of age in the late 1960s when youth culture dominated public life and a new freedom about sexuality prevailed.
      2. The introduction of "the pill" in 1960 both prevented pregnancy and made sex more convenient.
  B. The **sexual counterrevolution** began in 1980 as a conservative call for a return to "family values" by which sexual freedom was to be replaced by sexual responsibility.
  C. Although general public attitudes remain divided on premarital sex, this behavior is broadly accepted among young people.
  D. The frequency of sexual activity varies widely in the U.S. population. It is married people who have sex with partners the most and report the highest level of satisfaction.
  E. Extramarital sex is widely condemned. But extramarital sexual activity is more common than people say it should be.

III. Sexual Orientation.
  A. Sexual orientation refers to a person's preference in terms of sexual partners.
      1. The norm in all societies is **heterosexuality**, meaning sexual attraction to someone of the other sex.
      2. **Homosexuality** is sexual attraction to someone of the same sex.
      3. **Bisexuality** refers to sexual attraction to people of both sexes.
      4. **Asexuality** means no sexual attraction to people of either sex.

B. What gives us a sexual orientation?

    1. Sexual orientation: a product of society.

    2. Sexual orientation: a product of biology.

    3. Critical evaluation. Sexual orientation is most likely derived from both society and biology.

C. How many gay people? In light of the Kinsey studies, many social scientists estimate that 10 percent of the population are gay.

D. The gay rights movement.

    1. In recent decades, the public attitude toward homosexuality has been moving toward greater acceptance due to the gay rights movement that arose in the middle of the twentieth century.

    2. The gay rights movement also began using the term **homophobia** to describe the dread of close personal interaction with people thought to be gay, lesbian, or bisexual.

IV.   **Sexual Controversies.**

A. Teen pregnancy.

    1. Surveys indicate that while 1 million U.S. teens become pregnant each year, most did not intend to. Today, most teenagers who become pregnant are not married.

    2. SEEING OURSELVES—National Map 9-1: Teenage Pregnancy Rates Across the United States.

    3. CRITICAL THINKING BOX—Sex Education: Problem or Solution?

B. Pornography.

    1. **Pornography** refers to sexually explicit material that causes sexual arousal. Pornography is popular in the United States.

    2. Traditionally, people have criticized pornography on moral grounds.

    3. Other critics see pornography as a cause of violence against women.

    4. Pressure to restrict pornography is building from a coalition of conserrvatives (who oppose on moral grounds) and progressives (who condemn it for political reasons).

C. Prostitution.

    1. **Prostitution** is the selling of sexual services.

    2. WINDOW ON THE WORLD—Global Map 9-1: Prostitution in Global Perspective. In general, prostitution is widespread in societies of the world where women have low standing in relation to men.

    3. Prostitutes fall into different categories, from call girls to street walkers.

    4. Prostitution is against the law almost everywhere in the United States, but many people consider it a victimless crime.

    5. GLOBAL SOCIOLOGY BOX—Sexual Slavery: A Report from Thailand.

D. Sexual violence and abuse.

    1. Rape is actually an expression of power.

    2. Date rape refers to forcible sexual violence against women by men they know.

      a. CRITICAL THINKING BOX—Date Rape: Exposing Dangerous Myths.

V.   **Theoretical Analysis of Sexuality.**

A. Structural-functional analysis.

    1. The need to regulate sexuality. From a biological perspective, sex allows our species to reproduce. But culture and social institutions regulate with whom and when people reproduce.

    2. Latent functions: the case of prostitution. According to Kingsley Davis, prostitution is widespread because of its latent functions.

3. Critical evaluation. This approach ignores the great diversity of sexual ideas and practices found within every society. Moreover, sexual patterns change over time, just as they differ around the world.

   B. Symbolic-interaction analysis.

        1. The social construction of sexuality. Almost all social patterns involving sexuality have seen considerable change over the course of the twentieth century.

        2. Global comparisons. The broader our view, the more variation we see in the meanings people attach to sexuality.

        3. Critical evaluation. The strength of the symbolic-interaction paradigm lies in revealing the constructed character of familiar social patterns. One limitation to this approach is that not everything is so variable.

   C. Social-conflict analysis.

        1. Sexuality: reflecting social inequality. We might wonder if so many women would be involved in prostitution at all if they had economic opportunities equal to those of men.

        2. Sexuality: creating sexual inequality. Defining women in sexual terms amounts to devaluing them from full human beings into objects of men's interest and attention.

        3. **Queer theory** refers to a growing body of knowledge that challenges an allegedly heterosexual bias in sociology.

        4. Critical evaluation. Applying the social-conflict paradigm shows how sexuality is both a cause and effect of inequality. But this approach overlooks the fact that sexuality is not a power issue for everyone. And this paradigm ignores the progress our society has made toward eliminating injustice.

   D. CONTROVERSY AND DEBATE BOX—The Abortion Controversy.

Chapter Objectives

1) Define sex.

2) Define sex from a biological perspective.

3) Define sex from a cultural perspective.

4) Summarize the profound changes in sexual attitudes and practices during the last century, noting in particular, the sexual revolution and the sexual counter-revolution.

5) Summarize research findings on sexual behavior in the United States with regard to premarital sex, sex among adults, and extramarital sex.

6) Identify and define four sexual orientations along the sexual orientation continuum.

7) Present the two arguments on how people come to have a sexual orientation.

8) Discuss the role of the gay rights movement in moving the public attitude toward homosexuality toward greater acceptance.

9) Discuss the issues surrounding the high rate of teenage pregnancy.

10) What are the objections to pornography?

11) Examine types of prostitution and the extent of prostitution around the world.

12) Discuss the range of sexual violence and abuse in the United States.

13) Examine human sexuality by applying sociology's three major theoretical paradigms.

Essay Topics

1) Explain how sexuality is a cultural issue.

2) Do you think that the United States is a restrictive or permissive society when it comes to sexuality?

3) Debate one side of the argument on how people come to have a sexual orientation. Defend your position.

4) Can you think of any other movements that have used terminology to change public opinion?

5) What type of sex education programming do you think would be effective in reducing the high rate of teenage pregnancy?

6) Where do you stand on this issue?

7) Do you think prostitution is a "victimless crime?" Why or why not?

8) Compare and contrast sociology's three major paradigms in their application to the study of sexuality.

9) Identify "rape myths" from the text. Does this change your understanding of what rape is? If so, how?

10) The conservative pro-life people view abortion as a moral issue, while liberal pro-choice people view abortion as a power issue. How do you view abortion?

Integrative Supplement Guide

1. ABC Videos:

1. Welfare for Unwed Teen Mothers (*World News Tonight/AA*, 2/9/95)
2. The Law and Gay Rights in America (*Nightline*, 10/9/95)
3. Supreme Court Studies Sexual Harassment (*This Week with Sam & Cokie*, 4/26/98)

2. Transparencies - Series V:
• T-46 Prostitution in Global Perspective
• T-73 Measuring Sexual Orientation

Supplemental Lecture Material
Sex on the Net: Tracking Cyberporn

As the Internet has expanded beyond the Defense Department and industrial laboratories and into dormitories, children's bedrooms, and homeoffices, its content has evolved as well. Highly graphic sexual material such as hard-core commercial photos and video shorts, sex-themed live "chat" rooms, and explicit pay-per-view videoteleconferencing have all become more common. Anecdotal reports and casual browsing can lead to the impression that there is a lot of pornographic material on the Internet.

Some intriguing work has confirmed such suspicions. Researchers at Carnegie Mellon University took advantage of the consumer-tracking potential of the Internet, and over an eighteen-month period studied what pornographic material was actually being consumed at a number of Usenet newsgroups. They reached a number of conclusions:

- There is a great deal of online pornography. On the newsgroups with image files, some 83 percent of the images were pornographic in nature, and in total the researchers examined over 900,000 explicitly written video, and photographic materials.
- According to the researchers, pornography probably represents "one of the largest (if not the largest) recreational applications of computer networks."
- Pornography is quite lucrative for its purveyors. The top five subscriptions-based adult bulletin-board services (BBS) of the many thousands in the market all make over one million dollars annually.
- Pornographic consumers are widespread. In keeping with the Internet's decentralized nature, the researchers tracked clients from every state in America and over forty countries, some of which ban all forms of explicit material.
- Most consumers are men. BBS operators estimate that some 98.9 of their clients are

men; at least some of the women who can be found in chat rooms are paid to be there.

- Online pornography is quite varied in its content. "Perhaps because hard-core sex pictures are so widely available elsewhere, the adult BBS market seems to be driven largely by a demand for images that can't be found in the average magazine rack: pedophilia (nude photos of children), hebephilia (youths), and what the researchers call paraphilia — a grab bag of 'deviant' material that includes images of bondage, sadomasochism, urination, defecation, and sex acts with a barnyard full of animals."

For perspective, the Usenet is probably only about 10 percent of the whole of the Internet, and while explicit files are obviously popular, they also represent no more than about 3 percent of the content of the Usenet.

Still, pornography has long presented challenges to American culture. Defining what pornography is, regulating its consumption and distribution, and limiting its subject matter have all been the subjects of complex legal and moral arguments. And the Internet is proving to be a fruitful new ground for those arguments. Should the Internet be treated like a print medium, which would give it strong precedence for legal protections under the First Amendment? Or is the Internet like a broadcast medium, like television or radio, whose content can be regulated? Perhaps just as relevant is how the content on the Internet could be regulated, which presents difficult technical issues.

One kind of solution is growing up from the base of Internet users. Several companies offer software that, once a parent or teacher has subscribed to the service, regularly updates a list of explicit sites on the subscriber's computer and prevents users from visiting those sites. But based on past legal cases alone, it seems likely that solutions from above — from Congress, the Supreme Court, and perhaps even other countries — will be attempted in order to regulate the flow of pornography.

Source

Elmer-Dewitt, Philip. "On a Screen Near You: Cyberporn." *Time* (July 3, 1995):38-45.

Discussion Questions

1) Do you feel that the Internet should be treated like a print media or a broadcast media? Why? How do you think it will be treated?

2) Do you think the content of the Internet should be regulated? Why? How should it be regulated?

3) What does pornography on the Internet tell us about American sexual behaviors and attitudes? Does the Internet seem likely to maintain pre-Internet attitudes about sex, or will it cause Americans to view sex in a fundamentally new way?

Supplemental Lecture Material
Teaching Schoolchildren about Homosexuality

As public awareness concerning nontraditional sexual orientations has escalated, an increasing number of proposals have been made to include information about gay and lesbian lifestyles in public school curricula. Such proposals have aroused substantial controversy.

Some opposition comes from parents who feel that under no circumstances should schools mention what parents regard as morally unacceptable behavior. They argue that teaching about homosexuality has the effect of condoning such behavior. Other parents are concerned because they believe that this topic is being introduced too early. When the New York city school district developed a program entitled "Children of the Rainbow," designed to promote acceptance of a wide variety of diverse lifestyles, many parents and local school boards objected because a unit in which teachers urged their students "to view lesbians/gays as real people to be respected and appreciated" was originally targeted for the first grade. Chancellor Joseph Fernandez eventually backed off, agreeing that consideration of sexual orientation could be delayed until the fifth or sixth grade.

Opponents to inclusive curricula have also been concerned about the placement of books such as *Heather Has Two Mommies, Daddy's Roommate,* and *Gloria Goes to Gay Pride* in school libraries, even if such books are not on required reading lists.

Many school districts allow students to be excused from classes in which homosexuality is discussed, although few parents take advantage of this option — only 1.5 percent in Fairfax County, Virginia, did so.

Advocates of such inclusive programs in the curriculum stress that accurate information about gay lifestyles is especially important in an era when misinformation concerning AIDS is widespread and gay-bashing incidents remain common. They also emphasize the importance of such instruction in helping gay students recognize and come to grips with their own sexual orientation.

Source

Lacayo, Richard. "Jack and Jack and Jill and Jill," *Time* Vol. 140 No. 24 (December 14, 1992):52-53.

Discussion Questions

1) Were you taught about gay and lesbian lifestyles in school? If so, how did you and other students react to this instruction?

2) Do you think that inclusion of a unit on homosexuality in the public school curriculum amounts to condoning this behavior? Why or why not?

Supplemental Lecture Material
Legal Rights for Same-Sex Couples

It may well be a decision by Canada's Supreme Court that breaks the ice in granting legal rights to same-sex couples. The ruling, which centered on the case of an Ontario woman seeking financial support from her former female partner, does not address the issue of homosexual marriages. The 8-1 ruling that the heterosexual definition of spouse is unconstitutional may, however, give same-sex partners all the legal benefits of a common-law marriage.

The court gave Ontario six months to amend its laws, noting that dozens of its laws use the heterosexual definition. Because of the decision, the Canadian federal government and other provinces also were required to come into accordance with the ruling or face lawsuits, and several provincial premiers have already said their laws would change.

The Supreme Court decision is the result of an appeal of a 1995 decision that upheld a Toronto lesbian woman's efforts to receive alimony from her ex-partner. Two lower courts agreed with her argument that a spouse is not necessarily someone of the opposite sex. The Supreme Court's ruling backed the lower courts, saying, "It is clear that the human dignity of individuals in same-sex relationships is violated by the definition of 'spouse'." The court's ruling also said "The exclusion of same-sex partners (from the benefits of spousal support) promotes the view that… individuals in same-sex relationships generally are less worthy of recognition and protection." (U.S. courts have and continue to consider similar cases.)

Since the ruling does not recognize same-sex marriages, it does not mean same-sex couples in the U.S. could cross the border to get married. It does mean, however, that large parts of Canadian law, including tax code, health care, and insurance benefits, will need to be rewritten.

(It should be noted that the two women involved in the case, who had lived together for more than five years, had settled the dispute out of court, but the high courts review of the law continued.)

Source

Associated Press Release. Newsday.com (May 24, 1999).

Discussion Questions

1) British Columbia's premier, Glen Clark, has stated that "…its time that we treated people with equality and dignity regardless of their sexual orientation." Do you agree or disagree? Why or why not?

2) To date, the legitimacy of homosexual marriages has not been established in either the U.S. or Canada. Is this an example of culture lag? Explain your position on the subject.

Supplemental Lecture Material
"Facts & Stats on Teen Pregnancy"

Some questions we need to ponder on teen pregnancy in the U.S. today:

How bad is the problem?
- The United States has the highest rates of teen pregnancy and births in the western industrialized world. In 1997, teen pregnancy cost the U.S. at least 7 billion.
- More than 4 out of 10 young women become pregnant at least once before they reach the age of 20 — nearly one million a year. Eight in ten of these pregnancies are unintended and 80 percent are to unmarried teens.
- The teen birth rate has actually undergone a gradual decline from 1991 to 1996 with an overall decline of 12 percent for those aged 15 to 19. The largest decline since 1991 by race or ethnicity was for black women. (The birth rate for black teens aged 15 to 19 fell 21 percent between 1991 and 1996 [Hispanic teen birth rates declined 5 percent between 1995 and 1996.] Hispanic teens now have the highest birth rates.)

Who suffers the consequences?
- Only one-third of teen mothers receives a high school diploma.
- Nearly 80 percent of teen mothers end up on welfare.
- The children of teenage mothers have lower birth weights, are more likely to perform poorly in school, and are at greater risk of abuse or neglect.
- The sons of teen mothers are 13 percent more likely to end up in prison while teen daughters are 22 percent more likely to become teen mothers themselves.

What helps prevent teen pregnancy?
- Religious or moral values.
- Fear of contracting a sexually transmitted disease.
- Not having met the appropriate partner.
- Strong emotional attachments to parents.
- Being raised by both parents (biological or adoptive) from birth. (At age 16, 22 percent of girls from intact families and 44 percent of other girls have had sex at least once.)

Source

National Campaign to Prevent Teen Pregnancy. "Whatever Happened to Childhood? The Problem of Teen Pregnancy in the U.S." Washington, D.C. (1997).

Discussion Questions

1) Seven in ten teens interviewed said they were ready to listen to things parents thought they weren't ready to hear. In addition, asked about the reasons why teenage girls have babies, 78 percent white and 70 percent of African-American teenagers reported the lack of communica-tion between a girl and her parents to be a major factor. What can be done to improve adolescent-parent lines of communication?

2) A majority of sexually active teenage boys and girls who were sexually active said that they wish they had waited. Discuss the factors that encourage sexual activity among teens.

Chapter 10

Social Stratification

I. Social stratification refers to a system by which a society ranks categories of people in a hierarchy. There are four basic principles of stratification:
  A. Social stratification is a trait of society, not simply a function of individual differences.
  B. Social stratification persists over generations.
    1. However, most societies allow some social mobility or changes in people's position in a system of social stratification.
      a. Social mobility may be upward, downward, or horizontal.
  C. Social stratification is universal but variable.
  D. Social stratification involves not just inequality but beliefs.

II. Caste and Class Systems.
  A. A **caste system** is social stratification based on ascription.
    1. Two Illustrations: India and South Africa.
    2. GLOBAL SOCIOLOGY BOX—Race as Caste: A Report from South Africa. Under the apartheid system, South African blacks were treated as a subordinate caste.
    3. Caste systems shape people's lives in four crucial ways:
      a. Caste largely determines occupation.
      b. Caste systems generally mandate endogamy.
      c. Powerful cultural beliefs underlie caste systems.
      d. Caste systems limit outgroup social contacts.
    4. Caste systems are typical of agrarian societies because the lifelong routines of agriculture depend on a rigid sense of duty and discipline.
  B. In a **class system,** social stratification is based on both birth and individual achievement.
    1. Industrial societies move towards **meritocracy,** social stratification based on personal merit.
    2. In class systems, **status consistency,** the degree of consistency of a person's social standing across various dimensions of social inequality, is lower than in caste systems.
  C. Birth and Achievement: The United Kingdom.
    1. The estate system. During the feudal era, British society was divided into three estates:
      a. The first estate was the hereditary nobility.
      b. The second estate was the clergy.
      c. The third estate was the commoners.
    2. The United Kingdom today is a class society, but it retains important elements of its former caste system.

D. Another example: Japan.
    1. Feudal Japan was divided into several castes as well:
        a. Nobility.
        b. Samurai or warriors.
        c. Commoners.
        d. The burakumin or outcasts.
    2. Japan today consists of "upper," "upper-middle," "lower-middle," and "lower" classes and people move between classes over time. But they may still size up one's social standing through the lens of caste.

E. The former Soviet Union.
    1. Although the former Soviet Union claimed to be classless, the jobs people held actually fell into four unequal categories:
        a. apparatchiks or high government officials.
        b. Soviet intelligentsia.
        c. manual workers.
        d. rural peasantry.
    2. The second Russian Revolution.
        a. Gorbachev introduced perestroika and in 1991, the Soviet Union collapsed.
        b. Social mobility is relatively common in the Soviet Union, especially **structural social mobility,** a shift in the social position of large numbers of people due more to changes in society itself than to individual efforts.

F. Stratification persists because it is backed up by an **ideology**, cultural beliefs that justify social stratification.
    1. Plato and Marx on ideology. Plato explained that every culture considers some type in inequality "fair." Marx understood this fact, although he was far more critical of inequality than Plato.
    2. Historical patterns of ideology. Ideology changes as a society's economy and technology change.
    3. CRITICAL THINKING BOX—Is Getting Rich "The Survival of the Fittest"? Spencer's view that people get more or less what they deserve in life remains part of our individualistic culture.

III. The Functions of Social Stratification.

A. The **Davis-Moore thesis** is the assertion that social stratification has beneficial consequences for the operations of a society.
B. Critical evaluation:
    1. It is difficult to specify the functional importance of a given occupation; some are clearly over- or under-rewarded.
        a. CRITICAL THINKING BOX—Big Bucks: Are the Rich Worth What They Earn?
    2. Davis-Moore ignores how social stratification can prevent the development of individual talents.
    3. The theory also ignores how social inequality may promote conflict and revolution.

IV. Stratification and Conflict.
  A. Karl Marx: class and conflict.
      1. Marx saw classes as defined by people's relationship to the means of production.
          a. Capitalists (or the *bourgeoisie*) are people who own factories and other productive businesses.
          b. The proletarians sell their productive labor to the capitalists.
      2. Critical evaluation:
          a. Marxism is revolutionary and highly controversial.
          b. Marxism has been criticized for failing to recognize that a system of unequal rewards may be necessary to motivate people to perform their social roles effectively.
          c. The revolutionary developments Marx considered inevitable within capitalist societies have failed to happen.
  B. These reasons are suggested for the failure of Western capitalism to experience a Marxist revolution:
      1. The capitalist class has fragmented and grown in size, giving more people a stake in the system.
      2. A higher standard of living has emerged.
          a. Blue-collar occupations, lower-prestige work involving mostly manual labor, have declined.
          b. White-collar occupations, higher-prestige work involving mostly mental activity, have expanded.
      3. Workers are better organized than they were in Marx's day, and their unions have been able to fight for reform.
      4. The government has extended various legal protections to workers.
      5. Supporters of Marxist thought respond:
          a. Wealth remains highly concentrated.
          b. White-collar jobs offer no more income, security or satisfaction than blue-collar jobs did a century ago.
          c. Class conflict continues between workers and management.
          d. The laws still protect the private property of the rich.
  C. Max Weber identified three distinct dimensions of stratification: class, status and power.
      1. Following Weber, many sociologists use the term **socioeconomic status,** a composite ranking based on various dimensions of social inequality.
      2. Inequality in history: Weber's view. Weber noted that each of his three dimensions of social inequality stands out at different points in the evolution of human societies.
      3. Critical evaluation.
          a. Although social class boundaries may have blurred, all industrial nations still show striking patterns of social inequality.
          b. Income inequality has increased in recent years. Because of this trend, some think Marx's view of the rich versus the poor is correct.

V. Stratification and Technology: A Global Perspective.

  A. Structured inequality is minimal in hunting and gathering cultures.

  B. A small elite controls most of the resources in horticultural, agrarian, and pastoral societies.

  C. Industrialization initially increases inequality, but over time social inequality declines somewhat.

  D. This historical progression is illustrated by the **Kuznet's Curve.**

  E. WINDOW ON THE WORLD—Global Map 10–1: Income Disparity in Global Perspective.

        1. Countries that have had centralized, socialist economies display the least income inequality, although their standard of living is relatively low.

        2. Industrial societies with predominantly capitalist economies have higher overall living standards, accompanied by severe income disparity.

        3. The low-income countries of Latin America and Africa exhibit the most pronounced inequality of income.

VI. Social Stratification: Facts and Values.

  A. Explanations of social stratification involve value judgments.

  B. CONTROVERSY AND DEBATE BOX—The Bell Curve Debate: Are Rich People Really Smarter?

Chapter Objectives

1) Define and state the four basic principles of social stratification.

2) Distinguish between caste and class systems.

3) Discuss how the mix of caste and meritocracy in class systems operates in the United Kingdom and in Japan.

4) Explain the role of ideology in social stratification.

5) Examine differences between the structural-functional and social conflict analyses of stratification.

6) Evaluate the Davis-Moore thesis.

7) Suggest reasons why a Marxist revolution has not occurred in the advanced capitalist societies.

8) Identify and describe Max Weber's three dimensions of inequality.

9) Examine how stratification changes as societies pass through the stages of sociocultural evolution as outlined by the Lenskis.

10) Discuss the role of politics and values in the study of inequality.

Essay Topics

1) Suggest some of the ways that an individual's position in the contemporary U.S. stratification system affects that person's life.

2) The negative consequences of living in a caste system are quite evident, especially to someone raised in a class society. Can you think of any positive consequences of caste?

3) What powerful ideologies exist in various societies that shape social stratification?

4) Do you feel that it would be either desirable or possible to establish a truly classless society? Why or why not?

5) Do you agree with Herbert Spencer's assertion that getting rich is all about "the survival of the fittest"? Why or why not?

6) Do you agree with the Davis-Moore thesis? Why or why not?

7) Do you believe that Marx's predictions that advanced capitalist societies would eventually experience revolutions were simply wrong, or has the revolution merely been postponed? Discuss.

8) What are the similarities and differences between Marx and Weber's social conflict views of stratification?

9) Analyze the relationship between a society's technology and its type of social stratification drawing on Gerhard Lenski and Jean Lenski's model of sociocultural evolution.

10) Do you agree with Hernstein and Murray's assertion that there is such a concept as "general intelligence?" Why or why not?

Integrative Supplement Guide

1. **Transparencies - Series V:**
- T-50 Economic Inequality in Selected Countries, 1980-1996
- T-51 Social Stratification and Technology Development: The Kuznets Curve
- T-52 Income Disparity in Global Perspective

Supplemental Lecture Material
Executive Pay

The U.S. is characterized by great extremes of wealth and poverty. The plight of the poor during the past few years is well known. How have the rich been faring? The case of Gilbert F. Amelio offers some insight. During his 17-month tenure as head of Apple Computer Inc., the company lost almost $2 billion. When the board dismissed him in 1997, Mr. Amelio received a severance pay of $6.7 million, in addition to his $2 million in salary and bonus for the year. (Carol Bowie, research director of executive Compensation advisory Services in Springfield, VA, concludes that "There is no longer any risk financially in being a CEO.") A recent survey of 352 CEO's showed that, in 1997, a year in which corporate profits increased by 8.9 percent, CEO salaries and bonuses increased 11.7 percent compared with 5.2 percent the year before. Their median compensation was $1,596,667. That's up from $1,471,250 in 1996.

Furthermore, note that in the long run stock options are more valuable than bonuses or pay raises so long as the market continues to rise. Because of the substantial size of some CEO options, their ultimate profits could well be astronomical.

"Risk-free" compensation takes many forms…inflated signing bonuses, guaranteed first year signing bonuses, colossal grants of stock options and restricted shares, midterm "retention" bonuses tied solely to longevity, and loans for share purchases that are insulated against plunging prices.

New York compensation consultants Wm. M. Mercer Inc.'s survey conducted for the Wall Street Journal tracked the value shares owned by CEO's at the end of their companies 1997 total shareholder return (i.e., the change in stock price plus declared dividends). The median value of CEOs stakes was nearly $8 million, while the median total shareholder return (or TSR) equaled 29.7%. The top earner among CEOs in 1997 was Sanford I. Weill, Travelers Groups, Inc., with total direct compensation of $230.5 million. (This figure includes a $220.2 million gain from exercising stock options and restricted stock valued $777,322 at the time of the grant.)

On the other hand, middle managers, lacking lavish stock options, actually saw their pay raises trailing inflation for the first time in a decade. Some even had to absorb pay cuts. Paychecks of non-union salaried workers grew a modest 4.2% in 1997 compared to 47% the year before. (Base pay for CEOs advanced 5.3% in 1997 compared to 5.1% the year before.) Overall U.S. wages went up an estimated 3.1% in 1997 compared with a 2.85 rise in 1996. It's when one adds in the windfall from stock option exercises, any comparison of CEOs with other American employees ends.

Shifting executive compensation from salaries and bonuses to stock options is often defended as a move toward pay-for-performance. In theory, CEOs will benefit if their corporations thrive and will lose money if they do not. However, there are at least two weaknesses in this argument. First, "most plans are additions to pay. This means most plans are all reward and no risk" (p.R6). Second, "stock plans also allow executives to benefit from a rising stock market, and not necessarily from superior corporate performance" (p.R6).

Sources

Bennett, Amanda. "Hard Times Trim CEO Pay Raises." *Wall Street Journal* (April 17, 1991).

Lubin, Joann S. "Executive Pay: Pay for No Performance." *Wall Street Journal* (April 9, 1998): R1 & R4.

Discussion Question

1) How would supporters of the Davis-Moore theory justify these levels of executive compensation in a society plagued by high rates of poverty and homelessness? Do you find the explanation convincing?

Supplemental Lecture Material
Russia's New Problem – Poverty

Prior to the dissolution of the Soviet Union in 1991, most people had a place to live and food to eat — for all means and purposes the system of resource distribution was working. Standards of living were below those in the west (particularly in housing) but daily life was predictable. The Soviet leadership was legitimately able to say that their form of socialism had succeeded in nearly eliminating the kind of poverty that existed in Czarist Russia.

But Russian citizens now live in different times. The country's transformation to a more open economic system has created (at least temporarily) a large new group of people in poverty. A September, 1997 census Brief based the measurement of poverty in Russia on identifying households with incomes below 50 percent of the median adjusted for household size and composition. It found that there has been an economic "free fall" during the transition from the economic system prior to 1992 to the one that exists today. According to official Russian estimates, more than one-third of Russia's people were living in poverty in 1992 (one year after the breakup of the Soviet Union. Consumer prices increased 26 times and earning power fell one-third in the first 12 months. By 1994, real income had fallen to 60 percent of 1991's level.

Of the groups studied (households with householders who were unemployed), women, people under age 64 and the least educated were the most likely to live in poverty. Educationally, those with the equivalent of a high school education or less are twice as likely to be poor as those with more schooling. (This finding may indicate that, in a more competitive society, levels of education are an important benchmark for economic success.

"Transfer of income" kept the elderly above poverty. The ability to access disability allowances, pensions, private gifts, stipends for dependent children and generally meager unemployment benefits give the elderly an advantage over younger workers. (Sixty percent of poor households with householders between 18 and 54 have no such supplemental income.)

By 1995, there were signs of economic improvement. The percent living in poverty in Russia (according to their official data) declined from 33.5 percent in 1992 to 24.7 percent in 1995. The likelihood of being in poverty fell from 1992 to 1995 for households with unemployed, female, or younger householders. Only among those with limited education does the outlook remain bleak. (Their limited ability to adapt to an economy that now requires the development of work skills only exacerbates their

already disadvantaged position in Russian society.)

Still, the surge of poverty is a new phenomenon for millions of Russians, and poses an obstacle to economic growth that will continue for years to come.

Source

Rubin, Marc (analyst). "Russia's New Problem – Poverty." U.S. Census Bureau. (Sept., 1998).

Discussion Questions

1) It has been speculated that the Russian revolution of 1917 resulted in the quality of life the average citizen reverted to the level some 50 years before the revolution. How long do you think that it will take Russia to return to the quality of life that existed in 1991 (Just prior to the demise of the USSR)?

2) The definition of poverty in Russia has been the subject of considerable debate. The fact that the definition of poverty in Russia does not include unofficial or black-market income, income is one hot topic of debate. What are some other factors that might distort determining the degree of poverty in Russia today?

Supplemental Lecture Material
Blue Bloods: Born or Bought

As you have learned from the textbook, the United Kingdom today is primarily a class system, though aspects of the caste system survive. Take the House of Lords, for example. "The upper chamber includes hereditary peers, who inherit the right to sit there along with their titles; life peers (appointed by the Queen on the recommendation of the Prime Minister), and 26 bishops and archbishops from the Church of England." (Darnton, p. 8) It will not come as a surprise that the body is overwhelmingly conservative.

The House of Lords does not have a great deal of political power, but it can delay bills passed by the House of Commons, and often acts to revise others.

Granted, some reforms have been enacted. In 1958 a law created those so-called life peerages mentioned above, which cannot be passed on to descendants, while also allowing women to take seats. Nonetheless, hereditary peers still make up about three-fifths of the active body, that means, those Lords have the right to vote simply through birth, nothing else. Which means that in a few years the House of Lords might well include a felon, the Marquess of Blandford, "who has a lengthy record of forgery, assaulting policemen, cocaine possession and failure to pay child support. Currently and tellingly bankruptcy is the only ground for losing the right to be a member.

Later attempts to undermine the power of the Lords have been unsuccessful. Even the Labor Party now in power is "backtracking from more radical pledges," such as turning the Lords into an elected body. (Ibid). Apparently no one knows what the House of Lords should become.

Those in support of keeping the current structure of Parliament maintain that the House of Lords functions as a sort of legislative pause, a chance to think through proposed bills and make needed amendments.

While the United Kingdom is struggling with how to change an anachronistic system, certain people in the United States seem to have a hankering to return to it, or at least some of its trappings. Whenever a British peer is willing to sell a title, citizens of the country priding itself on its democracy come running. Most of the buyers are still newly rich Britons; U.S. citizens are the largest group of buyers outside the country.

Take entrepreneur Douglas Hall for example. He purchased not just one, but two lordships, one for himself, one for his business associate. His stated motive? Making money from endorsing products or selling his own, such as a proposed Lord Threshfield restaurant with pictures of Threshfield, a place he's never even visited.

Joe Hardy, whose title "offers the right to preside over a medieval court leet, at which manor business is discussed and the villagers must ask the ford for permission to extend their hedges or erect new fences. 'I've got everything money could buy. . .,' Mr. Hardy said. . .'but this gives me the chance to play with people's lives.'" (McKee, p. 50) In spite of what Hardy said, he has been a benefactor to the village, and has since passed the title on to his daughter.

Sources
Darnton, Joe. "The Battle Cry 'Reform!' Rocks the House of Lords." *New York Times,* April 21, 1996, pp. 1 and 8.

McKee, Victoria. "Blue Blood and the Color of Money." *New York Times* (June 9, 1996):49-50.

Discussion Questions
1) Using social theory, speculate on what factors might be keeping the House of Lords in power.

2) What do you think about the rush of some U.S. citizens to buy a peerage? Do you think either motive of the two examples above is more understandable than the other? How can you explain either of them, keeping in mind the stratification of our society?

Executive Pay in Hard Times

The U.S. is characterized by great extremes of wealth and poverty. The plight of the poor during the difficult economic times of the past few years is well known. How have the rich been faring? A recent analysis in the Wall Street Journal suggests that the case of Barry Sullivan, CEO of the First Chicago corporation, may be typical.

First Chicago was hard hit by the economic turmoil of the times, and as a result, Mr. Sullivan was forced to forgo his entire bonus in 1991, cutting his salary by 50 percent to a measly $736,000. But before you start to organize a charity drive to assist the near-destitute Sullivan family, you should know that the company rushed to his rescue by giving him 65,000 stock options as well as 25,000 restricted shares valued at a total of $662,500.

Sullivan's case is typical. CEO salaries are still rising, on the average, but the rate of increase has been slowed. A survey of 352 CEO's showed that, in 1990, a year in which corporate profits declined by 6.8 percent, CEO salaries and bonuses increased 6.7 percent compared with 8 percent the year before. Their median compensation was $981,000. However, 101 of these men exercised stock options or stock appreciation rights for an additional median gain of $485,000, up from $428,000 the previous year. The median total CEO compensation in 1990 was, therefore, in excess of $1.4 million.

Furthermore, note that in the long run stock options are more valuable than bonuses or pay raises so long as the market continues to rise. Because of the substantial size of some CEO options, their ultimate profits could well be astronomical. Consider the admittedly extreme case of "the four-million share grant to H.J. Heinz Co., Chairman Anthony J.F. O'Reilly. With a grant price of $29.88, the face value of the grant was $119.5 million, or 115 times his annual pay. Each $1 rise in the price of the stock yields Mr. O'Reilly a $4 million gain on these options. With the stock trading above $39 this month, his paper profits already exceed $36 million..." (p. R6).

On the other hand, middle managers, lacking lavish stock options, actually saw their pay raises trailing inflation for the first time in a decade. Some even had to absorb pay cuts.

Shifting executive compensation from salaries and bonuses to stock options is often defended as a move toward pay-for-performance. In theory, CEO's will benefit if their corporations thrive and will lose money if they do not. However, there are at least two weaknesses in this argument. First, "most plans are additions to pay. This means most plans are all reward and no risk" (p. R6). Second, "stock plans also allow executives to benefit from a rising stock market, and not necessarily from superior corporate performance" (p. R6).

Source
Bennett, Amanda. "Hard Times Trim CEO Pay Raises." *Wall Street Journal* (April 17, 1991).

Discussion Question
1) How would supporters of the Davis-Moore theory justify these levels of executive compensation in a society plagued by high rates of poverty and homelessness? Do you find the explanation convincing?

Supplemental Lecture Material
Class Is in Session: The Stratifying Effects of Russia's New Economy

While the old Soviet Union was certainly not the classless society it pretended to be, the top and the bottom of its economic hierarchy were separated by fewer steps than most of Western Europe or the United States. The Soviet economy kept many from rising very high, but it also prevented many from falling too far. While homelessness existed, for instance, the communist system held out more safety nets than now exist in the United States. The death of the Soviet Union and the emergence of a more capitalist Russia, however, have changed the upper and lower limits of the socioeconomic scale.

Russia now has few places to catch its free-falling citizens ⌐ _ _ provide. British Charities Aid Association in the *Christian Science Monitor* suggest that as many as 4 million of Russia's total population of 148 million are homeless, compared to some 600,000 homeless in America (which has a population closer to 238 million). The same organization believes that there are between 300,000 and 1 million homeless children alone in Russia.

The loss of state-funded social supports, changes in the economy that leave the government unable to continue funding those services, and the dissolution of uncompetitive industries have created this new class of citizens.

An ever-increasing divorce rate that generates poverty-mired single-parent households is probably the biggest single cause of the number of homeless children. Ethnic unrest in old Soviet republics has also led to an enormous increase in the number of refugees in cities. Many refugees are unable to find housing under the Soviet-designed housing system.

The few shelters are overcrowded and offer grim living at best. Many children are faced with prostitution, begging, stealing, and living in train stations. In fact, many homeless or low-income parents send their children out to beg:

> To pay the rent, [seven-year-old] Nadia works with other children at a busy intersection, where they wait until the light turns red and then hustle cars for cash. The children, none of whom attends school, scamper in front of the vehicles, beating their small hands on the windows and breathing exhaust fumes for hours at a time. On a good day, Nadia earns . . . just enough to pay the rent [for the night at the welfare barracks] and eat. [Her mother] Galina, who works part-time at a book kiosk, would earn that much working full-time for a month. (Sloane, p. 10)

In contrast, prior to 1991 almost all Russian children were sent by the Soviet government to government-funded summer camps, and children were so valued that child labor of almost any kind was illegal.

But the picture is not bleak for everyone. "Car ownership has risen by 40 percent in Moscow [between 1992 and 1994] . . . . [and] living standards have actually improved," according to a 1994 article in *The Economist*. Government statistics in that year suggest that household incomes rose 18 percent in the first six months of 1994 alone. Western luxury goods can be readily had — at premium prices. Other estimates suggest that many Russians are moving out of poverty, and the government reports show that the number of people living below the poverty line fell by half between June 1993 and June 1994. In spite of arguments about the amount of corruption in the government and in business and the sense of mafia pervasiveness, many Russians are clearly benefiting from the booming new economy.

The future of those Russians left out of the boom is unclear. Russian charities, forbidden by the Soviet government as unnecessary in a communist system, have begun to develop, and foreign charities are doing what they can. But as the Russians emulate western forms of government and capitalism, they appear to be inevitably facing western problems of stratification on a Soviet scale.

Sources

"Russian Capitalism: Under New Management." *The Economist* (October 8, 1994) pp. 21–23.

Sloane, Wendy. "Hard Times for Russia's Children." *Christian Science Monitor* (August 22, 1994):9–11.

Discussion Questions

1) What types of class-related conflict seem likely to develop in Russia as a result of growing stratification?

2) What long-term problems can you envision for Russia's homeless? How do they differ from what you know about the homeless in the United States? Do prospects seem encouraging in Russia for the homeless?

Chapter 11

Social Class in the United States

I. Dimensions of Social Inequality.
   A. U.S. society is highly stratified, but many people underestimate the extent of structured inequality in U.S. society for the following reasons:
      1. In principle, the law gives equal standing to all.
      2. Our culture celebrates individual autonomy and achievement.
      3. We tend to interact with people like ourselves.
      4. The United States is an affluent society.
   B. **Income** consists of wages or salaries from work and earnings from investments. U.S. society has more income inequality than most other industrial societies.
   C. **Wealth** consists of the total amount of money and other assets, minus outstanding debts. It is distributed even less equally than income.
   D. Power is also unequally distributed.
   E. Occupational prestige. Occupation serves as a key source of social prestige since we commonly evaluate each other according to what we do.
   F. Schooling affects both occupation and income.

II. Social Stratification and Birth.
   A. Ancestry. Family is our point of entry into the social system.
   B. Gender. On average, women have less income, wealth, and occupational prestige than men.
   C. Race and ethnicity.
      1. Race is closely linked to social position in the United States.
      2. Historically, people of English ancestry have enjoyed the most wealth and wielded the greatest power in the United States.
      3. SOCIAL DIVERSITY BOX—The Color of Money: Being Rich in Black and White. The number of affluent African Americans has increased markedly in recent years, but well-to-do blacks differ from their white counterparts in significant ways.
   D. Religion.
      1. Throughout our history, upward mobility has sometimes meant converting to a higher-ranking religion.

III. Social Classes in the United States.
   A. The upper class. Historically, though less so today, the upper class has been composed of white Anglo-Saxon Protestants.
      1. The upper-upper class includes less than 1 percent of the U.S. population.

2. The lower-upper class are the "working rich"; earnings rather than inherited wealth are the primary source of their income.

3. CRITICAL THINKING BOX—Caste and Class in America: The *Social Register* and *Who's Who.*

B. The middle class includes 40 to 45 percent of the U.S. population and has a tremendous influence on our culture.

1. The upper-middle class have an above-average income in the range of $50,000 to $100,000 a year.

2. The average-middle class typically work in less prestigious white-collar occupations or in highly skilled blue-collar jobs. Household income is between $35,000 and $50,000 a year, which is about the national average.

C. The working class make up one-third of the population. Their blue-collar jobs yield an income of between $20,000 and $40,000 a year.

D. The lower class make up 20 percent of our population. Low income makes their lives unstable and insecure.

IV. The Difference Class Makes.

A. Health. Richer people live, on average, seven years longer because they eat more nutritious food, live in safer and less stressful environments, and receive better medical care.

B. Values. Affluent people with greater education and financial security are more tolerant of controversial behavior, while working-class people tend to be less tolerant.

C. Politics.

1. More privileged people support the Republican party, while people with fewer advantages favor the Democrats.

2. Well-off people tend to be more conservative on economic issues but more liberal on social issues. The reverse is true for those people of lower social standing.

3. Higher-income people are more likely to vote and join political organizations than people in the lower class.

D. Family and gender.

1. Most lower-class families are somewhat larger than middle-class families.

2. Working-class parents encourage conventional norms and respect to authorities; whereas parents of higher social standing transmit a different "cultural capital" to their children, stressing individuality and imagination.

V. Social Mobility.

A. **Intragenerational social mobility** is a change in social position occurring during a person's lifetime; **intergenerational social mobility** is upward or downward social mobility of children in relation to their parents.

B. Myth versus reality.

1. Four general conclusions about social mobility in the United States:

a. Social mobility, at least among men, has been fairly high.

b. The long-term trend in social mobility has been upward.

c. Within a single generation, social mobility is usually small.

d. Social mobility since the 1970s has been uneven.

C. Mobility varies by income level.

D. Mobility varies by race, ethnicity and gender.

E. The "American Dream:" Still a reality?

    1. For many workers, earnings have stalled.

    2. Multiple job holding is up.

    3. More jobs offer little income.

    4. Young people are remaining at home.

    5. SEEING OURSELVES—National Map 10–1. "Fear of Falling" across the United States.

F. The Global Economy and U.S. class structure. Much of the industrial production that gave U.S. workers high-paying jobs a generation ago has moved overseas. In their place, the economy now offers "service work," which often pays far less.

VI. Poverty in the United States.

A. **Relative poverty** refers to the deprivation of some people in relation to those who have more. **Absolute poverty** is a deprivation of resources that is life-threatening.

B. The extent of U.S. Poverty.

    1. In 1997, 13.3 percent of the U.S. population was tallied as poor.

    2. Another 12 million people were marginally poor—defined as living on income no greater than 125 percent of the poverty threshold.

C. Who are the poor?

    1. Age.

        a. Four in ten of the U.S. poor are children under the age of eighteen.

        b. SOCIAL DIVERSITY BOX—U.S. Children: Bearing the Burden of Poverty.

    2. Race and ethnicity. African Americans are about three times as likely as whites to be poor.

    3. Gender and family patterns.

        a. The **feminization of poverty** is the trend by which women represent an increasing proportion of the poor.

    4. Urban and rural poverty. The greatest concentration of poverty is found in central cities.

        a. SEEING OURSELVES—National Map 11–3: Median Household Income across the United States.

D. Explaining poverty.

    1. One view: The poor are mostly responsible for their own poverty.

        a. The poor become trapped in a culture of poverty, a lower-class subculture that can destroy people's ambition.

    2. Another view: Society is primarily responsible for poverty.

        a. Most of the evidence suggests that society rather than the individual is primarily responsible for poverty.

        b. CRITICAL THINKING BOX—When Work Disappears: The Result Is Poverty.

        c. Weighing the evidence. The reasons that people do not work seem consistent with the "blame society" position.

d. The working poor. Two-and-a-half percent of full-time workers earn so little that they remain poor.
E. Homelessness.
   1. Counting the homeless. As many as 1.5 million poeople are homeless at some time during the course of a year.
   2. Causes of homelessness:
      a. Personality traits.
      b. Societal factors.
F. CONTROVERSY AND DEBATE BOX—The Welfare Dilemma.

Chapter Objectives

1) Identify and describe the dimensions of social class in the United States.

2) Recognize the continuing importance of ascriptive factors such as ancestry, gender, race and ethnicity, and religion in determining an individual's class placement in the United States.

3) Characterize the four social classes in the United States.

4) Examine ways in which social standing is linked to health, values, politics, and family life.

5) Distinguish between intergenerational and intragenerational social mobility.

6) Discuss trends in social mobility in the United States.

7) Distinguish between absolute and relative poverty.

8) Discuss the extent of poverty in the United States.

9) Provide a profile of the poor in the United States.

10) Debate the issue of whether poverty is a result of individual or social factors.

11) Examine the causes and scope of the problem of homelessness.

Essay Topics

1) What are the dimensions of social class in the United States?

2) Distinguish between the upper-upper class and the lower-upper class.

3) Did any of the rankings of occupations reported in Table 11-1 surprise you? If so, what does this suggest concerning the differences between the criteria you consider important compared with those evidently employed by most Americans?

4) How is your social standing linked to your health, values, politics, and family life?

5) Has your family experienced significant upward or downward mobility over the past three or four generations? How do you think your values and behavior might differ had you experienced the opposite pattern of mobility?

6) How has the global economy impacted the U.S. class structure?

7) What are some of the possible implications of a major slowdown in the rate of upward social mobility in the U.S.? In particular, reflect upon how this might affect the core ideology used to legitimate our system of social stratification.

8) Do you think Temporary Assistance for Needy Families (TANF) will be a way to end welfare?

9) Most sociologists clearly believe that poverty is primarily a result of social forces, while most Americans explain poverty as a result of personal inadequacies among the poor. Why do you think that this is the case? What sorts of solutions to the problem of poverty follow logically from each position?

10) What are the causes of homelessness?

Integrative Supplement Guide

1. ABC Videos:
*   Whose Contract, Whose America? (*Nightline*, 4/7/95)
*   Working Off Welfare, Working on Welfare Reform (*Nightline*, 6/19/95)
    Middle Class-The Family Dream (*Nightline*, 1/6/95)
    The End of Welfare *(Nightline*, 10/17/96)
    Clinton Social Welfare Propositions (*This Week with Sam & Cokie*, 1/11/98)

2. Transparencies - Series V:
*   T-53 Distribution of Income and Wealth in the United States by Income
*   T-54 Distribution of Income and Wealth in the United States by Wealth
*   T-55 U.S. Family Income

*   T-56 Income Disparities for Selected Industrial Countries
*   T-57 Schooling of U.S. Adults, 1996 (age 25 and over)
*   T-58 Average Wealth, by Race and Ethnicity of the U.S. Population, 1996
*   T-59 Mean Income, U.S. Families, 1980-1996 (in 1996 dollars, adjusted for inflation)
*   T-60 "Fear of Falling" Across the United States
*   T-61 Median Income, U.S. Families, 1950-1996
*   T-62 The Poverty Rate in the United States, 1960-1996
*   T-63 Child Poverty Across the United States
*   T-64 Median Household Income Across the United States
*   T-65 Assessing the Causes of Poverty
*   T-66 Poverty Threshold for Family of Four

Supplemental Lecture Material
Solutions to the Wealthfare Problem

In 1992, a key part of the Clinton election platform was a promise to revamp welfare. This was accomplished in 1996 with the passage of the "Welfare Reform Act" that established a five year maximum for welfare eligibility, replaced Aid For Dependent Children (AFDC) with Temporary Assistance to Needy Families (TANF), and ended welfare's entitlement status and instead made it a grant-funded program administered by the individual states.

Corporate welfare is still alive and well however and now the question is what can be done to end tax rebates to a selected few that leads to higher taxes for others and cutbacks in essential services. To date, cooperative efforts among states to stop the war of economic incentives to attract corporations have not been effective.

A *Time* (November 30, 1998) special report offers five suggestions that address the corporate welfare (A.K.A. "wealthfare") problem. They are:

1) the levying of a federal excise tax on incentives. Under this proposal, Congress would enact a law imposing a tax equal to the incentives granted to a company. In other words, if New York City and State governments were to give $600 million to the New York Stock Exchange, the Federal government would hit the stock exchange with a $600 million federal tax. Thus, no more value to economic incentives. No more bidding wars among governments.

2) a lawsuit to have incentives declared unconstitutional. (Legal scholars believe the practice violates the Constitution's commerce laws. The Supreme Court would need to decide.)

3) The creation of a special commission that would study federal programs and propose which should be scrapped. That list would go to Congress, which would be forced to vote either to kill or preserve the programs listed. (Of course, any such effort will face stiff opposition from the agencies, departments and special-interest groups that profit from the existing system.)

4) Shut off the flow of low-cost loans from the Department of Housing and Urban Development (HUD) that have helped fuel the competition to "snag" companies. These loans date from the Housing and Community Development Act of 1974 and were aimed at eliminating slums and urban blight. Today, *Time* notes, HUD loans help to bankroll such projects as a waterfront restaurant in Jacksonville, Florida (that later went out of business), a downtown hotel in Philadelphia and an upscale fashion retailer in Spokane Washington. In that case, a $24 million HUD loan arranged by the city of Spokane to construct a new store and enlarge a parking garage for Nordstrom Inc.

5) Sue the worst offenders. This is the course advocated by Dwight D. Bannon, a Dayton lawyer, who sued state and local officials and a one-time Dayton-based company on behalf of its former workers. The company is Hobart Corp., part of an international conglomerate with sales of $2.4 billion in 1997. The company moved thirty miles north to Piqua, Ohio, which offered $2 million in incentives. Sixty-six hourly workers were given three days notice that their jobs would be terminated. (The average ages of workers who lost their jobs was 52. Their jobs were given to part-time workers – average age 34 – from a temporary firm.) Until governments figure out a way to end the practice of corporate welfare, practices such as these will undoubtedly continue.

Source

"Five Ways Out." *Time* (November 30, 1998): 66-67.

Discussion Questions

1) Corporations argue that corporate welfare is motivated by sound economic or operational rationale. Critics see the motivation as corporate greed. What do you think?

2) Why do you think corporate welfare has continued while individual welfare programs experienced a dramatic revision?

Supplemental Lecture Material
Are There Cultural Roots to Poverty?

The conventional diagnosis of the persistence of poverty has pointed to short-falls in education and skills, lack of opportunity, lack of capital, discrimination, and in the Third World, imperialism are all inadequate, according to Lawrence Harrison (a senior fellow at Harvard University's Academy for International and Area Studies).

Harrison believes that a crucial element that has been ignored is "cultural values and attitudes that stand in the way of progress." It makes many people uncomfortable to acknowledge that some cultures produce greater well-being than others. Cultural relativism — the view that cultures can be evaluated only on their own terms — in universities. Many economists believe that people respond to economic signals the same way, regardless of the culture. Harrison, however, points out that "the extraordinary achievements of Chinese, Korean, and Japanese immigrants in the U.S. — and elsewhere — belie these views. "He notes that a recent RAND Corp. Study, "Immigration in a Changing Economy", documents the rapid upward mobility of East Asian immigrants in sharp contrast with immigrants from Mexico and Central America. East Asians in the U.S. substantially exceed the national averages for years of education, while the Hispanic high-school dropout rate is about 30%.

In her 1970 book, "Mexican Americans, "Joan Moore wrote; "Jewish & Japanese children march off to school with enthusiasm. Mexican and Negro children are much less interested. Some sort of cultural factor works here." It could be argued that the Hispanic dropout rate reflects a culture that does not attach a high priority to education. Note the persistence of illiteracy in Latin America (10% in Mexico, more than

40% in Guatemala). The high school drop-out rate in most Latin American countries exceeds 50%.

Harrison contends that progress-prone cultures cross religious and racial lines. "In addition to the Confucian cultures of East Asia, they include Bosques, Sikhs, Jews, Mormons and Americans, not to mention the mainstream culture of the West." Such cultures share the belief that one's destiny can be influenced through considered action, and they attach a high value to work, education, and saving. Progress resistant cultures tend to be passive and fatalistic, less entrepreneurial, and less committed to education.

A growing number of Latin Americans (e.g., novelist Mario Vargas Llosa) have come to the conclusion that culture is at the root of the region's underdevelopment. Lionel Sosa, a Mexican-American advertising executive and author, has come to the same conclusion about Latin American underachievement in the U.S. In his book "*The American Dream*" he notes fatalism, the resignation of the poor and the low priority of education as major obstacles to social mobility. Similarly, Harvard sociologist Orlando Patterson has concluded that culture is the key to understanding the underachievement of African Americans. Harrison also believes that the cultural legacy of slavery, perpetuated by the isolation of Jim Crow and the ghetto, has greatly impacted on not only the persistence of poverty among blacks but also such recently highlighted phenomena as the gap in black-white test scores and the gap in computer usage by blacks relative to whites and Asians.

Still, culture is not destiny. Note the gains made by black Americans in the past several decades — sharply rising educational attainment, declining poverty and unemployment, reductions in crime, and the rapid growth of the middle-class. These trends reflect the escape from the traditional culture to the progressive national cultural mainstream. (In contrast, isolation from that mainstream largely explains the disproportionate poverty of American Indians, particularly the 1.2 million [of a total of 2 million] who live in or on reservations.)

Dallas Morning News columnist Richard Estrada has expressed a concern that the high volume of immigration in the U.S. impedes acculturation to the American mainstream. Multiculturalism — the rejection of mainstream Western culture and the assumption that all cultures are equal — also poses an obstacle to assimilation (to say nothing of its erosive effect on national unity).

Harrison concludes:

> The course of human progress demonstrates that some cultures produce greater good for greater numbers than others. Both home and in the Third World, the antipoverty agenda must address values and attitudes, as difficult and painful as it may be.

Source

Harrison, Lawrence K. *"The Cultural Roots of Poverty."* The Wall Street Journal (July 13, 1999).

Discussion Questions

1) Given the different levels of achievement by Asian immigrants compared to Hispanic immigrants, what are your feelings about reestablishing immigration quotas?

2) Discuss how slavery and Jim Crow laws exacerbated the mainstream acculturation problems of African Americans, compared to Hispanics and Asian immigrants.

3) Native American cultures, with their traditional cultures' emphasis on man's relationship with nature, incubate both a sense of fatalism and egalitarianism that in Harrison's words "discourages initiative and upward mobility". Discuss the cost to Native Americans of abandoning this traditional heritage in exchange for upward social mobility.

Supplemental Lecture Material
Japan: Welfare and Homelessness

Homelessness is an especially serious issue in the United States because of this country's failure to provide the minimum level of social welfare funding. Such a "safety net" feature would be taken for granted in virtually any other industrial democracy, but the problem is by no means unknown in other societies. Even Japan, despite its remarkable economic progress during the last several decades, has a significant population of homeless people.

Nobody knows how many people are without places of permanent residence in Japan, largely because it is very difficult to conduct an accurate census of this highly transient population. "Census takers found 191 homeless people in Yokohama [in October of 1990], but social workers think the number at its peak in the summer is twice that."

There are some marked similarities between the homeless in Japan and those in the United States. Alcoholism is a serious problem for the homeless in each society, and in both societies minorities are disproportionately represented on the streets. Japan's homeless are often Koreans, Filipinos, Bangladeshi and members of the indigenous lower-caste Burakumin ethnic group.

But there are also differences between the two nations. Although a significant percentage of the Japanese homeless are suffering from mental illness, there has been no large-scale deinstitutionalization of mental patients in recent decades such as that which has taken place in the United States. Drugs are a minor problem among the Japanese homeless. "And, unlike the United States, Japan is not faced with large numbers of entire families without homes or people with jobs who cannot find housing."

U.S. officials sometimes charge that many of the homeless are simply lazy people who prefer not to work, a claim that poverty advocates generally regard as grossly distorted. Similar themes are heard today in Japan: "'It may be an oversimplification, but I think most of the homeless are there because they want to enjoy their freedom,' says Yoshinori Shibuya, a senior official in the Yokohama social welfare bureau. 'We urge them to accept welfare payments or to go to the hospital, but 80 percent refuse.'"

However, it is far from easy to receive welfare benefits in Japan. In fact, only 0.7 percent of the population receives such benefits. Compare this to the 4.8 percent of U.S. population who get grants from Aid to Families With Dependent Children, or the 9.7 percent who are food stamp recipients. The reasons the disparity among the two nations is so large lie at the heart of their respective societies and cultures. In Japan, it is the responsibility of the family to take care of its own. Only if a welfare applicant can prove that he or she does not have family to help them will they receive any benefits at all. Nor are healthy people ever eligible, the argument being that they could find work if they wanted to since Japan has a much lower unemployment rate than the U.S.. Unwed mothers are also much rarer, one percent in Japan versus the U.S.'s 30 percent. Moreover, in most cases, most single mothers in Japan are divorced or widowed rather than never married. Because the majority of

those women live with parents or family members that can both support them and help supervise the children, they make up only 9 percent of the welfare roll. The vast majority of recipients are elderly (44 percent). Another 41 percent is made up of households with sick or handicapped persons.

Not only is the family the first source of assistance, the welfare applicant must prove he or she has no assets or savings. Nor are luxuries such as cars or air conditioning allowed once a person receives benefits. Caseworkers who have a much lighter case load than in the U.S. make periodic checks to ensure no one cheats. In fact, welfare fraud is extremely rare.

"Japan does have two elements of a social welfare program that far surpass anything in the United States: universal medical care and comprehensive day care. Everyone has access to doctors and hospitals at affordable prices, with the services free for the poor. And neighborhood nurseries throughout Japan provide excellent care for children. . . for a modest fee that is waived for low-income families." (Kristof p. 10)

In any event, the Japanese cultural emphasis on politeness and saving face impacts the way both homelessness and welfare are handled. As one volunteer worker put it regarding the homeless, "We are careful not to become too familiar with the people we help because it's a shameful thing for them. They get annoyed even if we ask their names. They generally want to be left alone." Similarly, in the government building that houses one welfare office on the sixth floor, a separate hidden elevator ensures that welfare applicants need not be embarrassed. In fact, many people who may well be applicable for welfare never apply at all because of this sense of shame.

Sources

Kristof, Nicholas D., "Welfare as Japan Knows It: A Family Affair." *New York Times,* (September 10, 1996):1 and 10.

Weisman, Steven R. "Japan's Homeless: Seen Yet Ignored." *New York Times,* (January 19, 1991).

Discussion Questions

1) Do you believe that a substantial percentage of the homeless in the United States choose to live on the streets? What makes you feel that this is the case?

2) Do you believe that a welfare system similar to that in Japan could work in the United States? Why or why not? Use whatever information you have learned so far regarding the cultural and societal structures of the two countries that would either make it possible or impossible.

3) **Activity:** Research newspaper articles discussing the pros and cons of the welfare reform bill signed in 1996. Educate yourself on the changes. How do *you* think they will impact the poor? The country?

Supplemental Lecture Material
Tripping on Our Bootstraps:
Single Parents and the Working Poor

The Austin Lounge Lizards, a music group based in Austin, Texas, jeer politicians highly critical of the poor in a song about "Teenage Immigrant Welfare Mothers." Throughout the Reagan, Bush, and Clinton administrations, many public figures have blamed the poor — particularly the heads of single-parent families — as the primary cause for social problems such as drug abuse, the predominance of illegitimacy, the persistence of poverty across generations, and the general decay of America's moral structure.

Some of these public officials have been legislating their opinions into action, trying to limit the number of children in single-parent households, to cut off benefits after a certain period, and to require at least some people receiving public assistance to work in exchange for their checks.

Much of the criticism has recently been levied on unwed mothers. Many reformers point out that almost one-third of children born in the United States each year are illegitimate, and unwed mothers are more than twice as likely to be on welfare as their married counterparts. Many critics of welfare also argue that because the government increases monthly payments as the number of children in a family increases, at least some unwed mothers are making babies for money — roughly an additional 70 dollars a month per child, on average.

Several states have passed so-called family cap laws that are designed to limit family size by not increasing monthly payments when women have more children. Unfortunately, no creditable research has been able to support the view that women are having children to earn money, which calls the effectiveness of these laws into question.

One study focused on New Jersey, the first state to pass such a law. Rutgers University researchers followed 4,428 mothers, some 2,999 of whom would be penalized under the state's family cap law, while the other 1,429 made up the control group who would not be affected. The researchers found "no reduction in the birthrate of welfare mothers attributable" to the new law. Many social workers who agree with these findings believe that far more complex issues than simple cash returns are at work with unwed mothers who continue to have children. Many opponents of family cap laws also believe that such regulations will actually create or perpetuate more severe poverty than now exists.

Why don't the poor improve their lot more often? Likely reasons the poor stay poor are the lack of inexpensive health-care benefits, the high cost of child care and housing, the decreasing number of good-paying jobs, and a lack of marketable job skills.

Government assistance is often an ineffective bridge to economic empowerment. The Urban Institute prepared a study in 1995 of a hypothetical unemployed Pennsylvania mother of two receiving 4,836 dollars from Aid to Families with Dependent Children (AFDC), 2,701 dollars in food stamps, and 3,000 dollars in Medicaid benefits; her total package of cash benefits was 10,527 dollars. Working at a full-time job for minimum wage would only pay 9,516 dollars before taxes, she would lose Medicaid, AFDC, and about one-third of her food stamps, and she would still need to pay (or at least arrange with a friend or relative) for day care.

Unfortunately, the many working poor, who receive few or no government assistance, also face an economically tenuous life threatened by the prospect of illness, disability, and lay-offs. About two-thirds of the Americans without health insurance work. Funds for job retraining and additional education are being cut back by the federal government, as is the earned-income tax credit (EITC), which was promoted by Ronald Reagan as one of the most promising ways in American history to assist the working poor. Ironically, now Republicans are trying to reduce the EITC.

While few Americans would argue about the need to reform the current welfare system, a lot of the changes being discussed in Washington and in state capitols around the country assume that many if not most of the poor have chosen or deserve their poverty.

Marc Boldt, a Congressional representative from Washington State, responded angrily and in writing to a constituent who asked him to help keep a family-education center in his district funded:

> If your situation is subject to so much financial instability, then why did you have three children? Why is your husband in a line of work that subjects him to "frequent layoffs"? Why, in the face of your husband's ability to parent as a result of his frequent layoffs, are you refusing to work outside of the home? Why should the taxpayer foot the bill [for such education programs as this center offers]?

Sources

Gibbs, Nancy. "Working Harder, Getting Nowhere." *Time* (June 20, 1994): 24–33.

Gibbs, Nancy. "The Vicious Cycle." *Time* (July 3, 1995):16–20.

Kramer, Michael. "The Myth about Welfare Moms." *Time* (July 3, 1995):21.

Discussion Questions

1) Do the family cap laws appear to be effective and appropriate? Will there be a widespread deterrent effect? Why?

2) Do you agree with Marc Boldt's letter? What has assumptions about poverty has he made? What effects could come about from policies he might support?

Supplemental Lecture Material
Scraping Bottom: The Poorest Place in America

The 1990 census found that Lake Providence, Louisiana, is probably the poorest place in the United States. Located in the northeast corner of the state near the Mississippi River, the area covered by the Census Bureau's Block 9903 includes about two-thirds of the city and all but one-quarter of its population. The median household income there is only 6,536 dollars, while the government-defined poverty line is more than twice as high at 14,764 dollars for a family of four. The Children's Defense Fund states that about 70 percent of the parish's residents under eighteen live under the poverty line, the highest rate in America. Not surprisingly, local rates of infant mortality, teenage pregnancy, illiteracy, drug use, and welfare dependency are also very high. Even the pawn shop closed down on the poor side of town.

How did Lake Providence get this way? The city — and region — probably represent an extreme example of the kind of poverty found throughout the rural South rather than some new or exceptional form. Most of the poverty is concentrated among the blacks in the city, who suffer many of the same kinds of oppression they faced when slavery was legal. The sharecropping system that replaced slavery after the Civil War indentured the black laborers to their own debt, and advances in farm machinery reduced the need for paid labor. Most local residents with the drive, resources, and desire to make changes made tracks and left town, further concentrating the sense of hopelessness, fear, and apathy.

Taken together, these forces have allowed property and power to remain concentrated in white hands. And although blacks outnumber whites two to one overall and in most local voting districts, many blacks still feel economically threatened by their white employers and unsure of their political voices: "We've still got a lot of people working in white folks' kitchens or driving tractors. They're afraid to speak up for themselves because they're afraid of losing their jobs. They still have to say, 'Yassir, whatever you say,'" says James W. Brown, Jr., mayor of Lake Providence.

In contrast, at least some of the whites consider themselves to be the productive glue that holds the regional society together in the face of government handouts. According to Captain Jack Wyly, a local lawyer, "We don't have any colored leadership. . . . They lost their work ethic; they lost their discipline with all this gimme stuff." Black amorality is the primary cause of black poverty in the eyes of many white residents.

What can change Lake Providence? The area applied in 1994 to become a federal economic empowerment zone to garner tax breaks and grants worth about 100 million dollars. With luck, such a status would bring new industry, economic opportunity, social revitalization, and hope. Jeff Schneider, the president of a local bank, says, "We ought to qualify if anyone does, since there's no place that's worse off than we are here."

Source
White, Jack E. "The Poorest Place in America." *Time* (August 15, 1994):35–36.

Discussion Questions
1) What role does the racism Wyly displays play in the continued poverty of Lake Providence?

2) Encouraging residents to remain in Lake Providence appears to be an important part of rejuvenating the community. How might this occur?

3) Is Lake Providence a relatively unique place in America, or are there many places similar to it?

Chapter 12

Global Stratification

I. Global Inequality: An Overview.
In global perspective, the distribution of wealth is extremely uneven.
   A. Different types of terminology have been used by scholars to divide the nations of the world into several broad categories based on their level of economic development. The traditional typology of the first, second and third worlds is no longer as valid as it once was.
   B. The **high-income countries** are the relatively rich, industrialized nations. They include most of Western Europe, Canada, the United States, Japan, Australia and New Zealand.
   C. The **middle-income countries** are characterized by per capita incomes between $2500 and $10,000 per year. They have experienced some industrialization, but agriculture remains important in their economies. These countries include:
      1. The former Soviet Union and the nations of Eastern Europe.
      2. The oil-producing nations of the Middle East.
      3. Venezuela and Brazil in South America.
      4. Algeria and Botswana in Africa.
   D. The **low-income countries** are primarily agrarian societies with little industry.
      1. Most of the people are very poor.
      2. These countries are found in Central and Eastern Africa and in Asia.

II. Global Wealth and Poverty.
   A. Poverty in poor countries is more severe than it is in the rich countries.
      1. This is partly a result of low economic productivity.
      2. Absolute poverty is a particularly serious problem in the poorest nations.
      3. Relative poverty is more salient in the more developed nations.
   B. Poverty in poor countries is more extensive than it is in rich nations such as the United States.
      1. This contributes to serious problems of hunger and starvation in these societies.
      2. WINDOW ON THE WORLD—Global Map 12–1: Median Age at Death in Global Perspective. In low-income countries, it is children who die, half of them never reaching their tenth birthday.
   C. The extent and severity of child poverty is greatest in the low-income countries.
   D. Women in the poorer nations experience particularly severe poverty.
      1. GLOBAL SOCIOLOGY BOX—"God Made Me to Be a Slave."
   E. Slavery still exists in four forms:
      1. In chattel slavery, one person owns another.
      2. Child slavery includes abandoned children or those living on the street.
      3. Debt bondage occurs where people are paid less than they are charged for food or shelter.

4. Servile forms of marriage are also considered slavery.
F. Correlates of global poverty in the poorest nations:
1. Technology is limited.
2. Population growth is dramatic.
3. Cultural patterns emphasize tradition.
   a. GLOBAL SOCIOLOGY BOX—A Different Kind of Poverty: A Report from India. Indian poverty is extremely severe, although most poor Indians are relatively accepting of their status.
4. Social stratification is very pronounced.
5. Gender inequalities are also dramatic.
6. Global power relations handicap the poorest nations.
   a. Historically, they were oppressed by **colonialism**, the process by which some nations enrich themselves through political and economic control of other countries.
   b. Now, **neocolonialism**, a new form of global power relationship that involves not direct political control, but economic exploitation by multinational corporations, is a more serious problem.
   c. **Multinational corporations** are large corporations that operate in many different countries.

III. Global Stratification: Theoretical Analysis.
A. **Modernization theory** is a model of economic and social change that explains global inequality in terms of differing levels of technological development among societies.
1. Historical perspective: The development of industrial technology has raised the standard of living of even poor people in high-income societies.
2. The importance of culture: Modernization theory identifies tradition as the greatest barrier to economic development.
3. Rostow's stages of modernization:
   a. Traditional stage.
   b. Take-off stage.
   c. Drive to technological maturity.
   d. High mass consumption.
4. The role of rich nations in global economic development:
   a. Helping control population.
   b. Increasing food production.
   c. Introducing industrial technology.
   d. Providing foreign aid.
5. GLOBAL SOCIOLOGY BOX—Modernization and Women: A Report From Rural Bangladesh.
6. Critical evaluation:
   a. Modernization theory has been widely supported among social scientists.
   b. It has heavily influenced the foreign policies of the richer nations.
   c. It has been attacked as a thinly veiled defense of capitalism.
   d. It ignores global forces that thwart the development of the poorer nations.

e. It largely ignores the way in which all nations are linked through the global economy.

f. It holds up the developed world as a model that all nations should emulate, reflecting an ethnocentric bias.

g. It blames victims for their own economic problems.

B. **Dependency theory** is a model of economic and social development that explains global inequality in terms of the historical exploitation of poor societies by rich ones.

1. Historical perspective: The economic success of many wealthier nations was achieved at the expense of the poorer countries.

2. Neocolonialism perpetuates economic relationships shaped under colonialism.

3. Wallerstein's capitalist world economy.

a. Rich nations are the core of the world economy.

b. Low-income nations are at the periphery of the world economy.

c. The dependency of the peripheral nations results from:

1) Narrow, export-oriented economies.

2) Lack of industrial capacity.

3) Foreign debt.

4. Rich nations have contributed to global inequality by their single-minded pursuit of profit.

5. Critical evaluation:

a. Dependency theory correctly emphasizes the interdependency of the world's societies.

b. It treats wealth as a zero-sum commodity.

c. This theory predicts that countries with the strongest ties to rich nations should be the poorest, but this is not the case.

d. Dependency theory ignores the role of traditional culture in maintaining poverty.

e. This theory downplays the economic dependency fostered by the former Soviet Union.

f. The policy implications of dependency theory are vague.

IV. Global Inequality: Looking Ahead.

A. Modernization theory is correct in arguing that world hunger is at least partly a problem of production and technology.

B. Dependency theory is correct in claiming that global inequality is also a problem of distribution and politics.

C. WINDOW ON THE WORLD—Global Map 12-2: Prosperity and Stagnation in Global Perspective.

D. CONTROVERSY AND DEBATE BOX—Will the World Starve?

Chapter Objectives

1) Distinguish between the high-income countries, the middle-income countries, and the low-income countries.

2) Examine the severity of global poverty.

3) Examine the special problems of women and children living in poverty in the world's less- and least-developed nations.

4) Identify correlates of global poverty.

5) Compare and contrast modernization theory and dependency theory.

6) Identify and describe Rostow's stages of modernization.

7) Discuss Wallerstein's model of the capitalist world economy.

Essay Topics

1) What accounts for severe and extensive poverty throughout much of the world?

2) Distinguish between relative and absolute poverty.

3) What are four types of slavery? Where do these occur?

4) What do you think are the main causes of global hunger?

5) Which theory do you think best addresses the issue of alleviating the problem of hunger in the world? Why?

6) What are the stages of modernization?

7) What role does modernization theory and dependency theory assign to rich nations?

8) Is it wise or even possible for Americans to insulate themselves and ignore what is happening beyond their borders?

9) What role can U.S. citizens play in attempting to ease the problems of global poverty? How would the answer of a modernization theorist to this question differ from the answer that might be given by a dependency theorist?

10) What are the weaknesses of modernization theory and dependency theory in solving global hunger?

Integrative Supplement Guide

1. **Transparencies - Series V:**
- T-67 Distribution of World Income
- T-68 The Relative Share of Income and Population by Level of Economic Development
- T-69 Median Age at Death in Global Perspective
- T-70 Percent of Births Attended by Trained Health Personnel
- T-71 Africa's Colonial History
- T-72 Prosperity and Stagnation in Global Perspective

Supplemental Lecture Material
Global Poverty

It appears that North Korea, the last Stalinist country in the world is facing dire economic problems. Its downward spiral started with the collapse of the Soviet Union in 1991 when large subsidies for Pyongyang ended. While little hard data is available, Washington Post reporter Keith Richburg reports from a trip to areas of North Korea most affected by famine. He contends that the country's problems are much deeper than a lack of food — they can be traced to the core of a socialist system "that simply has ceased to work."

Drought damage was apparent during Reichburg's tour — he points out that years of overuse of petroleum-based fertilizers have destroyed much of the arable land according to experts and hills stripped of their topsoil because farmers used it to cover paddy fields, causing increased flooding in the plain. But flooding and record high summer temperatures are only part of the problem. In reality, the food crisis is just part of an overall breakdown of the country's state controlled and centrally planned system. The problems of the country are exacerbated by the fact that the North Korean government has no strategy for how to stop the freefall.

Reichburg describes North Korea as a country that in many ways has reverted from a doctrinaire socialist state to more of a theocracy, with the country's late founder and revered "Great Leader", Kim Il Sung, as its high priest. It was his guiding philosophy called "juche" or self reliance that propelled the country's rush to industrialize in the 50s and 60s. (It has also made it more difficult for North Korea's secretive rulers to admit the extent of the problem to outsiders and to ask outsiders for help.)

On Oct. 8, 1997, three years after the death of Kim Il Sung, his son, Kim Jong Il officially took over leadership of the ruling Korean Workers Party. This has led to speculation that the younger Kim might be willing to break from some of the country's socialist practices and adopt the reforms necessary for the country to survive. (Some relief workers have claimed that they've seen signs of a departure from past practices as six foreign relief agencies based in Pyongyang and outlying provinces were estab-

lished within one year of Kim Jong Il's ascent to power.)

To date, however, most changes in North Korea are not changes coming from the top but from the base. While some North Korean farmers are said to be "double cropping", or planting twice each year (a practice long forbidden by Kim Il Sung) no one is predicting that hardships will lead to any popular disaffection with the regime — in fact, many in North Korea expect attitudes to harden. It appears that officials are trying to transfer some of the popular affection for Kim Il Sung from father to son.

In an interview with Foreign Minister Kim Yong Nam referred to Kim Jong Ii as "the peoples leader, who is acknowledged as a man of ability", a man "who has produced immortal exploits," a general who "enjoys the absolute trust and support of our people", and who embodies "the destiny of our nation as well as the future of our country." The last part of his statement may be the most accurate observation of all.

Source

Reichburg, Keith B. "Beyond a Wall of Secrecy, Devastation." *Washington Post* (Oct. 19, 1997):A1, A23.

Discussion Questions

1) While Deputy Foreign Minister Kim Gye Gwan warmly thanked Rep. Tony P. Hall (D. Ohio) for U.S. food aid, he also notes that North Korea and the United States "are in a state of hostile relations." The question is "Given the food supplies of the U.S. and its influence on U.N. policy, can North Korea afford to maintain such a political posture? Why or why not?

2) What impact might North Korea's

economic freefall during the past decade have on other nations in that part of the world?

3) Compare and contrast how dependency theory advocates and modernization theory supporters would explain North Korea's downward economic turn since 1991.

Supplemental Lecture Material
Debt Bondage and Global Slavery

Officially, foreigners are forbidden to visit the diamond mines of Congo, the former Zaire. Nonetheless, two journalists recently managed to get a look at a mining camp in the jungle of eastern Congo. No wonder the government doesn't tolerate outsiders, since conditions at the mine are not only extremely harsh, but amount to debt bondage, a form of slavery as explained in the textbook.

Here, about 120 miners dig from dawn to dusk at the bottom of sweltering pits in the thick rain forest. Young men wield shovels, the only tools available, to dig their individual plots, risking the occasional cave-in due to lack of equipment. And why? Because though the mine is privately owned, each man pays a small fee for the right to dig a plot of his own and whatever small diamonds he sifts out of the sand are his to keep. Should he be so lucky as to find a large one, he will have to share the profit of its sale with the owner of the mine. Such a find is the stuff dreams are made of, but it is rare.

In fact, everything around them seems to conspire to rob the miners of any hope for more stable work. Just traveling to the regional center to sell their small diamonds is hazardous. "Nearly all the men have stories about how the fruit of many months' toil was seized at gunpoint by

laughing soldiers." Even if they get to the center, the pay for the usual small diamonds is barely enough to buy food and clothes, trapping the miners in an endless cycle of digging and sifting until they are worn out with work and age.

Expanding the investigation of worker exploitation, Kevin Bales has found that a "new slavery" has been produced by modern day demographics and global capitalism. Mr. Bales, an American-born sociologist at the London campus of the University of Surrey, defines global slavery as "a relationship in which one person is completely controlled by another person through violence or the threat of violence for the purpose of economic exploitation." He believes that our understanding of slavery is "muddied" by the obsolete notion of "people as property" so entrenched in the American consciousness. Owning people is already illegal in most of the places where it flourishes, and so contemporary slavery is hardly susceptible to ablution by government frat (as it was in America). Bales points out that "Nowadays, the population explosion plus the globalization of the economy have pushed a lot of people into economic vulnerability." Bribery undermines labor laws, capital flows where labor is cheap, and workers are easily replaced (or in his term "disposable.)

Mr. Bales describes sex slavery that thrives in Thailand for cultural and economic reasons, slavery in India, Pakistan's lucrative manufacturing industries and a variety of forms of debit bondage in India.

In spite of the extent of the problem, Bales is optimistic that governments, corporations, and individuals can fight the problem. To attack overpopulation, he suggests improving education and fighting extreme poverty. To remove violence as a means of exploitation, he urges political leaders to enact and enforce civil protection. And to disable slavery's profit engine, he calls on consumers and investors to support international watchdog groups and to sever their links to the slave trade. This means lobbying for economic sanctions against offending countries, divesting from mutual and pension funds that won't promise to shun slave labor, and buying products certified to be slavery free (e.g., the Rugmark campaign aimed as South Asian Carpet makers).

Sources

Kristof, Nicholas D., "Mine Labor in Congo Dims Luster in Diamonds." *New York Times* (June 1, 1997):9.

Miller, D. W. "Citing Research 7 Morality, Sociologist Depicts New Slavery." *The Chronicle of Higher Education* (May 7, 1999):A21-22.

Discussion Questions

1) How does this example typify the dilemma of poverty in low-income countries? What is the solution to a problem such as this?

2) Discuss how today's slavery and debt bondage would be explained differently by both modernization theory and dependence theory? How might a combination of both address this issue?

Supplemental Lecture Material
Thailand and Child Prostitution

Thailand has become one of the most popular destinations for sexual tourists in the world in recent years. Pedophilic businessmen from Europe, Australia, Japan, the United States, and Taiwan know they can travel there to visit the estimated 200,000 to 400,000 boys and girls in the sex industry, which make up between two-fifths and one-half of the total share of prostitutes in the nation. A 1994 UNICEF report suggests that as many as one million children throughout Asia are sex workers, generally in "conditions that are indistinguishable from slavery."

The market in children is certainly not limited to foreigners in Thailand, however. The nation has numerous brothels, even in small villages to the north that are far away from tourist centers. The widespread use of prostitutes by Thai men has given the country one of the highest AIDS/HIV infection rates in the world, with at least 1 percent of the population now infected. Although the government requires the use of condoms in brothels, the law is infrequently applied. In fact, children are often preferred as partners because many clients of the sex industry believe that children are less likely to have AIDS/HIV. Studies suggest that the highest infection rate in Thailand is among prostitutes under sixteen.

International organized crime syndicates sponsor much of the sex industry in Asia. Local government enforcement of the few regulations surrounding the massage parlors and brothels are often subverted or ignored. While many girls within Asia are knowingly sold by their parents or other family members to traveling agents, others are misled into believing that their children are going to another city to work in manufacturing or as a domestic.

Perhaps most disturbing is the abduction of children. Reliable studies suggest that some gangs kidnap girls (and boys, though less frequently) for use as sexual slaves, chaining them in revolting conditions. Kidnappers work in countries such as the Philippines, Burma, Laos, Cambodia, China, and Vietnam, and the most powerful groups have been known to transport victims — including Americans — across the Pacific to Asia, Hawaii, and Canada.

Unfortunately, child prostitution is proving difficult to control, much less eradicate. Its international market and distribution channels require multinational responses, but many of the countries involved are embarrassed by the problem and minimize or ignore it. Corruption of government officials hampers enforcement and coordination as well, particularly at lower governmental levels.

Efforts, however, are being made. In Denmark, for example, every tourist traveling to a country with an active child sex industry receives a folder, informing them of dangers that sex with children involves, such as a high risk of contracting AIDS. When asked by the Danish Minister of Justice not to sell tours to places where child sex is widespread, all but one Danish travel agency complied.

In addition, several countries are cracking down on those committing sex crimes with children in foreign countries. Sweden was the first country to jail a national convicted of such charges. "Germany, France, Denmark, Ireland, Iceland, Italy, Switzerland and Norway have also passed or extended extraterritorial legislation to allow the prosecution of nationals for offenses committed overseas." (Tranberg)

Equally important to consider is the treatment of the victims of child prostitution. These children have suffered severe psychological and physical damage that will last well into adulthood. Many are infected with HIV/AIDS and other diseases. Clearly, the international response needs to encompass the medical community, psychologists, legal teams, and social services.

Sources

Santoli, Al. "Fighting Child Prostitution." *Freedom Review* (September/October 1994):5–8.

Tranberg, Pernille. "Nordic Authorities Working to Reduce Sexual Exploitation of Children in Poor Countries." *Earth Times News Service* (September 25, 1996).

Discussion Questions

1) How might curbing child prostitution require different strategies if it were not so international in its customer base or in its means of acquiring children? How can the domestic markets in host countries best be limited?

2) Should child prostitution be condoned to some degree since so many Asian cultures have long allowed the practice? Is fighting child prostitution ethnocentric?

3) What might be good strategies for controlling the spread of AIDS/HIV through child prostitutes? How does the problem differ from the spread of AIDS/HIV in the United States?

4) **Activity**: Conduct research to discover how the U.S. government treats citizens convicted of sex crimes against children overseas, then compare that to the stance taken by Europeans. What are the differences? How might they be explained? Which, in your opinion, is better?

Supplemental Lecture Material
Nigeria: Why Didn't It Develop?

Nigeria has always had great promise. Many of its native groups have a long tradition of trading, it holds promising universities and a widespread sense of the value of education, and its extensive oil and gas reserves should have made Nigeria into the economic powerhouse of Africa. But why hasn't Nigeria turned into a South Korea?

The reasons are complex and frustrating. Since Nigeria left the British Empire in 1960, it has had only nine years without a military government in power. Five military coups and four attempted coups have created a climate of crippling political instability. The current leader, General Ibrahim Badamasi Babangida, assumed control in 1985 with the vow to bring a more solid democracy to the country. His continuation in power despite elections shows a change of heart that has too much precedent. Worse, his presidency has moved Nigeria from the lists of middling but slowly developing countries to among the poorest on the continent.

Unlike the citizens of Somalia or Sudan, however, Nigeria's people have nothing to blame but their own government. Nigeria has become known worldwide as a place with endemic political corruption, nonfunctioning phones, intermittent electricity, rampant inefficiency, and grand public projects that are incomplete, over budget, and frequently useless. International investment has fallen away because of the weak and inflationary economy and the decaying infrastructure. Institutionalized bribery and embezzlement at every level of government rob oil revenues, taxes, and duties that would otherwise fund the budget and reduce the nation's debt.

Even if the economy was in sound shape, however, Nigeria would face difficult ethnic problems that challenge its very existence. There are three major tribes, located in separate regions of the country. Religious and cultural rivalries have festered since long before Nigeria's founding as a state, and the discovery of oil in a region dominated by one group, the Igbo, helped fuel a violent civil war in the 1960s. Government corruption that promotes the perception of tribal inequities, combined with the development of increasingly confrontational forms of Islam and Christianity, are feeding renewed feelings of mistrust, which are again coalescing into violence.

But Nigeria's political unrest may reflect a poorly laid foundation. The country's boundaries were defined by the British with little reference to cultural borders; colonial administrators were more concerned with controlling the native population as easily as possible rather than establishing a sustainable and rational basis for a nation-state. As one chief wrote in 1947, "Nigeria is not a nation. It is a geographic expression."

Nigeria does not seem likely to escape its problems any time soon, and many of its citizens are worried about the future. The nation "oscillates between military dictatorship and civilian chaos. We remain unable to establish a political order which can usher in stability and progress and take the occasional shock," says Ken Saro-Wari, a Nigerian writer. The road to development grows ever longer.

Source
"Anybody Seen a Giant?" *The Economist* (August 21, 1993): 3–14.

Discussion Questions
1) Why has Nigeria failed to develop when compared to other low-income countries in Africa? in Asia or South America?

2) Some of the other nations that were also British colonial administrative units broke up into smaller countries after independence. Southern Rhodesia, Northern Rhodesia, and Nyasaland have all disappeared. Would the break-up of Nigeria into a number of lesser states be an advantage to its peoples?

Chapter 13

Gender Stratification

I. Gender and Inequality

A. Gender stratification refers to the unequal distribution of wealth, power, and privilege between men and women.

B. Male-Female Differences. It is important not to think of social differences in biological terms.

C. Gender in Global Perspective.

    1. Sex is considered as irrelevant to most areas of life in the Israeli *kibbutzim*, yet traditional gender roles seem to be reasserting themselves there.

    2. Margaret Mead studied gender in three New Guinea societies:

        a. Among the Arapesh, both sexes would be described by U.S. citizens as feminine.

        b. Among the Mundugumor, both sexes would be described by U.S. citizens as masculine.

        c. Among the Tchambuli, gender roles reverse U.S. standards.

        d. Mead concluded that these case studies prove that gender does vary across cultures.

        e. Critics charge that Mead oversimplified.

    3. George Murdock surveyed over 200 societies and found substantial but not complete agreement concerning which tasks are feminine or masculine.

    4. In sum, what is considered to be female or male is mostly a creation of society.

D. Patriarchy and sexism.

    1. **Patriarchy** is a form of social organization in which males dominate females.

        a. WINDOW ON THE WORLD—Global Map 13-1: Women's Power in Global Perspective. In general, women fare better in rich nations than in poor countries.

    2. **Matriarchy** is a form of social organization in which females dominate males. No matriarchal societies are known to exist or to have existed.

    3. **Sexism** is the belief that one sex is innately superior to the other. It underlies patriarchy and harms men, women, and the society as a whole.

    4. Patriarchy is not inevitable because modern technology has eliminated most of the historic justifications for it.

II. Gender and Socialization.

A. **Gender roles** are attitudes and activities that a culture links to each sex.

B. Parents treat male and female children differently from birth.

C. Peer groups reinforce these differences.

    1. Boys and girls play different kinds of games and learn different styles of moral reasoning from games.

2. APPLYING SOCIOLOGY BOX—Masculinity as Content.
D. Curricula in schools further reinforce a culture's gender roles.
E. The mass media, especially television, also serve this function.
F. CRITICAL THINKING BOX—Pretty Is as Pretty Does: The Beauty Myth.

III. Gender and Social Stratification.

A. In the United States and other industrial societies, women working for income is now the rule rather than the exception. Sixty percent of U.S. married couples depend on two incomes.
B. Women continue to enter a narrow range of occupations, with almost half in clerical or service work. Furthermore, the greater a job's income and prestige, the more likely it is that the position will be held by a male.
C. WINDOW ON THE WORLD—Global Map 13–2: Women's Paid Employment in Global Perspective.
D. Women's entry into the labor market has not substantially reduced their involvement in housework as husbands have resisted increasing their participation in these tasks.
  1. WINDOW ON THE WORLD—Global Map 13-3: Housework in Global Perspective. Our society defines housework and child care as "feminine" activities, even though a majority of U.S. women work outside the home.
E. The average female full-time worker earns about 74 cents for every dollar earned by a male full-time employee.
  1. Most of this results from the different kinds of jobs held by men vs. women.
  2. The greater responsibility for family and childcare tasks that our society has traditionally assigned to women is another factor explaining the earning differential.
  3. Discrimination is a third critical factor.
F. Our society still defines high-paying professions as masculine; this helps to explain why an equal number of women and men begin most professional graduate programs, but women are less likely to complete their degrees.
G. Female involvement in politics is also increasing, although very slowly at the highest levels.
  1. SEEING OURSELVES—National Map 13-1: Women in State Government Across the United States.
H. As technology blurs the distinction between combat and non-combat personnel, women are taking on more more military assignments, though equality has not yet been achieved.
I. While women fit the definition of a minority group, most white women do not think of themselves this way.
J. Minority women are doubly disadvantaged.
K. Violence against women:
  1. Family violence is frequently directed against women.
  2. GLOBAL SOCIOLOGY BOX—Female Genital Mutiliation: Violence in the Name of Morality.

3. Sexual harassment consists of comments, gestures, or physical contact of a sexual nature that is deliberate, repeated and unwelcome.
    a. Women are more likely to be sexually harassed than are men.
    b. Some harassment is blatant but much of it is subtle.
4. Feminists define pornography as a form of sexual violence against women, arguing that it demeans women and promotes rape.

IV. Theoretical Analysis of Gender.

A. Structural-functional analysis suggests that traditional sex roles emerged in hunting and gathering societies where they promoted the efficient functioning of the family. Each sex played a role that complemented the role played by the other, with men taking the instrumental part and women the expressive.

    1. Talcott Parsons argues that gender role complementarity helps to integrate society; that girls and boys are socialized into expressive and instrumental roles respectively; and that social control reinforces gender-linked behavior.

    2. This view has been criticized as follows:
        a. It ignores the fact that many women have had to work outside the home due to necessity.
        b. It ignores the personal strains and social costs produced by rigid gender roles.
        c. It legitimizes the status quo.

B. Social-conflict analysis explains contemporary sex roles in terms of dominance, subordination and sexism.

    1. This perspective draws heavily on the work of Friedrich Engels who felt that capitalism intensified male domination.

    2. This view has been criticized as follows:
        a. It casts conventional families as morally evil.
        b. It minimizes the extent to which people live happily in families.
        c. It argues, perhaps falsely, that capitalism stands at the root of gender stratification.

V. Feminism.

A. **Feminism** is the advocacy of social equality for the sexes in opposition to patriarchy and sexism.

B. Basic Feminist Ideas:
    1. The importance of change.
    2. Expansion of human choice.
    3. Elimination of gender stratification.
    4. An end to sexual violence.
    5. Sexual autonomy.

C. Types of Feminism:
    1. Liberal feminism.
    2. Socialist feminism.
    3. Radical feminism.

D. Opposition to feminism.
   1. Opposition is primarily directed at its socialist and radical forms, while support for liberal feminism is widespread.
   2. There is a trend toward greater gender equality.

VI. Looking Ahead: Gender in the Twenty-first Century.
   A. While changes may be incremental, we are seeing movement toward a society in which women and men enjoy equal rights and opportunities.
   B. CONTROVERSY AND DEBATE BOX—Men's Rights! Are Men Really So Privileged?

Chapter Objectives

1) Define stratification.

2) Make global comparisons with regard to "masculinity" and "femininity."

3) Define the concepts of patriarchy, matriarchy, sexism, and institutionalized sexism.

4) Explain the concept of gender roles.

5) Discuss the role of the family, school, peer groups, and the mass media in the socialization of gender roles.

6) Define gender stratification.

7) Examine ways in which women experience inequality and discrimination in occupations, economics, education, politics, and the military.

8) Discuss the special problems of minority women.

9) Be familiar with some of the ways in which women are victimized through violence, sexual harassment, and pornography.

10) Compare and contrast the structural-functional and social-conflict paradigms with regard to gender.

11) List five general principles of feminism.

12) Identify and describe three types of feminism and discuss reasons why many people resist feminist change.

Essay Topics

1) Do you think most people agree with social scientists that many of the differences between masculine and feminine behavior are culturally rather than biologically defined? Why do many people resist accepting this perspective?

2) Analyze how your own gender role has been shaped by your family, peers, school, and the mass media. Which seems to have had the most impact on you?

3) What are some steps that might be taken to remedy the problem of economic gender inequality? Will equal pay for the same job be enough to solve the problem?

4) Why do you think it has been especially difficult to convince men to share the housework? How did your parents divide up housework? How do you plan to do this in your own marriage?

5) Did female candidates markedly improve their success rate in the 1992 elections? How would you explain this?

6) Many sociologists believe that it will be very difficult to eradicate sexual harassment from our culture. Why might this be the case? What steps would you suggest to work toward this goal?

7) Do you find the structural-functional or the social-conflict analysis of gender-role inequality more convincing? Why?

8) Is structural-functional or social-conflict analysis more optimistic concerning the prospects for gender equality? Discuss.

9) What factors are changing the U.S. labor force?

10) Why do you think many people in this society resist pressures for change in gender roles? Is the strongest opposition from men or women? Discuss.

Integrative Supplement Guide

1. **ABC Videos:**
- Heart to Heart - Real Life True Love Stories (*Day One*, 2/14/94)
- The Law and Gay Rights in America (*Nightline*, 10/9/95)
- They Need Not Apply - Discrimination Against White Men (*20/20*, 11/18/94)

2. **Transparencies - Series V:**
- T-74 Men and Women's Athletic Performance
- T-75 Women's Power in Global Perspective
- T-76 Men and Women in the U.S. Labor Force
- T-77 Women's Paid Employment in Global Perspective

- T-78 Housework in Global Perspective
- T-79 Women in State Government Across the United States
- T-80 Use of Contraception by Married Women of Childbearing Age

Supplemental Lecture Material
Comparable Worth

It appears that the feminists who supported President Clinton through the Monica Lewinsky affair have been rewarded. In February, 1999 Mr. Clinton announced the commitment of $14 million to establish an "Equal Pay Initiative" while also supporting Sen. Tom Daschle's proposed "Paycheck Fairness Act." Clinton explained these steps as proactive steps as an effort to prevent the expansion of a gap in pay between men and women that is reflected by the fact that in 1999, women earned "about 75 cents for every dollar a man earns." This attempt to codify the frequently discredited theory of comparable wealth under another name would be enforced by the Labor Department's Office of Federal Control Compliance.

Diana Furchtgott-Roth and Christine Stolba question the need for such action. They point out that it is already illegal to pay unequal wages to equally qualified men and women who do the same job. When this does occur, women sue and invariably win. But such discrimination is rare. "When adjustments are made for age, experience, education, occupation, and position, women earn approximately the same as men" Furchgott- Roth and Stolba point out.

They suggest that Mr. Clinton's claim that women earn only 75 cents to a man's dollar is based on a crude comparison: all women's salaries vs. all men's salaries. The reality is, however, that the average woman's salary is 75% of the average man's because the average woman has less work experience and is more likely to choose a job that gives her the flexibility to combine work and family and to take time out of the work force to bear and raise children. Rather than discrimination, it's greater choice for women.

In reality, the only way to get rid of the average pay gap is to mandate equal pay for different jobs (i.e., "comparable worth"). That's exactly what Clinton's proposal does, say Furchgott-Roth and Stolba. Since comparable worth has been rejected in courts all over the country, it would require enforcement by legislation-authorized bureaucratic intervention.

Under the Clinton plan, government bureaucrats would "objectively" determine a job's worth by considering working conditions and knowledge required to perform a task. "Neither experience or risk, two factors that increase men's average wages relative to those of women, are included as relevant job-related criteria" say Furchgott-Roth while also noting: "Thus – these criteria favor traditionally female occupations over male ones (secretaries over truck drivers), and white collar jobs requiring education over blue-collar work."

Advocates of comparable worth say that all they want to do is correct market flaws due to discrimination against women, but federal legislation, suggest the authors, is a big step toward an economy ruled by bureaucratic dictate. A philosophical problem of such action is that it suggests that women can't make it on their own. If feminist claims that "women can do any job" are valid, the principle of comparable worth works against women's interests. Logic also dictates that if employers had to pay women higher-than-market wages, fewer women would get hired in the first place.

As of February, 1999, unemployment for both men and women was near a 30-year-low; wages and force participation rates for women were at an all-time high; and the economy was expanding robustly. Furchtgott-Roth and Stolba contend that the best way to help women succeed economically is to keep the economy strong. This is something that in their opinion, Washington can't accomplish by giving bureaucrats more power over the market.

Sources

Furchtgott-Roth, Diane & Christine Stolba, " □Comparable Worth' Makes a Comeback", *New York Times* (February 4, 1999).

Discussion Questions

1) If a law that would sanction meddling with the market in order to achieve "gender justice" were passed, why shouldn't other groups demand a more equitable solution?

2) How would you feel if the Labor Department decided, under a Paycheck Fairness Act mandate, that administrative assistants should be paid as much as oil drillers and teachers as much as construction workers?

Supplemental Lecture Material
Women as High School Football Players

At Lincoln High School in Los Angeles, Luisana Cruz was listed on the Lincoln High Tigers football roster, served as the student body president for the 1999-2000 school year, and as a candidate for homecoming. Three other girls also were on the school football team (as special team players and backup position players) and their coach (Leo Castro) didn't hesitate to send them into a game. Their play is based on their work ethic and attitude, not their sex or gender. These four young women on the football team experienced resentment toward them by the cheerleaders and frequently ambivalent-at-best attitudes on the part of male football team members.

Cruz ended up playing in a losing effort (34-0) against her homecoming football opponent and losing the homecoming queen crown to another student. The question is "Does opting for participation in a traditionally male sport make a woman any less feminine and thus less legitimate a candidate for a traditionally feminine status (e.g., homecoming queen)?

Source

Cruz, Luisana, "A Fullback Picks Her Gown," *Time* (Nov. 15, 1999):17.

Discussion Questions

1) In 1998, 708 girls played high school football (according to the National Federation of State High School Associations). Do you think that this trend that escalate in the future or is it one that will "die a quiet death" as the novelty wears off?

2) What are your feelings about the participation of women in traditionally male sports at the collegiate level?

3) Does women's participation in traditionally male sports increase or decrease the likelihood of their being targets of sexual harassment in high school or on college campuses? Explain your answer.

Supplemental Lecture Material
Rape In South Africa

In a nation that might have the highest incidence of rape in the world, children have become a primary target. Reported cases of sexual assault against children under the age of 18 more than doubled between 1994 and 1998; experts believe the actual numbers may be even higher. In 1997, there were 120.6 rapes for every 100,000 women in South Africa; in the U.S. in 1996 is was 71.

The reasons for this explosion of violence against both women and female children in South Africa are many and varied. The success of the liberation movement left thousands of young South African men without a cause, undereducated, unemployed, and accustomed to violence. At the same time, the breakdown of the apartheid laws triggered widespread migration, with millions of blacks flocking from the homelands to squatter camps in the cities. "Privacy has become scarce among the shacks, alcoholism is rampant and law enforcement is erratic" writes Donna Ferrato, (a *New York Times* reporter). At the same time, it has become difficult for even the most attentive mother to watch over her children.

Add to that, the fact that women have traditionally been held in low regard, and children (in general) are taught to be extremely submissive to adults and sometimes, even strangers. Most recently, the fear of AIDS has made young girls attractive to predatory men; for a time, there was even a rumor that sex with a virgin would cure the disease.

The police are so understaffed that an accused rapist may not even be arrested until months after the crime is reported and the victim may live near him and see him every day. (One 1996 study found that nearly two-thirds of suspected offenders were never prosecuted; of those only 7 went to prison.)

In Soweto, police officers arrest child rapists in weekly roundups in a convoy of unmarked cars, rousting whole families to drag out the accused. (Arriving late at night increases the chances of catching the suspect at home).

As of May, 2000 the rape of young women in South Africa continues to be a major problem. The question is why?

Source

Daley, Suzanne. "Young Vulnerable, and Violated in the New South Africa." *New York Times* (July 12, 1998):31-32.

Discussion Question

1) Rape victims in South Africa are predominantly black women and their attackers are also primarily black. Why do you think that blacks are more prone to be both victims and perpetrators of these acts of violence in South Africa today? Why do you think that this is the case?

Chapter 14

Race and Ethnicity

I. The Social Significance of Race and Ethnicity.
  A. A **race** is a socially constructed category composed of people who share biologically transmitted traits that members of a society consider important. There are no biologically pure races. Race is a significant concept chiefly because most people consider it to be such.
  B. **Ethnicity** is a shared cultural heritage. Ethnicity involves even more variability and mixture than race because most people identify with more than one ethnic background.
  C. A **minority** is a category of people, distinguished by physical or cultural traits, who are socially disadvantaged.
       1. SEEING OURSELVES—National Map 14–1: Where the Minority-Majority Already Exists.
       2. Minorities have two major characteristics:
            a. They share a distinctive identity.
            b. They occupy a subordinate status.

II. Prejudice.
Prejudice is a rigid and irrational generalization about an entire category of people. Prejudices are prejudgments and they may be positive or negative.
  A. **Stereotypes** are exaggerated descriptions applied to every person in some category.
  B. SOCIAL DIVERSITY BOX—Hard Work: The Immigrant Life in the United States. Immigrants represent the bottom level of the national economy.
  C. **Racism** refers to the belief that one racial category is innately superior or inferior to another.
       1. CRITICAL THINKING BOX—Does Race Affect Intelligence?
  D. Theories of prejudice:
       1. **Scapegoat theory** holds that prejudice results from frustrations among people who are themselves disadvantaged.
            a. A **scapegoat** is a person or category of people, typically with little power, whom people unfairly blame for their own troubles.
       2. **Authoritarian personality theory** views prejudice as a personality trait in certain individuals.
       3. The **cultural theory of prejudice** argues that prejudice is embedded in culture.
       4. The **conflict theory of prejudice** proposes that powerful people use prejudice to justify oppressing others.

III. Discrimination

Discrimination is an action that involves treating various categories of people unequally. While prejudice refers to attitudes, discrimination is a matter of action. Like prejudice, it may be positive or negative.

    A. Prejudice and discrimination may combine in four ways, according to Robert Merton.
        1. Active bigotry.
        2. Timid bigotry.
        3. Fair-weather liberalism.
        4. All-weather liberalism.
    B. **Institutional prejudice and discrimination** refers to bias inherent in the operation of society's institutions.
    C. Prejudice and discrimination form a vicious cycle based on the Thomas theorem: situations defined as real become real in their consequences.

IV. Majority and Minority: Patterns of Interaction.

    A. **Pluralism** is a state in which racial and ethnic minorities are distinct, but have social parity.
    B. **Assimilation** is the process by which minorities gradually adopt patterns of the dominant culture.
    C. **Segregation** refers to the physical and social separation of categories of people. It may be voluntary, but is usually imposed.
    D. **Genocide** is the systematic annihilation of one category of people by another.

V. Race and Ethnicity in the United States.

    A. **Native Americans** were the original inhabitants of the Americas. Before European contact, they lived in hundreds of distinct societies. Between 1871 and 1934, they were subjected to a policy of forced assimilation. Now they are being encouraged to migrate from reservations to the cities in search of economic opportunity, but they remain far behind whites in educational and economic standing. Many tribes and individuals have recently come together to assert pride in their culture.
    1. SEEING OURSELVES—National Map 14-2: Land Controlled by American Indians, 1790-1998. Native Americans control just a small share of land in this country.
    B. **White Anglo-Saxon-Protestants** (WASPS), mostly of English origin, have dominated the U.S. since colonial days. Most came to this country highly skilled and motivated to achieve. Especially in the last century, many WASPs strongly opposed subsequent waves of non-Anglo immigrants. Their power is gradually declining as we enter the 21st century.
    1. SEEING OURSELVES—National Map 13-2: The Concentration of People of WASP Ancestry Across the United States. The highest concentrations of WASPs are in Utah, Appalachia and northern New England.
    C. **African Americans** came to this country as indentured servants or slaves. This denial of basic human rights was a sharp contradiction to the promise of the American republic, a fact which sociologist Gunnar Myrdal referred to as "the American dilemma." In 1865, the Thirteenth Amendment to the Constitution outlawed slavery but after Reconstruction, Jim Crow laws perpetuated the subordinate status of African Americans.

In the first part of the twentieth century, a mass migration of African Americans to the cities of the North occurred, followed by the civil rights movement of the 1960s. Even today African Americans continue to be economically disadvantaged as a group, a problem exacerbated by the loss of factory jobs that has accompanied America's move to a service economy. The educational gap between whites and African Americans has narrowed substantially in recent years. Political clout of African Americans has increased substantially in recent decades.

   D. Most Asian Americans make up 4 percent of the United States population. They have a "model minority" image.

      1. Chinese immigration started with the Gold Rush. When the economy soured, discrimination increased and harsh laws were enacted limiting further immigration. In response, most Chinese Americans clustered in closed ghettoes called Chinatowns. Assimilation and upward mobility marked the era that began with World War II. Chinese Americans currently outpace the national average economically and educationally, although many living in Chinatowns continue to experience poverty.

      2. Japanese Americans also came to this country in the last century to work, and soon experienced legal and social discrimination. During the Second World war many were confined in relocation camps. After the war, many made a dramatic economic recovery, and today this group is above the national average in financial standing. Their upward social mobility has also strongly encouraged cultural assimilation and interracial marriage.

      3. More recent Asian immigrants include Koreans and Filipinos.

         a. Large-scale Korean immigration followed the Korean War. Korean Americans often own and operate small businesses.

         b. Filipinos enjoy relatively high incomes.

  E. **Hispanic Americans** make up about 11 percent of the U.S. population.

      1. SEEING OURSELVES—National Map 14-4: The Concentration of Asian Americans, African Americans, and Hispanic/Latinos by County, Projections for 2001.

      2. Most Mexican Americans (or Chicanos) are recent immigrants, though some lived in Mexican territory annexed by the U.S. in the last century. They are well below the national average in economic and educational attainment.

      3. Puerto Ricans are American citizens and travel freely between the island and the mainland, especially New York City. They are the most socially disadvantaged Hispanic minority.

      4. Many Cubans fled the 1959 Marxist revolution and settled in Miami and other U.S. cities. Most were well educated business and professional people and have done relatively well in this country.

  F. **White ethnic Americans** come from European nations other than Britain. Most experienced substantial prejudice and discrimination when they arrived here in the 19th century. Many have now fully assimilated and achieved substantial success.

VI. Looking ahead.

    A. Immigration has generated striking cultural diversity.

B. Many arrivals have much the same prejudice and discrimination experienced by those who came before them.

C. CONTROVERSY AND DEBATE BOX—Affirmative Action: Problem or Solution?

Chapter Objectives

1) Define race, ethnicity, and minority.

2) Define the concepts of prejudice and discrimination and discuss how they are related to each other.

3) Explain how stereotypes contribute to prejudiced thinking.

4) Outline four theories of prejudice.

5) Identify and describe four patterns of minority-majority interaction.

6) Summarize the social histories of the major U.S. minority groups.

7) Present arguments for and against affirmative action.

Essay Topics

1) Based on the research evidence, what do you conclude about IQ test score disparities? What could be done to raise the IQ scores of children from disadvantaged environments?

2) Discuss how prejudice and discrimination can form a vicious cycle.

3) Biologists sometimes argue that, from their perspective, race is of little or no real significance. How would a sociologist respond to such a claim? Make reference to the Thomas theorem.

4) How would each of the four theories of the origins of prejudice outlined in the text suggest that we might best go about trying to reduce this type of thinking?

5) Do you regard pluralism or assimilation as a more desirable condition from the standpoint of a minority group?

6) What do members of minority groups gain and lose as they undergo a process of assimilation?

7) Some American minority group members on occasion voluntarily seek to segregate themselves, having become convinced that the dominant group will never allow them to live in peace otherwise. What are the arguments in favor of and against such voluntary segregation?

8) Develop two parallel arguments, one in favor of affirmative action for minorities and one in opposition to this practice. Take a position yourself.

9) Media commentators frequently argue that race relations in the United States have worsened considerably over the past decade. Do you think this is true? How might a sociologist go about investigating this claim? If indeed this is an accurate assessment, what are some of the factors that may have contributed to this trend?

10) What do you think might be some effective ways of attempting to improve contemporary American race relations?

Integrative Supplement Guide

1. ABC Videos:
- Cheyenne Warriors (*Day One,* 7/6/95)
- Million Man March on Washington (*Nightline*, 10/16/95)
- The Debate Over Affirmative Action (*Nightline*, 6/16/95)
- City at Peace (*Nightline*, 6/9/95)
- Solutions: Church Targets Racial Issues (*World News Tonight*, 9/18/96)
- America in Black and White: The Philadelphia Story (*Nightline*, 5/20/96)
- America in Black and White: What About Black Racism (*Nightline*, 5/23/96)
- America in Black and White: Race, Crime and Pizza (*Nightline*, 9/27/96)

2. Transparencies - Series V:
- T-81 Where the Minority – Majority Already Exists
- T-82 Patterns of Prejudice and Discrimination
- T-83 Prejudice and Discrimination in the Vicious Cycle
- T-84 The Social Standing of Native Americans, 1990
- T-85 The Concentration of People of WASP – Ancestry Across the U.S.
- T-86 The Social Standing of African Americans, 1990
- T-87 The Social Standing of Asian Americans, 1990
- T-88 The Concentration of Hispanics/Latino Americans by County, Projections for 2001
- T-89 The Concentration of African Americans, by County, Projections for 2001
- T-90 The Concentration of Asian Americans, by County, Projections for 2001
- T-91 Immigration to the United States, by Decade
- T-92 How Much Discrimination is There?
- T-93 U.S. Population by Race and Ethnicity, 1995 and 2020

Supplemental Lecture Material
Kids and Race

A 1997 Time/CNN poll of 1,282 adults and 601 teens (ages 12-17) found some dramatic changes among the views of both black and white youths on race from those held by their parents. They indicated in their survey responses that race is less important to them than to their parents, both on a personal level and as a social divide. More than half of both white and black teenage respondents still considered racism a "big problem" in America — however more than one-third classified it as a "small problem". Asked about the impact of racism in their own lives, 89% of black teens called it a "small problem" or "not a problem at all." In fact, white adults and white teens were more convinced than black teens that racism in America remained a dominant issue.

In addition, black teens were more reluctant than others to blame racism for problems. Nearly twice as many black respondents as white believe "failure to take advantage of available opportunities" is more a problem for blacks than discrimination. ("This is especially extraordinary given the fact that 40% of the black teens surveyed believed that STATs are loaded against them, and that blacks have to be better qualified than whites to get a job" according to *Time* Magazine's Christopher John Farley.)

Sociologist Joe Feagin views the reactions of teens to this survey on race as an indicator of hope (on one hand) and youthful naiveté (on the other). He points out that "One word explains it — experience... You have to be out looking for jobs and housing to know how much discrimination is out there. People doing that are usually over 19." (In support of this view, only 25% of black teens surveyed said they had been victims of discrimination, whereas half of black adults say they have.)

Farley points out that extensive interviews with children, parents, educators, researchers and law enforcement officials indicate that the new optimism among teens has occurred against a backdrop of a number of new challenges (e.g., the growing presence of hate groups on the Internet) and old ones (e.g., interracial dating and ethnic turf wars). The hope expressed by teens involved in the survey sometimes flies in the face of pessimism and racial intolerance teenagers hear expressed by their elders. At the same time, the continued deprivation of so many black families in wrecked city neighborhoods poses another challenge to improved relationships between whites and blacks.

While the results of this survey provide hope for the future, it is one that must be tempered by today's realities.

Source

Farley, Christopher John. "Kids and Race." *Time* (November 24, 1997):88-91.

Discussion Questions

1) People don't always level with pollsters; they're notorious in fact, for giving socially acceptable answers at the expense of revealing their true feelings. But teens are less likely to do so than adults. Why do you think that this is the case?

2) Does the disinclination to blame problems on racism mean a reduced sense of racial identity among blacks today? If not, why not?

Supplemental Lecture Material
Native Americans: Reclaiming Ethnic Identity

As Chapter 12 points out, minorities currently make up an increasingly larger proportion of the U.S. population. Based on census figures, no group has grown as rapidly in recent decades as Native Americans, whose numbers tripled between 1960 and 1990 and now stand at roughly 1.8 million. Preliminary figures from the 1990 census suggest a 38 percent growth rate over the past ten years alone.

This increase is less a result of natural growth than a consequence of a shift in the meaning attributed to being Native American. For centuries, the dominant culture regarded "Indians" as inferior. As a consequence many people with mixed Native American and white ancestry chose to identify themselves as white to census takers.

However, in recent years prejudice against Native Americans has waned in most parts of the country. Films like "Dances With Wolves" have lent a degree of glamour to Native American ethnicity and the spread of ecological consciousness has had a similar effect because many people believe (not altogether correctly) that traditional Native American cultures strove to live in harmony with nature rather than dominating and exploiting their environment. Thus hundreds of thousands of people with "Indian" ancestry are now openly claiming to be Native Americans when asked to classify themselves by the census.

It should be noted that most of these "new" Native Americans have substantial white ancestry. "Because about 50 percent of Indians marry non-Indians, demographers say, the number of people with some Indian ancestry increases as they have children, even as the number with mostly Indian ancestry declines."

The tribal rolls of Native American groups are also expanding, in part because Native American heritage qualifies an individual for a variety of government benefits including health care, financial aid for college, and special fishing and hunting rights. While the census does not ask respondents to document their ethnic background, the tribes do require proof of ancestry, but "the blood requirement differs from tribe to tribe, some requiring applicants to prove they are one-half Indian for acceptance, others recognizing as little as one-two thousandth."

The Bureau of Indian Affairs also requires supportive evidence before qualifying an individual for programs, grants or loans that are set aside for members of minority groups, but "in a few well-publicized cases, people with only a tiny percentage of Indian blood have been able to take advantage. For example, a California contractor, who is one sixty-fourth American Indian, obtained $19 million in contracts set aside for minority-owned companies on the rapid-transit system in Los Angeles, more than any other 'disadvantaged' company."

Source
Johnson, Dirk. "Census Finds Many Claiming New Identity: Indian." *New York Times* (March 5, 1991).

Discussion Question
1) Among your friends, is Native American ancestry seen as something to be proud of or something which would be better concealed? Why?

Supplemental Lecture Material
The Use of the Term Racism

Words are the primary weapons on the battlefield of ideas. This notion, central to Marxian conflict theory, has rarely been more obvious than in the context of the controversy currently swirling around the use of the term *racism*.

Traditionally the term has been used by sociologists as it is defined in this chapter — to denote a belief (or action based on belief) that one racial category is innately superior or inferior to another. Generally such beliefs have been bolstered by scientific, or more properly pseudo-scientific, claims based on the supposed biological differences between the races. Thus, for example, the arguments of Southern slaveholders that black people were constitutionally unable to accept the responsibilities inherent upon free men and women are rather easily classified as racist.

Since the civil rights and black liberation movements of the 1960s and early 1970s, however, usage of this term has been changing in at least two very different ways.

Advocates of minority liberation, following the lead of 1960s militant leader H. Rap Brown, (who declared that "racism is as American as apple pie,") have come to define as racist any pattern of thought or action that has negative consequences for a minority, whether or not these patterns are inspired by deliberate discriminatory intent. Thus, for example, the minimum height requirement for New York City firefighters, introduced years prior to the large-scale immigration of Puerto Ricans into the city, has been roundly denounced as racist (and eventually changed), because it had the practical consequence of disproportionately excluding Puerto Rican men, who tend to be shorter than Anglos, from being hired as firefighters. The intent of such uses of the term is to extend the public's negative feelings about racism to almost anything that in any way, deliberately or unintentionally, supports, condones, or perpetuates the dis-advantaged position of a minority.

Advocates of this position some-times deny that it is possible for members of a minority to act in a racist fashion. By de-fining racism exclusively as behavior or ac-tions that harm minorities, these activists exclude the possibility that attacks on whites by minority youths or the inflammatory anti-white rhetoric of leaders like Louis Farra-khan can be called racist. Their logic rests on the observation that the behavior of the minority which is by definition relatively powerless, cannot seriously harm the domi-nant community, while the attitudes of the dominant group, termed racist, frequently have devastating implications for the life chances of minor-ities. By denying the pos-sibility of minority racism, this rhetoric fo-cuses full attention on the behavior of the dominant group, which is seen as more or less entirely responsible for the minority's delimma.

In contrast, opponents of liberation movements have chosen to redefine racism in an entirely different way, a redefinition that has already had profound implications for our national policies regarding minori-ties. These opponents, mostly political con-servatives (strongly represented in the Reagan and Bush administrations), argue that any action that takes any recognition of race whatsoever is "racist," whether per-petuated by the dominant or the minority community. This definition of racism has been used to mount an intense and increas-ingly successful assault against the principle of affirmative action. Arguing against any policy that is not totally color-blind, advo-cates of this definition of racism oppose any form of racial quotas or goals for employ-ment or college admissions. Ignoring the fact that the lingering consequences of bla-tant historical discrimination have not yet been fully overcome, conservatives insist

that they are only trying to create a "level playing field" in which no one is given any advantages on the basis of racial identity. Recent decisions by an increasingly conser-vative Supreme Court clearly reflect accep-tance of this view.

Opponents of this position, while fully sensitive to the ultimate desirability of a truly colorblind society (at least as regards economic and social opportunity), respond that, given the present circumstances, a truly non-racist society, defined as the conserva-tives would define it, would be a society that in practice continued to discriminate against minorities, because it did not give them the assistance that they require to fully over-come the consequences of centuries of ex-ploitation and discrimination they or their ancestors experienced in this country.

Discussion Questions

1) Which of the definitions of racism dis-cussed here comes nearest to your own un-derstanding of the term?

2) Do you believe that it is possible for the members of minorities to be racist? If so why?

Supplemental Lecture Material
Arab Americans: A Brief Profile

Many negative stereotypes surround Arab Americans. The increasing prominence of Islamic fundamentalism in the Middle East, acts of terrorism by Arabs (such as the hos-tage crisis during the Carter administration or the recent bombing of the World Trade Center), the Gulf War, and the ongoing ten-sions between Israel and her neighbors have all contributed to a sense among some Americans that Arabs are intolerant of

American political and social systems as well as anticapitalist, extremist, and dangerous.

Indeed, many Arab Americans have suffered needlessly and regularly from simple discrimination or ethnocentric and misleading images, such as those perpetuated in the popular Disney film *Aladdin*. In a few cases, international events have even sparked unjust vigilante-style "retaliations" against Arab Americans.

These negative perceptions of Arab Americans are unfounded. In fact, "Arab" is a rather loose term that covers individuals tracing their ancestry to northern Africa and/or western and southwestern Asia and which includes a variety of ethnic and cultural groups and many languages. Most of these peoples consider themselves to share a certain "Arabic heritage" and at least some usage of the Arabic language. Stereotypically, Arabs are viewed as olive-skinned, but there is no definitive "look"; Arabs can have blue eyes and either white or black coloration.

Arab Americans have been immigrating to the United States in increasing numbers, although they still make up only about 3 percent of all immigrants here. Estimates of the size of the Arab-American population range between 870,000 from the Census Bureau and between one and three million from demographers who believe the U.S. census figures are inaccurate. Some 82 percent are citizens.

Studies of Arab Americans show them to be younger and more educated than the general population. The average Arab-American household earns 39,100 dollars, compared to the national average of just 30,100 dollars. They tend to be concentrated in urban areas, and over one-third of all Arab Americans live in just ten cities. By state, one-third are located in California, New York, and Michigan. Arab Americans are also more likely to

be self-employed than most Americans. About half consider themselves Christians; most of the rest are Moslems but a few are Jewish.

Most Arab Americans came to the United States to escape political unrest in their mother country. Turmoil in Palestine, Iran, Iraq, Syria, and Egypt over the past fifty years has contributed to the immigrant pool. Large numbers attended Western-style schools at home before immigrating and were fluent in English upon arrival.

Arab Americans have been identified by some companies as a distinct market. Arab-language TV stations are located in some areas, with at least six in the Dearborn and Detroit area. Arab-Net is an Arabic-language radio network that broadcasts in the Detroit, Chicago, Los Angeles, Pittsburgh, and Washington regions. There are also a number of Arab-language newspapers and magazines distributed widely across the country. One bank in East Dearborn, Michigan, targets the large local Arab-American population, uses Arabic-language advertising, and requires most of the staff to speak Arabic.

Ali Hashem came to America from Lebanon and moved to Detroit. After a few years, he started a business exporting used American clothing to people in the Middle East. "These are all things Americans no longer want. . . . My parents love it here. They can get anything they want from the old country right here in Detroit, and there are many Arab-American social organizations."

Abraham Osta, who immigrated from Jordan and now works for the Arab American Chamber of Commerce, says, "Many Arab Americans come from Middle Eastern countries where they had no political power. I wanted them to know that in this country, you have a right and a responsibility to be involved in politics. . . . Most of us come here with a language deficit and must struggle to catch up. But we are willing to invest the time to learn about this country. We appreciate this political system. We recognize its value."

Source
El-Badry, Samia. "The Arab-American Market." *American Demographics* (January 1994):22–27, 30–31.

Discussion Questions
1) Many Americans automatically assumed that the Oklahoma City bombing and the summer 1996 Atlanta Olympic bombings were the results of Islamic Arab fundamentalists. Were these reactions the result of racism?

2) Does the economic success of Arab Americans seem likely to result in the same kind of "success stereotype" experienced by Asian Americans?

Supplemental Lecture Material
On the Edge of Europe: The Gypsies in Finland

Romani is what the "Gypsies" call themselves in every country in which they are found, but *Gypsies*, an English word derived from the slurred *Egyptian*, referring to where the English thought the Romani must have originated.

And as might be guessed from their inaccurate English name, the Romani are seldom well understood or liked by their neighbors. The Romani have lived in Finland since the sixteenth century — some four hundred years — but they are still treated as outsiders by the "white" Finnish majority.

The Romani originated as a distinct group in what is now northern India. They have spent centuries wandering, and can be found in many parts of Asia and Europe,

particularly southeastern Europe. Many still speak the Romani language, which is distinct from any European language. The Romani have been able to retain a powerful, separate identity from many of their host cultures. They have occasionally been the object of extremely harsh persecution, and in some areas of Central Europe they were almost exterminated by the Nazis during World War II.

Most Romani prefer to dress in their traditional clothing. Men wear dark suits, while women wear hoop-skirts with aprons and ruffles. Most Romani have dark hair and olive complexions, and the denigrating term for the Romani, *mustalaisia*, derives from *musta* or black. Finland's best-known ethnic group, the indigenous Samis or Lapps, number only around 2,500. In contrast, the Romani population is probably somewhere between 6,500 and 10,000.

Finland is not generally well known as a country with widespread racism, but discrimination against the Romani has only recently been made illegal. As the targets of governmental efforts to "integrate" them into the larger population and culture, they have endured extreme measures, including the forced removal of Romani children from their homes for placement in state-run children's homes. This practice only ended in 1970. Not until 1992 were Finland's citizens guaranteed equal protection under the law or the right to their own culture.

The Romani in Finland tend to have lower literacy rates, less education and economic resources, and higher levels of poverty than white Finns; many depend on state-funded welfare. A director of a charitable organization for the Romani stated, "Most Finns say that the mustalaisia are lazy, that they don't want to work, and that they are not able to perform ordinary jobs. They say they're dishonest and irresponsible."

Heikki Lampela, who is only part Romani, faces this attitude directly and often: "In restaurants where I had never been before, people told me, 'Get out of here. We don't like Gypsies.'. . . People in Finland hate Gypsies. They don't want Gypsies to come into society because they don't like them. And Gypsies have their own society. The Finnish lifestyle and the Gypsy lifestyle are like day and night."

Recent legislation has made overt, formal racism less common, and many Romani hope that these changes will result in the material improvement of their lives. But many Romani also have their doubts about any economic or social improvement. As Lampela says, "If we're talking about a dog, does it matter what pedigree it is? People use their eyes here, they don't use their brains. They don't ask how you feel inside."

Source
Sloane, Wendy. "After Four Centuries in Finland, Gypsies Still Live on the Fringe." *Christian Science Monitor.* (June 14, 1995):11.

Discussion Questions
1) Have you seen signs of racism directed toward Romani in any countries you have traveled to?

2) Many Europeans who show disgust at the continuation of racism in the United States also exhibit apparently racist attitudes toward their nation's native Romanis. Are such attitudes hypocritical? Are there differences between American and European racism?

Supplemental Lecture Material
What Race?

Increasingly, when the question is asked, "What race are you?" people are likely to answer "other." In the 1990 census, almost 10 million people did just that, up 45 percent since 1980, causing the government to reconsider its racial categories for the 2000 census.

So, who is resisting being categorized, and why? Young adults, for one, are likely to object to racial categories. In 1990, the median age of those checking the "other race" category was about 24 years, while the national median was 33. Some of these young adults are of mixed race, like Brian Courtney who, in a recent *Newsweek* article, described his dilemma. As a child of a white mother and African American father, he is constantly having to make choices as to what "side" he is on, chided by blacks that he "talks too white," while told by his white friends that he is different from the other black people they know. Both statements display prejudice. As he says, "I do not blame my African American or white friends for the problems faced by biracial people in America. I blame society for not acknowledging us as a separate race" (Courtney, p. 16).

Others, who mark themselves as "other race," are recent immigrants because overall, younger Americans are more likely to be minorities. For example, according to the Census Bureau, nonwhite and Hispanic Americans will make up 28 percent of the total United States population, but will be 36 percent among those under 18 and 33 percent of young adults aged 18 to 34.

Given our society's goal to diminish prejudice and stereotyping, it isn't surprising that young people are resisting these racial categories, which appear to go counter to those efforts. Unfortunately, those statistics are needed precisely to fight racial discrimination since the data are used to enforce the Voting Rights Act, equal employment regulations, and affirmative action plans.

One suggestion has been to add a multi-racial category. That, however, still leaves one problem: "Most of the people who check 'other race' probably have a clear racial identity, because 98 percent claim Hispanic origin on the ethnicity question. In other words, over 40 percent of the nation's 22 million Hispanics aren't willing to identify themselves as black or white" (Sándor, pp. 38-39). Mexicans, for example, consider themselves a mix of Spanish and indigenous peoples. Many Latin Americans trace their ancestry to native Indians, Europeans and Africans. Therefore, Hispanics often did not check either the "white" or "black" categories.

Unfortunately, census results could be skewed when people checked off "other race," because a computer was given the task of fitting them into one of the four race categories. If, for example, a person wrote in "biracial," and checked off two races, the computer assigned them the first race they reported. If someone wrote in "Latino," the census computer went through the steps of checking the answers first of other members of the household and using the race checked by them, or, next, the neighbors. The problem is that the latter method assumed a certain amount of homogeneousness in neighborhoods, which is not always the case. If a Hispanic person happened to live next door to African Americans, the computer categorized them as "black."

So why not simply add categories until everyone is satisfied? The problem is statistical and known as the "primacy" and "recency" effects. In other words, if confronted with a long list of choices on a survey, respondents are likely to check off the first choice that might apply to them without reading through the whole list for the one that applies *best*. Therefore, a long list creates more distortions than a shorter one.

To deal with this problem, federal agencies conducted extensive surveys and interviews for the last couple of years to find the best way to ask race and ethnicity questions in the 2000 census. The final decision was made in 1997 and published in the *Federal Register*. The 2000 census will now have five categories for data on race: 1. American Indian or Alaska Native; 2. Asian; 3. Black or African American; 4. Native Hawaiian or Other Pacific Islander; and 5. White. There are two categories for data on ethnicity: 1. "Hispanic or Latino" or 2. "Not Hispanic or Latino."

As you can see, "multiracial" is not a category, but instructions for questions regarding race tell respondents that they should "Select one or more."

Sources

Federal Register. Vol. 62, No. 210 (October 30, 1997): 58781-58790.

Courtney, Brian. "Freedom from Choice." *Newsweek* (February 13, 1995):16

Evinger, Suzann. "How to Record Race." *American Demographics* (May 1996):36-41

Sándor, Gabrielle. "The Other Americans." *American Demographics* (June 1994):36-42.

Discussion Questions

1) What do you think about the government choice regarding race and ethnicity categories of the next census form? Keeping in mind their usage, do you think asking those questions is necessary or valid? Why or why not?

2) **Activity.** Find a biracial person and interview them regarding their experiences. Do those experiences mirror Brian Courtney's, or did the person in fact make a conscious choice to identify themselves with one of the two races? What insight do they feel their background has given them? Should there be a separate multiracial category?

Chapter 15

Aging and the Elderly

I. The Graying of the United States.
  A. The number of Americans aged 65 or over has been increasing twice as fast as the population as a whole.
  B. WINDOW ON THE WORLD—Global Map 15-1: The Elderly in Global Perspective, 2020.
  C. It is the rich nations where the share of elderly people is increasing most rapidly. Two factors help explain this trend:
    1. Low birthrates.
    2. Longevity.
  D. An Aging Society: cultural change.
    1. Age segregation will decline as this country's elderly population increases.
    2. SEEING OURSELVES—National Map 15–1: The Elderly Population of the United States. Most countries with high percentages of older people are in the Midwest.

II. Growing Old: Biology and Culture.
  A. **Gerontology** is the study of aging and the elderly.
  B. As we age, the body undergoes a series of biological changes, most of which are viewed negatively by our culture. Most elderly people are not disabled by their physical condition.
  C. Aging is also commonly accompanied by a few psychological changes.
  D. Aging and culture.
    1. WINDOW ON THE WORLD—Global Map 15–2: Life Expectancy in Global Perspective. Life expectancy has shot upward over the course of this century in industrial countries.
    2. **Global Sociology Box:** Growing (Very) Old: A Report from Abkhasia.
  E. **Age stratification** is defined as the unequal distribution of wealth, power and privileges among people at different stages in the life course.
    1. Hunting and gathering societies become less active and are considered an economic burden as they age.
    2. The most privileged members of pastoral, horticultural, and agrarian societies are typically the elderly, which gives rise to **gerontocracy**, a form of social organization in which the elderly have the most wealth, power, and prestige.
    3. Industrialization tends to erode the social standing of the elderly.
    4. Japanese society is, in some ways, an exception to this pattern.

III. Transitions and Challenges of Aging.
    A. Neugarten identifies four personality types that respond differently to the aging process.
        1. Disintegrated and disorganized personalities.
        2. Passive-dependent personalities.
        3. Defended personalities.
        4. Integrated personalities.
    B. Social isolation results from retirement and the death of significant others. It is an especially serious problem for women, who usually outlive their spouses.
    C. Retirement often entails a reduction in income, diminished social prestige, and a loss of purpose in life.
    D. Aging increases the risk of poverty, although in recent decades the poverty rate among the elderly has declined.
    E. **Caregiving** refers to informal and unpaid care provided to a dependent person by family members, other relatives, or friends.
        1. Eighty percent of caregiving to elders is provided by family members.
        2. Abuse of older people takes many forms.
    F. **Ageism** refers to prejudice and discrimination against the elderly.
        1. It may be blatant or subtle.
        2. Is based in stereotypes that are sometimes promoted by the media.
        3. There is disagreement as to whether the elderly are considered a minority.

IV. Theoretical Analyses of Aging.
    A. Structural-functional analysis: Aging and disengagement.
        1. **Disengagement theory** is the idea that society enhances its orderly operation by disengaging people from positions of responsibility as they reach old age.
        2. Critical evaluation.
            a. Disengagement creates major financial problems for the elderly in many cases.
            b. Many elderly people do not wish to disengage.
            c. The social disadvantages of disengagement usually outweigh its advantages.
    B. Symbolic-interaction analysis: Aging and activity.
        1. In opposition to disengagement theory, **activity theory** is the idea that a high level of activity enhances personal satisfaction in old age.
        2. Critical evaluation.
            a. Activity theory notes the diversity among the aged population.
            b. It tends to exaggerate the well-being and competence of the elderly.
    C. Social-conflict analysis: Aging and inequality.
        1. This perspective notes that in capitalist societies the aged often suffer discrimination at the hands of more powerful groups.
        2. Critical evaluation.
            a. It seems likely that the central problem is industrialization rather than capitalism.
            b. This view also overlooks recent improvements in the circumstances of the elderly.

V. Death and Dying.

A. Historical patterns of death. In the past, confronting death was commonplace.

B. The modern separation of life and death. Modern society fosters a desire for eternal youth and immortality. Death has become separated from life.

C. Ethical issues include determining the exact point of legal death and dealing with **euthanasia,** defined as assisting the death of a person suffering from an incurable disease.

   1. GLOBAL SOCIOLOGY BOX—Death on Demand: A Report From the Netherlands.

D. Bereavement.

   1. Bereavement may parallel the five stages by which, according to Elisabeth Kübler-Ross, we confront our own death: denial, anger, negotiation, resignation and acceptance.

   2. The hospice movement has developed to help people prepare for death.

VI. Looking Ahead: Aging in the Twenty-first Century.

A. The health of tomorrow's elderly people is better than ever.

B. Younger adults will face a mounting responsibility to care for aging parents.

C. An aging population will almost certainly change the way we view death.

D. CONTROVERSY AND DEBATE BOX—Setting Limits: Must We "Pull the Plug" on Old Age?

Chapter Objectives

1) Discuss the causes and consequences of the "graying" of the U.S. population.

2) Define gerontology.

3) Describe the biological and psychological changes that accompany aging, as well as the role of cultural factors in determining how aging is defined in any given society.

4) Examine how age stratification varies according to a society's level of technological development.

5) Identify and describe four personality types identified by Neugarten in their responses to the aging process.

6) Examine the transitions and challenges of aging, including social isolation, retirement, poverty, caregiving, and elder abuse.

7) Define ageism.

8) Discuss the extent to which the elderly can be analyzed as a minority group.

9) Compare and contrast three theoretical paradigms on the sociology of aging.

10) Compare and contrast historical patterns of death with the modern separation of life and death.

11) Discuss ethical issues surrounding death.

Essay Topics

1) What transitions and challenges of aging could be facilitated by cultural changes?

2) The chapter suggests several ways in which the aging of the U.S. will affect our social life in the next century. Can you think

of further implications of this change, perhaps in institutional areas such as religion, politics, and education?

3) Do we need to develop any formal programs to help people care for their aging parents or are such programs unneeded?

4) What steps could we take to enhance the esteem with which the elderly are regarded in this culture?

5) Presently the policy of mandatory retirement is quite controversial in U.S. society. Do you favor this policy, or should people be allowed to retire whenever they desire? Outline the arg͏͏ for and mandatory retirement.

6) Are disengagement and activity theories polar opposites, or is there some truth in each approach? Which is more accurate as a description of what actually occurs?

7) Outline some of the ageist stereotypes that you either have held or have seen in people around you. Do you think that such stereotypes will become more or less widely held as our society ages? Why?

8) Should the elderly be described as a minority group? Why or why not?

9) Reflect on how much direct exposure you have had to death and dying in your life. What positive and negative consequences might follow from narrowing the separation of the dying from the rest of us?

10) Debate the "right to die" issue. Defend your position.

Integrative Supplement Guide

1. **ABC Videos:**
- Age and Attitudes (*Prime Time Live,* 6/9/94)
- Will There Be Enough Money for Your Old Age? (*Nightline,* 9/18/95)

2. **Transparencies - Series V:**
- T-94   The Graying of U.S. Society
- T-95   The Elderly in Global Perspective
- T-96   The Elderly Population of the United States
- T-97   Life Expectancy in Global Perspective
- T-98   Living Arrangements of the Elderly, 1996
- T-99 U.S. Poverty Rates, by Age, 1996

Supplemental Lecture Material
The Consequences of a Graying Population

More seniors getting into traffic accidents has prompted several states to consider tougher driver licensing policies. Since 1987, fatal crashes involving drivers 70 and older have risen 42%, to some 4,928 in 1997. By 2019, the number of 70 plus drivers is expected to balloon to 30 million persons, and highway safety experts warn the number of people killed in crashes involving elderly motorists is likely to surpass the drunk-driving death toll. While it is true that drivers 60 and older have a lower accident rate than younger ones, and that some seniors drive safely into their 90s, others are impaired by such ailments as poor vision, slow reflexes, partial paralysis and dementia. Attempts to identify unfit drivers, moreover, have been haphazard. While some states require frequent vision tests for elderly drivers, others mandate nothing.

Mostly, the decision to give up the keys is left up to the elderly themselves. With limited transportation alternatives, seniors who can't drive often become housebound and depressed. While some communities offer low-cost vans and private-care services, for many, city buses and taxis are frequently all there is. "Losing a license is like a death sentence to most people" according to Time's Tammerlin Drummond. This is one reason why the adult children of elderly drivers will usually not intervene, even when an aging parent is a road menace.

Some seniors self-regulate their driving but increasingly, individual states (e.g., California and Florida) have proposed regulatory legislation that include requirements such as periodic mandatory vision exams as well as a written and road test every five years after age 80, every two years after 85 and annually after 90.

Senior citizens are not without their advocacy groups however. The American Association of Retired Persons has already pushed state lawmakers to defeat age-based driving bills in Florida, Texas, and California. As an alternative the AARP sponsors eight-hour driver refresher courses. In 1998, 700,000 people participated, lured in part by a 10% discount on their auto insurance.

Sources

Drummond, Tammerlin. "On the Road Too Long." *Time* (August 2, 1999):46.

Discussion Questions

1) The Federal Government recently conducted a study in Maryland on targeting problem motorists before they cause an accident. How do you feel about the Federal Government's monitoring of seniors who drive?

Supplemental Lecture Material
Elderscam

Scamming the elderly. Convictions for this particular crime are rare, and sentences often relatively mild. Yet criminals are preying on one of the more vulnerable segments of our society: the elderly. They often do so over the phone, donning a caring voice and exploiting the loneliness of widows or the precariousness of finances of a retirement budget. "The American Association of Retired People (A.A.R.P) figures that while anyone over 60 is likely to be on at least one "mooch" (sucker) list, a woman 75 or older is virtually guaranteed to be. . . .Such women are often widows, lonely and suffering from ills that make them desperate for someone to talk to. (p. 54)." And once on such a list, a person is likely to appear on others soon, as telemarketing firms buy and sell names for prices depending on just how gullible the person has proven to be in the past. The more often you have been cheated, the more your name is worth.

These criminals, usually telemarketers, are con artists cheating the elderly out of $40 billion a year, according to one FBI estimate. Initial phone calls might promise some grand prize if the person purchases essentially worthless junk. That cycle goes on endlessly without the grand prize ever appearing, of course. Fraud victims, afraid to tell others of their financial losses for fear of being declared incompetent and losing their independence, continue in hopes of recouping the money they have already lost. Of course, they never do and can wind up losing thousands of dollars in the process.

Telemarketers usually call out-of-state victims only, dodging prosecution by the simple expedient of being in a different jurisdiction. There are even specialties within the system. So-called "Fronters" make the initial contact, using either lists or scanning telephone books for old-fashioned first names. "Closers" make the follow-up calls. "Re-load men" call people who have fallen for other scams. "No-sales men" try to persuade the suspicious. Scams range from phony prizes to fake charities to fraudulent investments.

Unfortunately, the elderly are all the easier targets for the unscrupulous because they have been raised at a time when being polite was valued. In other words, they feel it is rude to simply hang up the telephone or slam a door.

Unfortunately, because often there are only two witnesses — the victim and the con-artist — it is difficult to prosecute these criminals. Even if they are convicted, prison terms are short, typically one to three years. A minimum sentence requirement passed by the House in 1997 consists of only six months, or 15 months if the victims are over 55.

However, efforts are being made to protect the elderly. Apart from education on how to avoid being scammed, state and local authorities are trying to step up prosecutions. In 1989, the Florida state attorney general's office, formed "Senior Sleuths," an organization employing 550 people "in sting operations to gather evidence against scammers (p. 57)."

One possible consolation: aging baby boomers will be much tougher targets, given they are more cynical and less trusting than their parents.

Source

Church, George J.. "Elderscam: Reach Out and Bilk Someone." *Time* (August 25, 1997): 54-57.

Discussion Questions

1) Do you think "scamming" the elderly is as easy in other cultures? Why or why not? What other solutions for preventing this crime apart from education and prosecution would you suggest?

2) Using Neugarten's classification of the elderly according to their coping skills, which types would be most vulnerable to scams and why?

Supplemental Lecture Material
Men & Midlife Crisis

Parenting is a long haul for everyone but some men have considerably lengthened their life course. Men who raise one family, then remarry and go on to raise another with a new set of biological children, are starting over in more ways than one. American Demographics columnist Joanne Cleaver points out that they must adjust to their new wife's expectations for how they'll share the parenting load. They also must explain to their older children that they're not being abandoned, even if it looks as though that's exactly what's happening. And for themselves, there's the need to come to grips with the fact that they've just taken on a 21-year commitment that completely alters their future.

For celebrities who become dads for a second time, the reality of being a father to two very diverse sets of children, who have dramatically different financial and emotional needs is often less of a challenge than the one faced by working class and middle class divorced fathers.

While exact figures on the population of older, second-generation dads is difficult to obtain, the number of second-generation dads is clearly growing. Numerous reports have examined the emotional complications of stepparenting, but few researchers have zeroed in on the equally "convoluted" relationships between fathers and two separate biological families. Elizabeth Cooksey (an associate professor at Ohio State University) and Patricia Craig (a Harvard researcher) however, gathered data on fathers who have one biological family (children between the ages of 0 & 17), then remarry and have another set of kids. One of their conclusions is that these fathers are actually far less likely to spend time with their first biological children.

In the May, 1998 issue of Demography, Cooksey wrote that "the arrival of a new baby may signal the beginning of the cooling of the relationship with the dad's first set of kids. The biological children they fathered at an earlier time tend to be displaced." Her data also suggests that two additional factors play into a dad's tendency to stay in close contact with his first generation family — residential proximity and the father's education level. (The higher the education level, the more likely he is to maintain close relationships with these children.)

"It's when [a father] settles down in the relationship and has new children with the new partner that crowding-out happens" says Cooksey. "We don't know why he's not seeing the first kids — we don't know how old the kids were when the relationship split or the nature of the relationship with the first partner."

However, one looks at the situation, one thing is certain: Dads with two biological families are stretched in two different directions. David Carnoy, the author of "Fathers of a Certain Age" (Fairview Press), interviewed 30 fathers who were at least 40 when they had biological children. He found that most of the men who fathered children at a later age did so out of love for their younger wives, not because they discovered late in life the need to be a father. Their wives usually had very different expectations for their husbands than did the first wives. (For one thing, they are usually working mothers, sociologists say, and fully expect their husbands to share equally with child-rearing tasks). North Carolina State University sociology professor, Barbara J. Risman, who has researched the changing patterns in American families, speculates that there's a "generational difference between husbands and wives. The husbands may have to learn the new way of raising children" she says.

Rachel Geller, chief strategic officer for a New York City marketing firm that specializes in children and teens has found that "Second-time dads feel that they used to be part of the old male model — you work, you support, you're the disciplinarian. They bonded with their sons more than their daughters. Now, they're grateful that they have a second chance, and that's not the same as the first." They're really patterning themselves after current models of fatherhood.

In the meantime, the first marriage children often experience a feeling of conflict because they feel that "all of a sudden, they're having to share what they thought was theirs." Here lies the prime irony of two-family dads: The unexpected blessing of the second family is inevitably accompanied by reduced expectations and a feeling of emotional and financial distance on the part of the first.

Source

Cleaver, Joanne. "Good Old Dad." *American Demographics* (June, 1999):59-63.

Discussion Questions

1) What are some forms of role conflict that two-family dads are likely to experience in addition to those cited in this abstract?

2) How might two-family dads accommodate the value-stretch involved in resolving the contradictory role expectations of fatherhood in their first and second family social settings?

3) Discuss how sociogenic aging and our cultural obsession with youthfulness contributes to men forty years of age and older remarrying younger women and assuming the role of fathers a second time.

Supplemental Lecture Material
Can America Survive the Aging of the Baby Boomers?

Thoughts of the Baby Boom generation growing old terrifies many. Current projections suggest that one in five Americans will be eighty-five or older by 2045, compared to one in ten in 1990, and now 45 percent of the oldest elderly require some assistance with personal care. How can our society withstand having 20 percent of its population elderly and dependent? Paying for personal-care assistance and health emergencies is of equal concern. Many Americans, notably a majority of those born after the Baby Boomers, doubt that the Social Security System can handle such a massive drain as the post-Boomer generations are much smaller and therefore less able to contribute in amounts capable of supporting the coming wave of retirees.

These and other fears have inspired grim visions of the United States after 2025 — millions of destitute seniors that are either homeless or living in thousands of squalid factory-like nursing facilities. However, most of the fears are based on what are likely to prove to be incorrect assumptions.

It is true that the numbers of the elderly in the United States will increase. The demand for long-term care and personal assistance and the demands on Social Security will all certainly grow as well, but many projections ignore generational effects — the potential changes in our society that will come about as specific generations age. The Baby Boomers have already effected numerous changes in our society, ranging from drug use and sexual behavior in the 1960s to the growth of on-site childcare in the workplace in the 1980s.

While the number of elderly dependent on assistance will increase, the percentage of the elderly needing assistance seems more likely to decrease as many of the Baby Boomers have lived healthier than their parents and grandparents. Per capita tobacco consumption, for instance, is 40 percent lower than in 1953. The consumption of whole milk and cream has declined about 25 percent, the use of saturated animal fats for cooking is 40 percent lower, and the per capita consumption of vegetable oils and fish has grown. In fact, the amount of chronic disability among seniors already dropped 4 percent between 1984 and 1989.

Furthermore, the Boomers promise to want to live as independently as their means and abilities will allow. Already, the number of elderly who choose to avoid both long-term residential care (such as a nursing home) and assisted home living has grown. More Americans are opting for tools and devices that will enable them to live at home as long as possible. Tools to modify phones, to regulate heating and lighting more easily, and to improve the safety of kitchens and bathrooms are becoming more common.

Medical technology to compensate for malfunctioning body parts promises to continue improving in quality. And because many female Boomers delayed marriage and childbearing relative to their parents, future senior women will have a higher degree of self-sufficiency in handling their finances, homes, and emergencies.

The future of Social Security is probably secure as well; it was rescued once from bankruptcy in the early 1980s, and broad bipartisan concern for the security of Social Security was discussed in the 1996 presidential election. While Americans often wait to react to a difficult problem until shortly before it becomes a serious threat, Social Security is popular and important enough to avoid expiring.

Taken together, the elderly of the next century will face and present a number of critical issues in the next century. But advances in technology, changes in society, and the creativity of the electorate promise to equal the problems behind those issues.

Source

Longino, Charles F., Jr. "Myths of an Aging America." *American Demographics* (August 1994):36–42.

Discussion Questions

1) What do you think will happen with the Social Security System by the time you retire?

2) Do you know people — friends, colleagues, instructors, parents, or yourself — who are concerned enough about the Social Security System to have changed how they prepare for retirement?

3) Are you likely to become responsible for the care of any relatives as they age? When might this occur? What would you like to have happen at that point? What are you afraid will happen?

Chapter 16

The Economy and Work

I. The Economy: Historical Overview.
  A. The **economy** is the social institution that organizes a society's production, distribution and consumption of goods and services.
  B. The agricultural revolution led to a dramatic expansion of the economy as a result of:
      1. New agricultural technology.
      2. Productive specialization.
      3. Permanent settlements.
      4. Trade.
  C. The industrial revolution.
      1. Industrialization changed the economy in five ways.
          a. New forms of energy.
          b. Centralization of work in factories.
          c. Manufacturing and mass production.
          d. Specialization.
          e. Wage labor.
      2. SOCIAL DIVERSITY BOX—Women in the Mills of Lowell, Massachusetts.
  D. The **Information Revolution** and the **postindustrial society**.
      1. A **postindustrial economy** refers to a productive system based on service work and extensive use of information technology.
      2. Since 1950, the Information Revolution has dramatically transformed U.S. society.
          a. From tangible products to ideas.
          b. From mechanical skills to literacy skills.
          c. From factories to almost anywhere.
  E. Sectors of the economy:
      1. The **primary sector** is the part of the economy that generates raw materials directly from the natural environment.
      2. The **secondary sector** is the part of the economy that transforms raw materials into manufactured goods.
      3. The **tertiary sector** is the part of the economy involved in services rather than goods.
  F. Recent decades have witnessed the emergence of a **global economy,** expanding economic activity with little regard for national borders. The development of a global economy has four major consequences:

1. There is a global division of labor by which each region of the world specializes in particular kinds of economic activity:
   a. WINDOW ON THE WORLD—Global Map 16–1: Agricultural Employment in Global Perspective. The primary sector of the economy predominates in societies that are least developed.
   b. WINDOW ON THE WORLD—Global Map 16–2: Industrial Employment in Global Perspective. Because the world's poor societies have yet to industrialize for the most part, a small proportion of their labor force engages in industrial work.
2. An increasing number of products pass through the economies of more than one nation.
3. Governments can no longer fully control the economic activity that takes place within their borders.
4. A small number of businesses control a vast share of the world's economic activities.

II. Economic Systems: Paths to Justice

A. **Capitalism** is an economic system in which natural resources and the means of producing goods and services are privately owned. Ideally, capitalism has these features:
   1. Private ownership of property.
   2. Pursuit of personal profit.
   3. Competition and consumer sovereignty.
B. **Socialism** is an economic system in which natural resources and the means of producing goods and services are collectively owned. Ideally, socialism has these features:
   1. Collective ownership of property.
   2. Pursuit of collective goals.
   3. Government control of the economy.
C. **Communism** is a hypothetical economic and political system in which all members of society are socially equal. No society has ever achieved true communism.
D. **Welfare capitalism** is an economic and political system that combines an economic and political system that combines a mostly market-based economy with extensive social welfare programs. It is found in some European nations.
E. **State capitalism** is an economic and political system in which companies are privately owned although they cooperate closely with the government.
F. Relative advantages of capitalism and socialism:
   1. Capitalist societies are considerably more economically productive.
   2. Socialist societies display considerably less income and wealth disparity.
   3. Statistics are not enough to compare overall well-being in either system.
   4. Capitalist countries are characterized by more civil liberties and political freedom.
G. Recently the socialist societies have undergone sweeping changes. Among the reasons:
   1. Their economies were unable to produce enough to allow their citizens an adequate standard of living.
   2. Their governments were heavy-handed and unresponsive.

III. Work in the Postindustrial Economy.

A. SEEING OURSELVES—National Map 16-1: Labor Force Participation Across the United States.

B. The decline of agricultural work. The family farms of yesterday have been replaced by corporate agribusinesses.

C. From factory work to service work. Many jobs in this postindustrial era provide only a modest standard of living.

D. The dual labor market:

   1. The **primary labor market** includes jobs that provide extensive benefits to workers.

   2. The **secondary labor market** includes jobs that provide minimal benefits to workers.

E. **Labor unions** are organizations of workers that seek to improve wages and working conditions by using various strategies, including negotiations and strikes.

   1. American unions have been losing members in recent years and are much weaker than their counterparts in other advanced societies.

F. A **profession** is a prestigious, white-collar occupation that requires extensive formal education. Professions display the following characteristics:

   1. Theoretical knowledge.
   2. Self-regulated practice.
   3. Authority over clients.
   4. Community orientation rather than self-interest.

G. Self-employment, once common in the U.S., is now rare.

H. Unemployment is a major problem in postindustrial societies.

I. The **underground economy** is economic activity involving income that one does not report to the government as required by law.

J. American workplaces are becoming much more socially diverse.

   1. SOCIAL DIVERSITY BOX—Diversity in the New Century: Changes in the Workplace. An upward trend in the U.S. minority population is changing the workplace.

K. Computers are altering the character of work in several ways:

   1. Computers are deskilling labor.
   2. Computers are making work more abstract.
   3. Computers limit workplace interaction.
   4. Computers enhance employers' control of workers.

IV. Corporations.

A. At the core of today's capitalist economy lies the **corporation**, an organization with a legal existence, including rights and liabilities, apart from those of their members.

B. The corporate economy is highly concentrated, with a few large firms holding most assets and earning most of the profits.

C. Conglomerates and corporate linkages.

   1. **Conglomerates** are giant corporations composed of many smaller corporations.

   2. An **interlocking directorate** is a social network of people who serve simultaneously on the boards of directors of many corporations.

Chapter Objectives

1) Define the economy.

2) Identify and discuss ways that the Industrial Revolution changed the economy.

3) Trace the changes that occurred as the economy moved from an industrial to a postindustrial model.

4) Identify and define three sectors of a modern economy.

5) Compare and contrast the two economic models of capitalism and socialism.

6) Distinguish between socialism and communism.

7) Examine the relative advantages of capitalism and socialism, especially with regard to productivity and the distribution of income.

8) Discuss some of the recent trends in the composition of the labor force.

9) Be familiar with the major changes occurring in the U.S. labor market, especially the decline of the agriculture and the shift toward the service sector.

10) Distinguish between the primary and secondary labor markets.

11) Understand some of the reasons why labor unions are presently in decline.

12) Identify the characteristics of a profession and discuss the contemporary trend toward professionalization.

13) Examine the severity of unemployment.

14) Discuss the segments of contributors to the underground economy.

15) Identify ways that computers are changing the workplace.

16) Recognize the extent of economic concentration in the contemporary United States.

17) Explain how large corporations are linked, including conglomerate formation and interlocking directorates.

18) Define the concepts of monopoly and oligopoly and discuss the extent to which large corporations are no longer engaged in competitive economic activity.

19) Examine the global scale on which megacorporations currently operate.

Essay Topics

1) How effectively do you think that the U.S. work force is presently being prepared to work in the evolving postindustrial economy?

2) Given the collapse of the majority of the world's socialist societies, is there still any purpose in learning about non-capitalist economic systems? Defend your position.

3) To what extent does the contemporary U.S. economy reflect the ideal type capitalist model?

4) Given the discussion of the comparative advantages of capitalism and socialism, consider what the U.S. might gain and lose by moving toward a democratic socialist system.

5) What are some consequences of the decline of the family farm and the rise of agribusiness?

6) Consider some of the consequences for the U.S. that follow the fact that most new jobs currently being created are part of the secondary rather than the primary labor market.

7) Do you think that the union movement will continue to decline or can this current trend be reversed? Do workers still need unions? What would happen if there were no unions?

8) Supporters call government aid to corporations "public-private partnerships." Critics call these arrangements "corporate welfare." What do you think? Defend your position.

9) What is the impact of multinationals on poor societies?

10) What are some of the positive and negative consequences of the dramatic concentration of economic power in the U.S. into the hands of the directors of the top corporations?

Integrative Supplement Guide

1. **ABC Videos:**
   - If the Economy Is So Good, Why Do We Feel So Bad? (*Nightline*, 10/27/95)
   - Changes in the Workplace (*World News Tonight/American Agenda*, 12/27/95)
   - Good Economics or Good Politics? (Nightline, 8/5/96)

2. **Transparencies - Series V:**
   - T-100 The Size of Economic Sectors by Income Level of Country
   - T-101 Agricultural Employment in Global Perspective
   - T-102 Industrial Employment in Global Perspective
   - T-103 Participation in the Labor Force by Sex, Race, and Ethnicity, 1997

Supplemental Lecture Material
Forced Labor in the Postindustrial Society

Each year, according to the combined figures of the Justice, Labor, and State departments, more than 100,000 people are forced into servitude in the U.S. Their ranks include both immigrants and U.S. citizens who are forced to work in factories, small businesses and service industries, private homes, and on farms. Of major concern is the fact that their numbers are rising.

The Justice, Labor and State departments response initially was the creation of the National Worker Exploitation Task Force in 1998. To accelerate the effort, they opened a hotline to take calls from anyone to report cases of servitude or worker exploitation in February, 2000.

The Justice Department defines involuntary servitude as "using physical force, threats of force or legal coercion (such as threats of arrest or incarceration) to keep someone working for you." A common example would be an employer threatening to turn in an illegal immigrant.

In most cases, the Immigration and Naturalization service (TNS) says, the victims had been lured to the United States by false promises. This problem arising now (135 years after the passage of the 13th amendment, banning slavery and involuntary servitude) is due to the better reporting of abuses as our perception of what is 'unacceptable' evolves. Keep in mind that slavery wasn't seen as bad for 200 years in this country and even child labor was legal prior to Fair Labor Standards Act in 1938.

Other contributing factors converged in the 1980s. Civil wars and collapsing economies in Third World countries created a flood of new immigrants to the U.S.; lax U.S. border controls made it easier to enter the country illegally; and a massive crackdown on drug traffickers led some to switch to smuggling immigrants. The result was a steep increase in illegal immigrants who entered the country indebted to and exploited by criminals.

There's no doubt that a business gains a competitive edge by using labor supplied by smugglers. Secretary of Labor Alexis Herman points out that: "There's no way a business paying the minimum wage and taxes required by law can compete with one using involuntary help."

By the mid-1980s, international rings of immigrant smugglers were charging up to $35,000 for passage and false papers. When the immigrants were unable to pay, they become indentured to or victimized by their traffickers. (A Rutgers University survey of 300 such Chinese immigrants found that many had been tortured before paying off their debts.

By the 1990s, INS Commissioner Doris Messner noted that sophisticated smugglers were demanding their fees in advance from employers, who passed on the cost to workers by withholding their pay.

A clearer picture of the problem emerged in 1999, when 18 persons pleaded guilty to running a $200 million smuggling ring. Recently, immigrants from China have promised smugglers as much as $50,000 in future wages to stow away in metal cargo containers on giant freighters (Parade Magazine, Feb. 20, 2000). American citizens have also been the victims of exploitation since the 1980s, when Congress passed the Migrant and Seasonal Agricultural Worker Act; things improved even more in 1996 when with overwhelming bipartisan support, congress passed the Illegal Immigration Reform Act that made the trafficking in humans a felony punishable by up to 15 years. Rep. Lamar Smith (R-Wyo.) noted that "we inadvertently created an imbalance in the penal code that made smuggling more appealing than drug trafficking. This law redresses that."

Victims have also begun to fight back as they have taken some aggressive steps to make it apparent to corporations that they are victims too, as they sue former and current employers in federal court and thus make it more difficult for such exploitation to ever happen again.

Sources

Gordy, Molly. "A Call to Fight Forced Labor." *Parade Magazine* (February 20, 2000):4-5.

Discussion Questions

1) Do you know of any cases of forced labor? If so describe it and discuss what steps you have taken to eliminate such exploitation.

2) Discuss how the globalization of the economy contributed to the increase in forced labor both in the U.S. and other industrialized countries.

3) In both New York and California, we have seen the emergence of a class of indentured garment workers; in New York, forced subway peddlers. What are some other examples of forced labor that you are aware of in your geographic area?

Supplemental Lecture Material
Changing Workplace Trends

Recent data suggests that American managers and professionals putting in ever-increasing work hours is a trend that is coming to an end. For years, the proportion of Americans working very long weeks was on the rise. In all occupations, the share of people putting in more than 49 hours a week on the job rose significantly in the late 1980s and early 1990s, accord-ing to the Bureau of Labor Statistics. Leading the trend and posting the longest hours were the highest-paid workers, managers and professionals, with as many as 29.5% logging marathon workweeks in the 1980s and early 1990s, compared with about 24% in the early 1980s.

But Randy Ilg, an economist with the Labor Department's Division of Labor Force Statistics, says that the past several years data suggest the share of workers putting in 49 hours or more a week "has plateaued." Managers and professionals working 49-plus hours fell to 27.9% in 1998.

That doesn't mean, however, that U.S. workers are taking fewer and shorter vacations, and also that they are working more hours over the course of a year. As a result, the U.S. has even surpassed Japan (the stolid capital of overwork) as the leader among major developed nations in annual hours worked per person, according to the International Labor Organization.

Also, the proportion of women entering the workforce continues to rise, and more of them are working in occupations that demand long hours. Women now hold 49% of management and professional jobs (up from 45.2% in 1989.) That means that more households, as a whole, are focused more intensely on work, fostering stress. The Economic Policy Institute says that annual hours worked by all household members in the average U.S. family have continued to rise steadily, posting gains of about 6% in the last 20 years.

Sue Shellengerger, in a Wall Street Journal column, however, indicates that there are signs that "workplace trendsetters are putting al lid on hours." One reason is the aging of the workforce. It's median age has risen nearly 10% since 1985, to 39.1 years (from 35.7). Workers aged 24 to 54 typically work the longest hours, and the oldest members of the baby boom generation are moving out of that group.

"Many employees are working smarter" writes Shellenberger. More employees are challenging the popular wisdom that anyone holding "a real management job" needs to put in 45 to 60 hours a week. The issue is more whether or not one gets the job done more than how many hours per week they work. Others want schedules that can be sustained over the "long-haul" as four-day-a-week schedules are increasing in popularity, as family responsibilities are becoming more of a priority. Clearly the values of workers are changing.

"Only time will tell whether Americans have indeed turned a corner from the stressed-out, overworked archetypes that are part of our national self-image" says Shellenberger. "But it's starting to look as though more of us are assigning our time the high value it deserves and allocating it, in measured fashion, to what matters most."

Source

Shellenberger, Sue. "The American Way of Work (More!) May Be Easing Up." *The New York Times* (Jan. 19, 2000):B1.

Discussion Questions

1) If work hours are topping out in many occupations, will workers stress levels top out too? Why or why not?

2) What factors, in addition to the length of the workweek, cause stress for workers? (Where would you rank such factors as urgency and the lack of control over one's work schedule on a list of workplace stressors?)

Chapter 17

Politics and Government

I. Power and Authority.
  A. **Politics** is the social institution that distributes power, sets a society's agenda, and makes decisions.
  B. According to Max Weber, **power** is the ability to achieve desired ends despite resistance from others. Power is wielded by **government**, which is defined as a formal organization that directs the political life of a society.
  C. **Authority** is power that people perceive as legitimate rather than coercive.
    1. **Traditional authority** is power legitimized by respect for long-established cultural patterns. Its importance declines as societies industrialize.
    2. **Rational-legal authority** is power legitimized by legally enacted rules and regulations.
    3. **Charismatic authority** is power legitimized through extraordinary personal abilities that inspire devotion and obedience.
      a. Because it is inherently unstable, charismatic authority must undergo a process of **routinization of charisma** in which it is transformed into a combination of traditional and rational-legal authority.

II. Politics in Global Perspective.
  A. As the political institution expanded, the political state emerged.
    1. The earliest political states were city states.
    2. The modern world is characterized by nation states.
  B. **Monarchy** is a type of political system that transfers power from generation to generation in a single family. Earlier monarchies were absolute. Modern ones are generally constitutional, with the monarch being little more than a symbolic head of state.
  C. **Democracy** is a political system in which power is exercised by the people as a whole. Democracies are generally representative rather than fully participatory. Affluent industrial societies tend to be democracies. Modern democracies are characterized by extensive bureaucracies and economic inequalities.
    1. Democracy and freedom: Contrasting approaches.
      a. Capitalist societies define freedom as political liberty.
      b. Socialist societies see freedom as satisfaction of basic economic needs.
    2. WINDOW ON THE WORLD—Global Map 17–1: Political Freedom in Global Perspective. In 1999, 88 of the world's nations, containing 40 percent of all people, were politically "free."
  D. **Authoritarianism** is a political system that denies popular participation in government.
    1. GLOBAL SOCIOLOGY BOX—"Soft Authoritarianism" or Planned Prosperity? A Report from Singapore.

E. **Totalitarianism** is a political system that extensively regulates people's lives.

F. The rise of multinational corporations, the information revolution, and the growth of non-governmental organizations all suggest that a global political system may be emerging.

III. Politics in the United States.

A. Our cultural emphasis on individualism implies the desirability of a small government, but in recent decades the U.S. government has expanded into a vast **welfare state**, a range of government agencies and programs that provides benefits to the population.

B. The political spectrum.

    1. Economic issues. Economic liberals expect government to maintain a healthy economy, whereas economic conservatives counter that government intervention inhibits economic productivity.

    2. Social issues. The Republican party is more conservative on both economic and social issues, while the Democratic Party takes a more liberal stand.

    3. Mixed positions. Most people do not hold the same positions on economic and social issues.

    4. Party identification in the United States is weak.

C. **Special-interest groups** are political alliances of people interested in some economic or social issue. Many employ lobbyists.

    1. **Political action committees** are organizations formed by a special-interest group, independent of political parties, to pursue political aims by raising and spending money.

D. Voter apathy is widespread in the United States. Gender, age and ethnicity are all correlated with likelihood of voting. Conservatives attribute apathy to indifference to politics; liberals attribute it to alienation from politics.

    1. SEEING OURSELVES—National Map 17–1: Political Apathy among Young People across the United States. Of all age categories, young people are the least likely to vote in national elections.

IV. Theoretical Analysis of Power in Society.

A. The **pluralist model** is an analysis of politics that views power as dispersed among many competing interest groups. It is compatible with the structural-functional paradigm.

    1. Pluralists claim that politics is an arena of negotiation and that it has many sources.

B. The **power-elite model** is an analysis of politics that views power as concentrated among the rich. It is linked with the social-conflict paradigm.

    1. C. Wright Mills developed this view.

C. The **Marxist political-economy model** is an analysis that explains politics in terms of the operation of a society's economic system.

D. Critical evaluation: Research by Nelson Polsby supports the pluralist model; Research by Robert Lynd and Helen Lynd as well as Floyd Hunter supports the power-elite model; However, in the end, how one views this country's political system is as much a matter of political values as scientific fact.

V. Power Beyond the Rules.
  A. **Political revolution** is the overthrow of one political system in order to establish another. Most revolutions share the following patterns:
      1. Rising expectations.
      2. Unresponsive government.
      3. Radical leadership by intellectuals.
      4. Establishing a new legitimacy.
  B. **Terrorism** constitutes random acts of violence or the threat of such violence used by an individual or group as a political strategy. Terrorism has four distinguishing characteristics:
      1. Terrorists try to paint violence as a legitimate political tactic.
      2. Terrorism is used not just by groups but also by governments against their own people.
      3. Democratic societies reject terrorism in principle, but they are especially vulnerable to terrorists because they afford extensive civil liberties to their people and have less extensive police networks.
      4. Terrorism is always a matter of definition.

VI. War and Peace.
War is armed conflict among the people of various societies, directed by their governments.
  A. The Causes of War:
      1. Perceived threats.
      2. Social problems.
      3. Political objectives.
      4. Moral objectives.
      5. The absence of alternatives.
  B. GLOBAL SOCIOLOGY BOX—Violence Beyond the Rules: A Report from Yugoslavia.
  C. The costs and causes of militarism:
      1. Defense spending diverts resources from the struggle for survival by millions of poor people throughout the world.
      2. The **military-industrial complex** is the close association among the federal government, the military and defense industries.
  D. Nuclear weapons and war.
      1. **Nuclear proliferation** is the acquisition of nuclear weapons by more and more nations.
  E. Pursuing peace. Here are the most recent approaches to peace:
      1. Deterrence.
      2. High-technology defense.
      3. Diplomacy and disarmament.
      4. Resolving underlying conflict.
  F. CRITICAL THINKING BOX—Information Warfare: Let Your Fingers Do the Fighting.

VII. Looking Ahead: Politics in the Twenty-First Century.
A. Several problems and trends:
1. Inconsistency between our democratic ideals and low public participation in politics.
2. The Information Revolution is changing politics.
3. Analysts envision a broader range of political systems, linking government to economic production in various ways.
4. There is the danger of war in many parts of the world.
B. CONTROVERSY AND DEBATE BOX—"On-line" Democracy:" Can Computers In crease Political Participation?

Chapter Objectives

1) Define politics.

2) Distinguish between power and authority.

3) Identify and define Max Weber's three ideal types of authority.

4) Describe the four basic types of contemporary political systems: monarchy, democracy, authoritarianism, and totalitarianism.

5) Discuss the extent to which a global political system is beginning to emerge.

6) Summarize attitudes and party identification that form the political spectrum.

7) Understand the role of special interest groups and political action committees in the U.S. political system.

8) Discuss the problem of voter apathy and interpretations of this phenomenon.

9) Compare and contrast three models of power in the United States.

10) Characterize successful political revolutions.

11) Outline four distinguishing characteristics of terrorism.

12) Name five factors that promote war.

13) Explain how the military-industrial complex fueled the arms race during the Cold War.

14) Examine the continuing dangers associated with nuclear proliferation.

15) Summarize four recent approaches to peace.

16) Outline several problems and trends of political systems in the twenty-first century.

Essay Topics

1) Compare and contrast the three models of U.S. politics with regard to power distribution.

2) What are some of the beneficial and the negative characteristics of charismatic authority?

3) Which of the three different models of the U.S. political system do you believe is correct?

4) Of the four approaches to peace, what do you think is the best way to reduce the danger of war?

5) What are your positions along the political spectrum with regard to economic and social issues? What are some of the sociological factors which explain your style of political thinking?

6) Do you think that the power of special-interest groups and PACs improves or corrupts the U.S. political system? How, if at all, would you control or restrict their power?

7) Do you think that political apathy is due to indifference or alienation? Discuss.

8) What are the problems which result from widespread political apathy? Are there any positive consequences of such apathy?

9) Outline what you regard as some of the positive and negative consequences of the concentration of political power at the national level in the hands of a coherent power-elite or military-industrial complex.

10) In what way is the Information Revolution changing politics?

Integrative Supplement Guide

1. ABC Videos:
*   The Debate Over Affirmative Action (*Nightline*, 6/16/95)
*   Working Off Welfare, Working on Welfare Reform (*Nightline*, 6/19/95)
*   America's Fight Against Terrorism (*This Week with Sam & Cokie*, 8/23/98)
*   Good Economics or Good Politics? (*Nightline*, 8/5/96)

2. Transparencies - Series V:
*   T-112 Political Freedom in Global Perspective
*   T-113 The Size of Government: Tax Revenues as Share of Gross Domestic Product, 1994
*   T-114 Voter Turnout Across the United States
*   T-115 Political Apathy by Income Level
*   T-116 Deaths of Americans in Ten U.S. Wars
*   T-117 Members of Congress by Race

Supplemental Lecture Material
The Size & Scope of the Federal Government in the U.S. Today

Our cultural emphasis on individualism implies the desirability of a small government. Statistics however, suggest that government may be bigger than we think. "Debate over the size & scope of government has long been the stuff of politics" notes Paul C. Light (a senior fellow at the Brooburgs Institution) and this assessment held true for the 2000 presidential race.

In 1996, President Clinton declared that the era of big government was over. Critics point out, however, that it was only by using the most narrow head count of civil service employment that Mr. Clinton could make his claim about cutting big government. To see the true picture, Light argues that "one must count all the heads, including full-time federal civil servants, uniformed military personnel, postal workers and people who deliver goods and services on behalf of the federal government under contracts, grants and mandates to state and local government."

When all those numbers are added together, the federal government appears to be very large indeed. In 1996 (the most recent years for which good numbers are available), the true size of government was almost 17 million people — most off the books. Light estimates that "a high shadow workforce that accounted for 64 jobs per 1000 Americans in 1996 — not the 11 per 1,000 Americans advertised in that year's federal budget."

During then Vice President Al Gore's presidential campaign, he claimed that the total federal work force was almost 750,000 smaller in 1996 than it had been in 1993 and continued its decline through the end of 1998. Yet most of those cuts came from Pentagon downsizing that began at the end of the Vietnam and accelerated under President George Bush.

Mr. Light points out that the key question in debating the size of government "is not why the shadow of government is so large, but why the federal civil service is so small." He believes that the answer resides in the incentives for both the democrats and Republicans to "create an illusion of small-ness." Democrats use the illusion to protect a more activist government, and Republicans to hide their reluctance to change the basic mission of government. And both parties cater to a public that wants a federal government that looks smaller, but delivers at least as much as it always has.

Light concludes that "it is impossible to have an honest debate about the proper size of government without accurate estimates of the true size of government." As much as the numbers might unsettle presidential candidates, they might help the public recognize just how big government must be to deliver the things they want. Indeed, everything has its price.

Source

Light, Paul C. "Big Government Is Bigger Than You Think." *The New York Times* (Jan. 13, 1999):A22.

Discussion Questions

1) The financial costs of big government are obvious. The question is what are the social costs of reducing or eliminating the services that big government has come to provide?

2) It has been argued that the key issue in the debate about big government is what the government does, not how many people do it. What are your feelings on this issue?

Supplemental Lecture Material
Political Action Committees

The 2000 presidential campaign has been marked by the emergence of "stealth PACs' — a new breed of political attack operations that work largely in secret. Using deliberately bland names like "Shape the Debate" or "coalition to Protect Americans Now," these groups take advantage of loop-holes in campaign and tax laws that allow them to legally raise millions from individuals and corporations for openly partisan purposes without revealing where the money comes from.

Both parties long ago mastered the art of accessing millions in unlimited soft money from wealthy donors and companies to be used to promote the party and pay for issues ads. In April, 2000, the GOP raised $21.3 million at a single fund-raising dinner (a new record). A few weeks later, Bill Clinton and Al Gore helped the party raise $26.5 million at a ribs-and-chicken fund-raising event featuring Robin Williams and pop singer Le Ann Rimes. Major contributors include AT&T, Lockheed, Martin, and Westinghouse. At both events, all monies raised had to be disclosed. The new groups, however, aren't required to report any of their activities to the public or the Federal Election Commission.

Both Democrats and political-watch-dog groups have lodged protests against these "stealth PACs," complaining that the anonymous operations are the final collapse of decades-old campaign reform laws designed to limit the influence of special interests. Newsweek's Michael Isikoff points out that voters who turn on their television sets and see an attack ad produced by one of these groups, have no way of knowing who paid for it – or what political favors the group might expect in return.

But as much as Democrats complain about the groups, campaign finance experts say it may have been Clinton himself who led the way during his 1996 campaign. Critics contend that the president stretched the limits of the law as never before, taking money intended for party-boosting "issue ads" and using it instead for a multi-million dollar blitz promoting his own re-election.

As the barrier between "issue ads" and "candidate ads" collapsed, political operatives for both parties saw an opportunity to push the boundaries even more. Isikoff reports that the AFL-CIO spent $35 million on attack ads against Republicans in 1996. The same year, the liberal Sierra club found a loophole in the tax laws. By registering with the IRS under section 527 of the tax code, the group was able to set up a separate "political committee" — and avoid reporting its activities to the federal election Committee. The Seirra Club used the gimmick to pay for $3.5 million in pro-environment ads targeting Republicans and in the 2000 presidential campaign, spent over $8 million for an ad campaign that in part bashed George W. Bush's environmental record in Texas.

Stealth PACs are careful not to violate two rules: like political parties, they aren't allowed to use the words "vote for" or "vote against" in their ads and they can't coordinate their activities with the politicians who

benefit from their ads. They often, however, come very close to the line.

Source

Isikoff, Michael. "The Secret Money Chase." *Newsweek* (June 5, 2000):23-25.

Discussion Question

1) Given the secretive nature of "527s", how can their activities be monitored (or can they be monitored at all)?

Supplemental Lecture Material
The Political Spectrum: A Closer Look

As noted in Chapter 16, the conventional liberal-to-conservative political spectrum is too crude a conceptual tool to accurately capture the true diversity of the political attitudes of U.S. voters. As a result, political scientists have constructed a number of more sophisticated topologies.

The following schema was developed on the basis of surveys taken by the Times Mirror Center for the People and the Press, combined with a cluster analysis of U.S. demographic characteristics:

CORE DEMOCRATIC GROUPS
'60s Democrats: 9 percent of the adult population, up 1 percentage point since 1987. This well-educated, heavily female group has a strong belief in social justice. These mainstream Democrats are highly tolerant of views and lifestyles they do not share. They favor most forms of social spending.

New Dealers: 7 percent of the adult population, down 4 percentage points since 1987. Older, blue-collar, and religious. The roots of this aging group of traditional Democrats can be traced back to the New Deal. Although supportive of many social-spending issues, New Dealers are intolerant on social issues and somewhat hawkish on defense.

God and Country Democrats: 8 percent of the adult population, up 1 percentage point since 1987. This group is older, poor, and disproportionately black with high numbers concentrated in the South. The God and Country Democrats have a strong faith in America and are highly religious. They favor social spending and are moderately intolerant.

Partisan Poor: 10 percent of the adult population, up 1 percentage point since 1987. Very low income, relatively high proportions of blacks, and poorly educated. This traditionally loyal Democratic group has a strong faith in its party's ability to achieve social justice. The Partisan Poor firmly support all forms of social spending, yet they are conservative on some social issues.

DEMOCRATIC-LEANING GROUPS
Followers: 5 percent of the adult population, down 2 percentage points since 1987. Young, poorly educated, and disproportionately black. This group shows little interest in politics and is very persuadable and unpredictable. Although they are not critical of government or big business, Followers do not have much faith in America.

Seculars: 7 percent of the adult population, down 1 percentage point since 1987. This group is uniquely characterized by its lack of religious belief. In addition, Seculars are strongly committed to personal freedom and are dovish on defense issues. Their level of participation in politics, however, is not as high as one might expect, given their education and political sophistication.

CORE REPUBLICAN GROUPS
Enterprisers: 12 percent of the adult population, up 2 percentage points since 1987. Affluent, well-educated, and predominantly male. This classic Republican group is mainly characterized by its pro-business and anti-government attitudes. Enterprisers are moderate on questions of personal freedom but oppose increased spending on most social issues.

Moralists: 11 percent of the adult population, unchanged since 1987. Middle-aged and middle income, this core Republican group is militantly anti-Communist and restrictive on personal freedom issues.

REPUBLICAN-LEANING GROUPS
Upbeats: 8 percent of the adult population, down 2 percentage points since 1987. Young and optimistic, the members of this group are firm believers in America and in the country's government. Upbeats are moderate in their political attitudes but were strongly pro-Reagan.

Disaffecteds: 12 percent of the adult population, up 3 percentage points since 1987. Alienated, pessimistic, and financially pressured, this group leans toward the GOP camp, but it has had historical ties to the Democratic party. Disaffecteds are skeptical of both big government and big business, but are pro-military.

LOW-INCOME GROUP
Bystanders: 12 percent of the adult population, up 1 percentage point since 1987. The members of this group are young, predominantly white, and poorly educated. They neither participate in politics nor show any interest in current affairs. They lean toward Republicanism.

Source

"Eleven Ways to Vote," *American Demographics* Vol. 13 No. 11 (November l991):35.

Discussion Questions
1) With which of these groups do you most closely identify? Which are most visible in your home community?

2) Can you think of any groups of people whose views do not seem to be addressed in this typology?

Supplemental Lecture Material
Women in Politics

In 1994 only 868 of the 12,800 candidates running in Brazil's general election were women. That changed in 1996, when a new quota law mandating that 20 percent of the candidates of each party be women came into effect. An amendment to raise that quota to 30 percent has been introduced. In conjunction with legislation, Brazil's government launched an aggressive media and education campaign to encourage women to stand for election. Thousands of handbooks with tips on how to raise money, organize a campaign committee, and develop campaign literature were distributed. The book also encourages women to form alliances with other female candidates no matter what parties they belong to, since practical support such as adequate funds for campaign expenses or availability of daycare is often lacking, making it difficult for many women to run unless they do so on a combined platform emphasizing issues such as family planning, equal pay, abortion, and daycare.

Critics contend that these measures are a kind of reverse discrimination and will also cause unqualified candidates to be put up for election by the parties. Supporters respond that in the end voters will have the last word

and choose whom they consider best suited anyway.

In general, laws granting women equal rights have been slow to emerge in Brazil. It wasn't until 1988 that the right of husbands to prevent wives from accepting employment was annulled. So, some might say, the lack of female representation in government should come as no surprise. Consider, however, the fact that the United States ranks number 54 in the percentage (only 11.7%) of women in legislature, behind most of Europe.

In 1997, Scandinavian countries such as Sweden (40.4 %), Norway (39.4 %), Finland (33.5 %), Denmark (33 %), and the Netherlands (31.3 %) led the way, making up the top five of a list of top ten countries with the most women in their national legislatures, lower or single house. New Zealand, Seychelles, Austria, Germany and Iceland rounded out that list. Generally, those countries have some sort of rules and quotas in place to ensure women candidates run.

That same year, Britain followed suit. "In the May 1 election, British voters nearly doubled the representation of women in Parliament, thanks to the Labour Party's decision to field women for a quarter of all seats." (Chaddock, p.1) This happened only, however, after a 1987 Labour loss had analysts conclude they needed the vote of women to win the next election. The result was quotas requiring 40 percent representation of women at all levels of the party. A suit by two male candidates charging sexual discrimination came late enough in the process that despite a victory of quota opponents in court, too many women had already been designated to change course. In addition, many local parties selected women as a protest against the court ruling.

France, on the other hand, is resisting quotas that might encourage more women to enter politics. Just last year, "75 percent of

French deputies said they opposed the principle of parity between men and women in the legislature." (Chaddock, p. 7) As a result, only 45 women will run for the 577 seats available, or 7.8 percent of the candidates for the two major parties.

Though some in France claim that women simply will not vote for women, others dispute such a charge, and polls appear to support the latter. In 1996, 82 percent of French people said they favored sexual parity in politics.

"Worldwide, women constitute 11.7 percent of the world's parliamentarians. 'Political life is still dominated by men, and the majority of parliamentary assemblies are still overwhelmingly or entirely composed of men,' concluded women legislators from 75 countries meeting in Seoul." (Chaddock, p. 7).

Sources

Chaddock, Gail Russell. "British Election As Model: Quotas Boost Women Pols," *Christian Science Monitor* (May 14, 1997):1 and 7.

Epestein, Jack. "'Lipstick Lobby' Puts 75,000 Women On the Ballot in Patriarchal Brazil," *Christian Science Monitor* (September 10, 1996):1 and 7.

Discussion Questions

1) What is your opinion on quotas to ensure women have a chance to be elected to public office? Would they work in the United States? Why or why not? Are there other strategies that might increase female representation?

2) Would a greater representation of women in government alter our society in a significant way? How?

3) **Activity.** Research your state legislature to find out the percentage of women, then research their voting records compared to that of men. Do you see any trends?

Supplemental Lecture Material
Family and Friendship Guide Japanese Voting

"Giri" is a Japanese word that describes the sense of being in debt or under obligation to someone. The concept not only plays a role in private relationships, but also in politics, especially in smaller communities.

"Giri" explains why an employee votes for the candidate his or her corporation supports and asks *them* to support as many firms do. It explains why wives and parents go along to vote the same. After all, the company gives the employee a job, income, and benefits. This entitles them to loyalty and support, according to Japanese culture. The same goes for a local politician having provided some benefit to the town, such as allocating funds to build a bridge or a road, or the son who inherits his father's seat in Parliament.

At the root of this attitude, however, is not just "giri," but also a sense that elections don't make a difference at all in real life. While the Japanese are more likely to vote than U.S. citizens, issues hardly seem to matter at all.

"Of course, that may not be just apathy but also shrewd observation. Politicians are rarely agents of change in Japan and the real decisions are typically made by bureaucrats in government ministries. Even then, the decision-making process tends to be based less on leadership than on consensus."

Source

Kristof, Nicholas D.. "Family and Friendship Guide Japanese Voting," *New York Times* (October 13, 1996):1 and 10.

Discussion Question
1) Although the concept of "giri" might initially strike you as alien, do you see any similarities in certain aspects of our political system?

Chapter 18

Family

I. The Family: Basic Concepts.
  A. The **family** is a social institution, found in all societies, that unites individuals into cooperative groups that oversee the bearing and raising of children.
  B. Families are structured around **kinship,** a social bond, based on blood, marriage, or adoption, that joins individuals into families.
  C. The **family unit** consists of a social group of two or more people, related by blood, marriage, or adoption, who usually live together.
    1. The **family of orientation** is the family into which a person is born and from whom s/he receives early socialization.
    2. The **family of procreation** is a family in which people have or adopt children of their own.
  D. In most societies, families are formed by **marriage**, a legally-sanctioned relationship involving economic cooperation as well as normative sexual activity and childbearing, that people expect to be enduring.
  E. In practice, the definition of a family is becoming more inclusive, with many people accepting the concept of **families of affinity,** people with or without legal or blood ties who feel they belong together and who want to define themselves as a family.

II. The Family: Global Variations.
  A. The **extended family** is a family unit including parents, children, and also other kin. It is also called the consanguine family.
    1. Industrialization tends to promote the decline of the extended family and the rise of the **nuclear** or **conjugal family,** a family unit composed of one or two parents and their children.
    2. GLOBAL SOCIOLOGY BOX—The Weakest Families on Earth? A Report from Sweden. David Popenoe argues that one drawback of an expanding welfare state is that the family unit weakens.
  B. Marriage patterns:
    1. **Endogamy** is marriage between people of the same social category.
    2. **Exogamy** is marriage between people of different social categories.
    3. Industrial societies favor **monogamy**, a form of marriage involving only two partners.
    4. Most preindustrial cultures allow **polygamy**, a type of marriage uniting three or more people.
      a. **Polygyny** is a type of marriage uniting one male to two or more females.
      b. **Polyandry** is a type of marriage joining one female with two or more males.

5. WINDOW ON THE WORLD—Global Map 18–1: Marital Forms in Global Perspective.

C. Residential patterns:

   1. **Patrilocality** is a residential pattern by which a married couple lives with or near the husband's family.

   2. **Matrilocality** is a residential pattern by which a married couple lives with or near the wife's family.

   3. More common in industrial societies, **neolocality** is a residential pattern in which a married couple lives apart from both sets of parents.

D. **Descent** refers to the system by which members of a society trace kinship over generations.

   1. **Patrilineal descent** is a system tracing kinship through males.

   2. **Matrilineal descent** is a system tracing kinship through females.

   3. Industrial societies with greater gender equality usually display **bilateral descent,** a system tracing kinship through both men and women.

E. Virtually all family systems worldwide are **patriarchies**.

III. Theoretical Analysis of the Family.

A. Functions of the family: Structural-functional analysis.

   1. Socialization.

   2. Regulation of sexual activity through the **incest taboo,** a cultural norm forbidding sexual relations or marriage between certain kin.

   3. Social placement.

   4. Material and emotional security.

   5. Critical evaluation.

      a. This approach demonstrates why society depends on the families.

      b. It pays little attention to the fact that other institutions can provide key familial functions.

      c. It ignores the diversity of family life in the U.S.

      d. It overlooks the problems of family life.

B. Inequality and the family: Social-conflict analysis.

   1. Family structure promotes inequality in several ways:

      a. Because property is inherited through the family, it perpetuates class inequality.

      b. The family is generally patriarchal, perpetuating gender inequality.

      c. Endogamous marriage also perpetuates racial and ethnic inequality.

   2. Critical evaluation. This approach fails to account for the existence of family problems in noncapitalist societies.

C. Constructing family life: micro-level analysis.

   1. As families share activities, they build emotional bonds.

   2. Family life can also be analyzed using social-exchange theory.

   3. Critical evaluation. These perspectives ignore the fact that family life is similar for people affected by any given set of structural and cultural forces.

IV. Stages of Family Life.

A. Courtship.
    1. Arranged marriages were common in preindustrial cultures.
    2. With industrialization, romantic love becomes a central criterion in mate choice.
    3. All societies promote **homogamy**, marriage between people with the same social characteristics.
    4. GLOBAL SOCIOLOGY BOX—Early to Wed: A Report from Rural India.

B. Settling in: Ideal and real marriage. Newly married couples often have to scale down their expectations.

C. Child rearing has changed since industrialization. Children are now seen as economic liabilities rather than as assets. Congress passed the Family and Medical Leave Act in 1993 to help ease the conflict between family and job responsibilities.
    1. APPLYLING SOCIOLOGY—Critical Thinking Box: Who's Minding the Kids? Working parents are increasingly relying on daycare programs for their children.

D. Marriages between the elderly usually stress companionship. Retirement and the death of a spouse disrupt families in later life.

V. U.S. Families: Class, Race and Gender.

A. Social class heavily influences partners' expectations regarding marriage; and the same holds true for children.

B. Ethnicity and race also strongly affect the family.
    1. Hispanic families tend to enjoy the support of extended families, to exercise a good deal of control over their children's courtship, and to promote machismo.
    2. African-American families, facing serious economic problems, are especially likely to be single-parent and female-headed.
    3. The number of racially mixed marriages is rising steadily.

C. Women and men experience marriage differently, with men clearly benefiting more than women, according to Jesse Bernard.

VI. Transition and Problems in Family Life.

A. The United States has the highest divorce rate in the world. The divorce rate has risen rapidly this century and at present about half of all couples are expected to divorce.
    1. The high U.S. divorce rate has many causes:
        a. Individualism is on the rise.
        b. Romantic love often subsides.
        c. Women are now less dependent on men.
        d. Many of today's marriages are stressful.
        e. Divorce is more socially acceptable.
        f. Legally, divorce is easier to get.
    2. Who divorces? At greatest risk of divorce are young spouses with little money, who have yet to mature emotionally.
        a. SEEING OURSELVES—National Map 18–1: Divorced People Across the United States. About 11 percent of the U.S. population aged fifeen and over are divorced or separated.
        b. CRITICAL THINKING BOX—Which Will It Be: Real Marriage or Marriage "Lite"?

    B. Nationwide, almost half of all marriages are now remarriages for at least one partner. Remarriage often creates blended families.

    C. **Family violence** is the emotional, physical or sexual abuse of one family member by another.

        1. Violence against women includes spouse battering and marital rape, problems which are receiving increased attention in modern society.

        2. Violence against children is also a widespread problem.

VII. Alternative Family Forms.

    A. One-parent families tend to face serious financial problems.

    B. **Cohabitation** is the sharing of a household by an unmarried couple .

    C. Gay and lesbian couples continue to face opposition from most Americans.

    D. An increasingly large number of people are voluntarily choosing temporary or permanent singlehood.

    E. CONTROVERSY AND DEBATE BOX—Should We Save the Traditional Families?

VIII. New Reproductive Technology and the Family.

    A. Recent medical advances involving *in vitro* fertilization.

IX. Looking Ahead: Family in the Twenty-First Century.

    A. The high divorce rate is unlikely to decline.

    B. Family life in the future will be highly variable.

    C. Most children will probably continue to grow up with only weak ties to their fathers.

    D. Two-career couples will continue to be common.

    E. The importance of the new reproductive technologies will increase.

Chapter Objectives

1) Define kinship, marriage, and the family.

2) Distinguish between nuclear and extended families.

3) Distinguish between endogamy and exogamy.

4) Describe the two basic types of marriages (monogamous and polygamous) and with the two types of polygamy (polygyny and polyandry).

5) Identify and discuss three residential patterns of marriage.

6) Distinguish between bilateral, patrilineal, and matrilineal descent.

7) Summarize how the structural-functional, social-conflict, symbolic-interactionist, and social-exchange paradigms direct our attention to different aspects of the sociology of the family.

8) Identify the social functions of the family.

9) Identify how the family perpetuates social inequality.

10) Identify and describe the four stages of family life.

11) Discuss how variables of class, race and gender influence family patterns.

12) Identify causes for the high U.S. divorce rate.

13) Identify risk factors for divorce.

14) Discuss the scope of the problem of family violence.

15) Examine alternative family forms currently gaining popularity in the United States.

16) Realize why some of the new reproductive technologies are causing controversy.

Essay Topics

1) Do you believe that the traditional family should be saved? Why or why not?

2) Do you think that Congress has done enough to ease the conflict between family and job responsibilities by passing the Family and Medical Leave Act or should more laws be enacted? What would you propose?

3) What are some positive and negative consequences of the Swedish de-emphasis of the family? Should the United States move in this direction? Why or why not?

4) Do you think most people have unrealistically high expectations regarding marriage? Where do these expectations come from?

5) What are some of the ways in which society might respond to help reduce the problems that arise when both parents work? Should these responses be the responsibility of the parents, the employer, or the government?

6) Is divorce best viewed as a problem, a solution, or a symptom?

7) After reflecting on the text's explanation for our high rate of divorce, do you think that a substantial reduction of this rate is likely in the foreseeable future? How might we attempt to attain such a reduction? Would the social consequences of such a program be, on the whole, socially beneficial?

8) How serious a problem is single-parent childrearing? How ought our society respond to this concern?

9) Should we allow gay and lesbian couples complete legal equality with heterosexual couples? Discuss.

10) How is new reproductive technology changing families? What ethical concerns do you have about such medical advances?

Integrative Supplement Guide

1. **ABC Videos:**
- Middle Class - The Family Dream (*Nightline*, 1/6/95)
- Soft on Domestic Violence (*Day One*, 2/2/95)
- That's Not My Job - Division of Parenting Duties (*20/20*, 9/23/94)
- Family Matters (*Prime Time Live*, 3/22/95)
- Where Are the Fathers? Welfare and Unwed Mothers (*20/20*, 4/15/94)
  Solutions: Managing Family Time (*World News Tonight*, 9/12/96)

- Faceless, Nameless Fathers (*20/20*, 1/19/98)
- One Big Happy Family (*20/20*, 6/19/98)

2. Transparencies - Series V:
- T-118 Marital Form in Global Perspective
- T-119 Percentage of College Students Who Express a Willingness to Marry Without Romantic Love
- T-120 Family Form in the United States, 1996
- T-121 The Divorce Rate for the United States, 1890-1996
- T-122 Divorced People Across the United States
- T-123 Payment of Child Support Following Divorce
- T-124 Percent of Births to Unmarried Women, 1994
- T-125 Multicultural Marriages in the United States
- T-126 Children Living with Married Couples

Supplemental Lecture Material
Birth Order and the Baby Boom

According to Massachusetts Institute of Technology scientist Frank J. Sullivan, birth order makes all the difference in personality and openess to change. Firstborns tend to identify with authority and uphold the status quo, while laterborns identify with the underdog and challenge establishment. This is not just interesting on a personal level, but has larger implications for society. During the 1930s, families had an average of 2.5 children, so firstborns made up 41 percent of children born then. This group has been known as the Silent generation, generally conservative and defending the status quo.

On the other hand, in the baby boom of the post-war years, families had three or four children on average, and the percentage of firstborns shrank in proportion.

Since the older boomers, who are more likely to be firstborns, are now at the prime age for positions in power in business and politics, this is a possible explanation for such conservative movements as the rise of the religious right, welfare reform, and the crackdown on drugs and cigarette smoking.

But younger baby boomers, of whom many are younger siblings, will follow on the heels of their older brothers and sisters. "Their openess to change and their acceptance of new ideas could provide the impetus to reinvent Social Security, health care, and other societal systems." Lastborns, in particular tend to be daring and liberal.

So, what does all this mean for the not-so-near future? Baby boomers themselves have tended to have smaller families of less than two children, with firstborns once again at a higher 43 percent. Since those children tend to follow the lead of their parents, it will matter tremendously which set of baby boomers they have been raised by, the more conservative, or the more liberal.   " The firstborn of the firstborn boomers may try to counteract some of the changes instituted by laterborn boomers. But their younger siblings along with the firstborns of laterborn boomers, will soon come along to stir things up."

Most notably, what is going to be lacking, is a lack of middleborns, who tend to mediate and compromise. Therefore, "in the future, the contrast between firstborns and lastborns could become stark indeed."

Source

Russell, Cheryl. "Birth Order and the Baby Boom," *American Demographics,* Vol. 19, No. 3 (March 1997):10-12.

Discussion Question

1) Do you think this birth order principle holds true globally? Why or why not?

Supplemental Lecture Material
Cohabitation

The National Marriage Project on the negative effects of cohabitation, co-authored by Rutgers University sociologist David Popenoe and Barbara Dafoe Whitehead, challenges much of the conventional wisdom on the subject.

In an interview with David Boldt of the Philadelphia Inquirer, Popenoe points out that living together may do no harm if the two people involved are clearly intent on getting married, and if the male partner is "mature and honorable." The problem is that these circumstances don't always exist. Surveys show that women frequently imagine that the man they are living with has more serious intentions than he does.

Further, there is no evidence that living together before marriage improves the couple's chances for a successful marriage. A growing amount of evidence suggests that living together can reduce their chances, probably by diminishing their respect for the institution of marriage.

This is nothing new, but in the past a number of researchers (including Popenoe) have minimized it on the grounds that people who live together include a large percentage of unconventional, free-spirited types more likely to get divorced anyway which may skew the statistics.

This new report dismisses that interpretation. It can't stand up to findings like the 1992 study in the Journal of Marriage & the Family of 3,300 married couples who had lived together "has a 46 percent greater hazard" of breaking up than those who had not.

The report is certainly not "draconian" in its prescriptions. "Principles" suggested as a guideline include "consider not living together". Others suggest reducing the duration and frequency of such living arrangements.

The only absolutist prescription is that couples should not cohabit if there are children involved. Cohabitors increased likelihood of breaking up (compared to married couples) hurts children in many ways. There is also a greater chance of child abuse in many ways. There is also a greater chance of child abuse in a household where the adults are living together rather than married, according to the report.

In fact, the most dangerous family structure for a small child is to be in a household where the child's mother is living with a man other than its father. Survey data indicates that there is a 3,000 percent greater likelihood to batter a baby in the home than is the father's biological father.

Boldt cites a conversation with his 27-year old son who lived with a woman until they broke up. His son pointed out that "...everyone in my generation is scared to death of getting divorced. They either come from a broken home, or know someone who did and know what the pain is like. Everyone says ☐I'm only going to get married once, and it's going to be the perfect person.' "

The reality is, however, the important thing isn't finding the perfect person, its being able to work things out.

Source

Boldt, David. "Dangers of Cohabiting Before Marriage." Philadelphia Inquirer Commentary (Feb. 16, 1999):A11.

Discussion Questions

1) While many persons that cohabit do so as a prelude to getting married, but others cohabit for a variety of other reasons. What are some of them?

2) Discuss the similarities and the differences between being married and living in a cohabitative relationship.

Supplemental Lecture Material
Negotiated Marriage

As the roles of men and women in American society have changed in recent decades, couples are finding it harder than ever to stay together. Census Bureau statisticians project that at least four out of every ten marriages that occur today will end in divorce. Those that do stay together will do so not because of luck, but because of hard work and skill. In this age of "negotiated marriage" couples must determine "Who takes off work when a child is sick?" and "Who handles family finances?" Howard Markham, a psychologist at the University of Denver, points out that "We've gone from marriages where very little needed to be negotiated to ones where nearly everything needs to be negotiated." It's the success or failure of that process that often determines the durability of relationships. This is one of the reasons for programs like PAIRS (Practical Application of Intimate Skills Relationships) which has counseled 30,000 people in the last 10 years who have enrolled in the 16-week class.

A series of polls conducted by the Washington Post, Harvard University, and the Henry J. Kaiser Family Foundation, highlights the challenges couples face managing careers, raising families, sharing responsibilities and keeping their identities intact. Washington Post Staff Writers Kevin Merida and Barbara Vebejda note however, that while changing gender roles have con-siderably altered the ways that men and women relate to each other in schools, on dates, in the workplace, and in the confines of home life, the shifts have not been so dramatic. The surveys portray an America where married couples have the same "bifurcated" lives that their parents and grandparents had, where men are the primary breadwinners and women (now forces in the workplace) continue to run the household.

From cooking and washing clothes to paying the bills and taking children to the doctor, women are carrying the heaviest loads at home. Studies show that men are doing more around the house but Andrew Cherlin, a John's Hopkins sociologist, believes that "It may be that men are still able to use their greater economic power to opt out of doing work at home, or it may be that people's preferences are in reality less egalitarian than we thought."

Among the Post survey of couples are the following findings:

• More women than men are bothered by the traditional division of duties. (e.g., 38 percent of women compared to 24 percent of men have a problem with the amount of housework their spouses do.)

• Overwhelming majorities of both sexes say they are satisfied with how affectionate and attentive their spouse is, with the money their families earn and with the amount of time they spend together as partners.

• Significant differences exist in the importance men and women place on what's important to them as individuals and in how they handle their relationship problems. Women placed greater importance on being able to talk to friends about what's happening in their lives than men did while married men placed a premium on having ample time to relax and pursue hobbies away from their mate.

As marriages have become more complex and more difficult to hold together, many couples are finding help in places that didn't exist when their parents and grandparents were starting out. Once, there was only psychologist or clergymen to visit. Now, there are weekend retreats, marriage education conferences, videos, board games, and Internet chat rooms.

Diane Sollee, director of the Coalition for Marriage, Family and Couples Education believes that in the past, when marriage counselors ascribed marital problems to childhood character disorders or faulty personality traits, they were on the wrong track. Sollee believes that "The difference between couples who stay happy and those who crash and burn are skills. The notion of luck, finding Mr. or Mrs. Right is overrated. It's a skills game."

Source

Merida, Kevin & Barbara Vebejda. "Battles on the Home Front: Couples in Conflict Over Roles." *Washington Post* (March 25, 1998): A1, A14-A15.

Discussion Questions

1) Couples with young children at home surveyed indicated that they were less satisfied with the state of their relationship over-all. Why do you think this was the case? What might they do to improve their relationship?

2) Among those surveyed, the sexes agreed that women are more likely than men to under-stand the problems faced by the opposite sex. Why do you think this is the case?

Supplemental Lecture Material

Black Children, White Parents: The Politics of Adoption

The adoption of black children by white parents has long been controversial. About 20,000 of the children in the foster-care system are eligible for adoption. Although 44 percent of them are white and the 43 percent are black, 67 percent of the families who want to adopt children are white. Many of these families are willing to adopt black children, but they face serious institutional obstacles.

In at least forty states, government agencies prefer same-race adoptions, although each state varies in the degree to which it will pursue such policies. In Arkansas, California, and Minnesota, matching the race of the child and adopting family is legally preferred.

In fact, such policies can lead agencies to take what appear to be extreme measures to avoid interracial adoption. In Texas, Lou Ann and Scott Mullen, both of whom are white, had been the foster parents of two black brothers, ages two and six, since their infancies. The Mullens tried to adopt but claim that the state agency delayed action on the adoption in order to find a suitable black family instead.

Robyn was three days old when she was abandoned in San Francisco in 1991. She had been born addicted to crack cocaine. Patricia and Bill Mandel cared for her for fourteen months when they applied for adoption. Because of the difference in race, the adoption agency attempted to remove Robyn from their care. After some two years of legal struggle, the Mandels were finally declared eligible to adopt Robyn.

The history of such policies is long and complicated. Black groups against interracial adoptions have probably been the most important factor. The National Association of Black Social Workers (NABSW), for instance, called the adoption of black children under white parents "cultural genocide" in the 1970s. Although the group has toned down its opposition in recent years, the NABSW still prefers same-race adoptions.

Much of the opposition to race-blind adoption is based on fear that the racial identity of black children will be erased, distorted, or at least greatly limited by being raised by white parents. Interracial adoption is a "major, major assault on black families," says Ruth-Arlene Howe, a law professor at Boston College.

But the deficit between the number of black children waiting to be adopted and the number of black adults seeking to adopt has caused more individuals and groups to support interracial adoptions. "Leaving African-American kids in foster care rather than allowing them to be adopted by loving parents inflicts very serious harm on children," says Laurence Tribe, a Harvard law professor. Randall Kennedy, another Harvard law professor, states, "I'm sure there's a difference between the way Jesse Jackson raises his kids, Louis Farrakhan raises his kids, and my parents raised me."

Research conducted by Rita Simon, an American University sociologist, provides an useful perspective. She followed about two hundred parents and children in interracial families for twenty years. Most of the children felt as teenagers that their parents were "very, very committed" to discussing black issues with them. According to Simon, the children would say, "My God, not every dinner conversation has to be about black history." When grown, the children felt that they had a strong sense of racial identity that had not suffered from having adopted white parents. Her study provides more support to those white parents who want to take black children into their homes.

Source

Smolowe, Bill. "Adoption in Black and White." *Time* (August 14, 1995):50–51.

Discussion Questions

1. What if any threats to racial identity does interracial adoption pose? Is there anything wrong with a black family adopting a white child?

2. Should the government seek to restrict or encourage interracial adoption? Should the government do nothing?

Supplemental Lecture Material
A Pro-Gay, Pro-Family Policy

In a 1994 article, author Jonathan Rauch charged Republicans with the task of building truly pro-family policies by embracing responsible adults, no matter whether heterosexual or homosexual as the basis of families. Currently, "family values," he argued, are often coupled with intolerance, which claims that homosexuals are a threat to the family. "But this is canard. Divorce, illegitimacy and infidelity are the enemies of the family. . . . To see it as a threat to the family, you need to believe that millions of heterosexual Americans will turn gay if not actively restrained — an absurd notion. And it is perfectly possible to venerate the traditional family without despising those who are, for whatever reason, unable to have one."

As you learned from the textbook, in 1997 about 4 in 10 marriages ended in divorce and nearly 1 in 3 children were born to single mothers, raising their chances of growing up poor. This, Rauch argues, is what is killing the family. Being pro-family, ought to mean being pro-responsibility, not anti-gay. By definition, gays don't put illegitimate children into this world, and so long as homosexuals are monogamous, faithful and responsible, they should be welcomed to form families. Acting responsibly means caring for children and keeping the burden of support off society's shoulders.

This stance means that unmarried heterosexual partners should not get benefits, because homosexuals are not allowed to be married, they should receive partner benefits to encourage them to settle down. This "holds that the two-parent family is special and should be favored by public policy — not at the expense of homosexuals per se, but at the expense of single people (including homosexuals) and childless couples (again including homosexuals)." If the focus remains on the straight versus gay issue, we are avoiding the real problems dogging the family today.

Rauch wrote his article in 1994, but two years later, the United States Congress rejected same-sex marriages. Although Hawaii and some cities grant limited marital benefits on homosexual couples, marriages between gays and lesbians are prohibited in all 50 states.

Source
Rauch, Jonathan. "A Pro-Gay, Pro-Family Policy," *New York Times* (November 29, 1994):A22.

Discussion Questions
1) Where do you stand on this issue, and why?

2) Do you think same-sex marriages will ultimately become acceptable in the United States? Why or why not? What will their effect be on the family?

3) **Activity.** Conduct some library research to find articles or studies regarding same-sex marriages in countries such as Denmark or Norway. How do their attitudes toward homosexuals differ from ours? How about their attitudes toward the family?

Chapter 19

Religion

I. Religion: Basic Concepts.
  A. **Religion** is a social institution involving beliefs and practices based upon a conception of the sacred.
  B. According to Durkheim, the **sacred** is that which is defined as extraordinary, inspiring a sense of awe, reverence and even fear. In distinction, the **profane** consists of ordinary elements of everyday life.
  C. Religions involve **ritual**, formal ceremonial behavior.
  D. Sociology can investigate the social consequences of religious activity, but can never assess the validity of any religious doctrine because religion involves **faith**, belief anchored in conviction rather than scientific evidence.

II. Theoretical Analysis of Religion.
  A. Functions of religion: Structural-functional analysis.
      1. Durkheim understood religion as the symbolic celebration of the power of society over the individual.
      2. Durkheim noted three major functions of religion for the operation of a society:
          a. Social cohesion.
          b. Social control.
          c. Providing meaning and purpose.
      4. Critical evaluation. This approach downplays the dysfunctional consequences of religion, especially the fact that strongly held beliefs can generate social conflict.
  B. The social construction of the sacred: Symbolic-interaction analysis.
      1. Peter Berger argues that religion places life in a "cosmic frame of reference."
      2. Critical evaluation. This approach pays little attention to religion's link with inequality.
  C. Inequality and religion: Social-conflict analysis.
      1. Marx noted that religion tends to legitimize inequality and the status quo. It also endorses patriarchy.
      2. Critical evaluation. This approach ignores religion's ability to promote change and social equality.
      3. SOCIAL DIVERSITY BOX—Religion and Patriarchy: Does God Favor Males?

III. Religion and Social Change.
  A. Max Weber's Protestant ethic thesis is an important example of how religion can promote social change, in this instance the growth of capitalism.
  B. **Liberation theology** is a fusion of Christian principles with political activism, often Marxist in character. It has been important in much of Latin America.

IV. Types of Religious Organization.
   A. A **church** is a type of religious organization well integrated into the larger society. There are two types of churches.
      1. A state church is a church formally allied with the state.
      2. A **denomination** is a church, independent of the state, that accepts religious pluralism.
   B. A **sect** is a type of religious organization that stands apart from the larger society. In comparison with churches, sects display the following characteristics:
      1. They are less formal, more emotional, less intellectualized.
      2. Their leaders display **charisma**, extraordinary personal qualities that can turn an audience into followers.
      3. They rely on active **proselytization**, recruiting many members through a process of **conversion**, a personal transformation or rebirth resulting from adopting new religious beliefs.
      4. They usually attract lower-class members.
   C. A **cult** is a religious organization that is substantially outside the cultural traditions of a society.

V. Religion in History.
   A. Religion in preindustrial societies.
      1. Hunting and gathering cultures often embrace **animism**, the belief that elements of the natural world are conscious life forms that affect humanity.
      2. Among pastoral and horticultural people, there arose a belief in a single divine power.
      3. In agrarian societies, religion becomes more important, with a specialized priesthood in charge of religious organizations.
   B. Religion in industrial societies.
      1. People generally look to physicians and scientists for the comfort and certainty members of their society had previously sought from religious leaders.
      2. Religious thought persists simply because science is powerless to address issues of ultimate meaning in human life.

VI. World Religions.
   A. **Christianity** is the world's most widespread religion. It grew out of Judaism.
      1. Christianity is an example of **monotheism,** or belief in a single divine power. Many other religions are **polytheistic**, believing in many gods.
      2. **Global Map 19–1:** Christianity in Global Perspective.
   B. **Islam** is centered in the Middle East but spreads throughout much of the world. Moslem beliefs center around the "five pillars of Islam."
      1. **Global Map 19–2:** Islam in Global Perspective.
   C. **Judaism** is the smallest of the world religions. It centers around the concept of the covenant and is divided into three main denominations: Orthodox, Reform, and Conservative.
   D. **Hinduism** is the oldest of the world's great religions and is mostly practiced in India and Pakistan. Key Hindu concepts include dharma, karma, reincarnation and nirvana. It includes some polytheistic elements.

      1. WINDOW ON THE WORLD—Global Map 19–3: Hinduism in Global Perspective.

  E. **Buddhism** also arose in India and is now spread through much of Asia.

      1. WINDOW ON THE WORLD—Global Map 19–4: Buddhism in Global Perspective.

  F. **Confucianism** was the state religion of China for over two millennia. A central concept is jen, meaning "humaneness." It lacks a clear sense of the sacred.

  G. Western religions (Christianity, Islam, and Judaism) are typically deity-based, with one clear focus on God. Eastern religions (Hinduism, Buddhism, Confucianism) tend to be more like ethical codes that make a less clear-cut distinction between sacred and secular.

VII. Religion in the United States.

  A. SEEING OURSELVES—National 19–1: The Religious Diversity Across the United States.

  B. SEEING OURSELVES—National Map 19-2: Religious Diversity Across the United States.

  C. Religious affiliation. Eighty-six percent of U.S. adults claim a religious preference.

  D. **Religiosity** is the importance of religion in a person's life. It is multidimensional and high by most measures in the contemporary U.S.

  E. Religion and social stratification.

      1. Religion varies by social class.

      2. Religion is frequently related to ethnicity and race.

VIII. Religion in a Changing Society.

  A. **Secularization** is the historical decline in importance of the supernatural and the sacred. It is widespread in the modern world, but this does not suggest that religion is likely to fade away completely.

      1. GLOBAL SOCIOLOGY BOX—The Changing Face of Religion: A Report from Great Britain.

  B. **Civil religion** is a quasi-religious loyalty binding individuals in a basically secular society.

  C. There has been a marked revival of **fundamentalist** religions in the U.S., which feature a conservative religious doctrine that opposes intellectualism and worldly accommodation in favor of restoring traditional, other-worldly spirituality.

      1. Fundamentalism is distinctive in the following ways:

         a. Fundamentalists interpret sacred texts literally.

         b. Fundamentalists reject religious pluralism.

         c. Fundamentalists pursue the personal experience of God's presence.

         d. Fundamentalism opposes "secular humanism."

         e. Many fundamentalists endorse conservative political goals.

      2. Some fundamentalist religions take the form of electronic churches.

      3. CRITICAL THINKING BOX—Should Students Pray in School?

      4. APPLYING SOCIOLOGY BOX—The Cyber-Church: Logging On to Religion.

IX. Looking Ahead: Religion in the Twenty-First Century.

A. Religion will remain a central element of society.
B. Immigration will intensify and diversify the religious character of U.S. society.
C. CONTROVERSY AND DEBATE BOX—Does Science Threaten Religion?

Chapter Objectives

1) Define basic concepts of religion.

2) Examine how each of the three theoretical paradigms directs us toward different social aspects of religion.

3) Provide examples of how religion has promoted dramatic social transformation.

4) Distinguish between church and sect.

5) Explain how religion changes as a society undergoes industrialization.

6) Identify characteristics of six world religions.

7) Identify and define five dimensions of religiosity.

8) Examine how religion varies by class and ethnicity and race.

9) Discuss the extent to which U.S. religion has become secularized.

10) Recognize the existence of U.S. civil religion.

11) Examine the growth of fundamentalism in the United States.

Essay Topics

1) What are two general differences between the belief systems of Eastern and Western societies?

2) How religious is our nation?

3) What are some of the sacred things, places, persons and ideas in contemporary American society? Are all of these sacred elements connected with what we normally regard as religions?

4) What are examples of secularization in our nation? Do you think secularization is good or bad? Why?

5) Can you think of any additional social functions of religion beyond the three outlined in the chapter?

6) How are an increasing number of religious organizations using computer technology to spread their message? How effective are these efforts?

7) Provide examples of religion's ability to promote significant social change.

8) Analyze a religion with which you are personally familiar with the beliefs. Analyze this religion among the ideal-type continuum from church to sect.

9) How are cults and sects different from each other? In what ways are they similar?

10) Most 19th century social thinkers assumed that secularization was an irresistible tide that would eventually sweep away all religious activity. Modern sociologists are far less likely to expect religion to fade away. Can you envision a society without religion? Explain.

Integrative Supplement Guide

1. Transparencies - Series V:
- T-127 Christianity in Global Perspective
- T-128 Islam in Global Perspective
- T-129 Hinduism in Global Perspective
- T-130 Buddhism in Global Perspective
- T-131 Religiosity in Global Perspective
- T-132 Religious Diversity Across the United States

Supplemental Lecture Material
Gender Friendly Religion —"Women of Faith"

"Women of Faith" are adherents of an evangelical Christian movement that is rapidly becoming both a complement and antidote to the all-male "Promise Keepers." Rather than trading promises or admonishments, "Women of Faith" swap stories and compliments. Since this for-profit enterprise was founded in 1996, predominantly white women of all Christian denominations have been attending revivals staged in churches and small-to-moderate size sports arenas across the United States.

Other similar Christian groups have emerged, including the women's ministry of James Dobson's "Focus on Family". But WOF has attracted many more followers than its competitors. Attendance grew from 36,000 in 1996 to 156,000 in 1998 to over 350,000 in 1998. It is a subsidiary of New Life Clinics, a private company that is the largest Christian counseling chain in the U.S. WOF has its headquarters in Plano, Texas as well as its own management, its revenues (which come largely from fees and souvenir sales) totaled $6.1 million in 1997 and have more than doubled since then. Its appeals is "old-fashioned therapy, cloaked in

the Ten Commandments" according to Time Magazine's Nadya Labi.

The idea is the "brain-child" of Stephen Arterburn who believed that the key to maximizing interest in the organization was to ask the question "What can we do for you?"" speakers like Sheila Walsh (author of "Never give It Up") and Barbara Johnson (author of "Where Does a Mother Go To Resign?") have eschewed the talk-and-run approach customary at most mass gatherings and instead listens intently to soft Christian rock and tales of hard knocks. "Women of Faith" advocates "warm hugs, not revolution". Says Ms. Labi, WOF Christie Barnes has been silent on the issue of women's subservience to their husbands (as Southern Baptists have recommended in the past). "We don't make comments about the whole submission issue, we just believe God will bring everything to light." (i.e., Keep it light on the sermons, heavy on the anecdotes, and they will come.) In Portland, Oregon, Walsh brushed up against the issue of abortion, revealing her feeling on bearing a child with Down Syndrome, then retreated from taking any political position. Johnson talked about her son's homosexuality but stopped short of promoting or disapproving of gay rights.

Such circumspection has helped forestall criticisms. Mainline Protestant organizations that have been critical of Promise Keepers have reserved judgement on Women of Faith; at the same time, members of the religious right haven't had a problem with WOF's nonactivist stance.

Recently WOF has held mass meetings for couples and is moving toward targeting children as well. Is it too much too soon? Only time will tell.

Source

Labi, Nadya & Richard Ostling. "Female of the Species." *Time* (July 13, 1998):62-63.

Discussion Questions

1) The "Promise Keepers" created a sensation at an enormous get-together in Washington in October of 1997 but within a year, its future was very much in jeopardy. With the cost of their stadium rallies exceeding $1 million, things are not what they once were. What do you project for "Women of Faith" in the next five years? Discuss the parallels and differences between them and their male counterparts in "Promise Keepers."

2) What are your thoughts on "for-profit" religious organizations?

Supplemental Lecture Material
The Growth of Christian Colleges

Evangelical Christian Colleges, where the belief that the Bible is inerrant is woven into academic and social programs, are becoming increasingly popular. Enrollments have surged during the 1990s, dramatically outpacing the average increase at secular institutions.

From 1990 to 1996, undergraduate enrollment increased by only 5 percent at private institutions, and 4 percent at public colleges, compared with a 24 percent increase at the 90 U.S. evangelical institutions that are members of the Council for Christian Colleges and Universities. (About 129,000 undergraduates are enrolled at the colleges that are part of the council, which is based in Washington.)

Officials at Christian colleges point to factors to explain their growth. The first is demographics — Christian elementary and secondary schools, home schooling, and youth ministries are all thriving. The second is a desire by students (many from home

schooling or church-run schools), to avoid the life styles found at secular institutions. Some experts think that the lack of diversity — stifles student's critical thinking skills. Richard T. Hughes, a professor of religion at Pepperdine University, has stated that "Some of these smaller, really conservative schools look more like a church than a university. If you're a student there, you haven't been exposed to the larger world, and more importantly, you may never have been force to think through issues that really challenge your faith and intellect." In a speech at a conference in San Diego in February, 1999, Mr. Hughes said that hundreds of institutions had tried, but failed, to synthesize faith and learning. "Some of these schools succeeded wonderfully well as outposts of Christian conviction, but never amounted to much academically." Still, Huges notes, a few Christian colleges have been able to successfully "open the door to more serious academic inquiry and radical kinds of questioning."

Calvin College is a case in point. One of the best-regarded-and least traditional Christian colleges in the council, Calvin allows its students who are of legal drinking age to consume alcohol (although not on campus). It has no prohibitions on smoking (except in buildings) and allows openly gay students to enroll and also has support groups for them. Thomas E. McWherter, vice president of enrollment and external studies, says "The watchword here is responsible freedom." He also notes that "a lot of the colleges within the Christian college orbit have gotten better in the last 15 or 20 years, if you look at the percentage of faculty with Ph.D. degrees and the success of graduates in both career and graduate school placement."

Source

Reisberg, Leo. "Enrollments Surge at Christian Colleges." The Chronicle of Higher Education (March 5, 1999): Vol. XLV, No. 20: A42-43.

Discussion Questions

1) Separation of church and state has always been a hotly debated issue. What are your feelings about religion and education? Should they also be kept separate from one another or is it appropriate to combine the two in the case of church-sponsored schools?

2) James Barnes, the president of Indiana Wesleyan, says the university is trying to recruit more minority students, but it isn't interested in diversifying in other ways. Like many Christian institutions, it does not permit gay and lesbian students to enroll and those who openly express their homosexuality are asked to leave. How do you feel about such a policy?

Supplemental Lecture Material
The Price of Success: Jews in America

A Jewish settler wrote to Germany from the colony of Virginia in 1791 that "one can make a good living here [in America, but]. . . I know that you will not want me to bring up my children like Gentiles. Here they cannot be anything else." Such a view of being Jewish in America seems prophetic to Seymore Martin Lipset and Earl Raab in *Jews and the New American Scene.* While Jews may have found security and prosperity in America, Lipset and Raab believe Jews have also found their religion and distinctness as an ethnic group dissolving in their success.

"Jews achieve higher levels of education, professional status, and income than all other [religious and ethnic] subgroups," say Lipset and Raab. They are certainly the most economically successful of all of immigrant groups. And this economic success reflects a relatively high degree of ethnic, political, and religious toleration. In the United States, "everyone is treated according to the logic of the marketplace, that is, without reference to inherited traits."

But Lipset and Raab argue that the same "logic of the marketplace" has also removed some of the external forces that promoted Jewish identity, religious and social cohesiveness, and cultural continuity. For most Jews, "identification with the tribe no longer provides members with a life meaning that can compete with the fruits of individual accomplishment." Throughout their history in North America, Jews have been steadily lessening the degree to which they adhere to dietary laws, speak Hebrew, study the Talmud, or center their lives on the synagogue. Perhaps even more significant, 57 percent of American Jews intermarry, and the current birthrate is far under replacement levels.

Lipset and Raab cite three forces supporting the current degree of cohesion among American Jews: opposition to anti-Semitism in America and Europe, concern for the survival of Israel, and the assumption of politically liberal values. However, all three of these forces are weakening. Anti-Semitism is not a serious problem in the United States in spite of the vocalizations of some fringe groups. Further, most Jews have been less and less worried about Israel's stability and long-term viability, and few perceive pressing threats to it as a nation. Perhaps even more significant, most concern about Israel in recent decades has been based on humanitarian grounds rather than Zionist or religious motivations.

Lipset and Raab believe that liberalism, too, is in decline as a unitary force. With the exception of African Americans, Jews have been the most consistently liberal ethnic or major religious group in the United States. Liberalism has been bolstered somewhat by the growing empowerment of right-wing Christian groups, but to date liberal ideologies have supplied only weak support for Jewish identity.

The future of American Jews seems empty to Lipset and Raab, who see in American history a slow dissolution and fading of Jewishness. They advocate a return to ethnic and religious self-awareness and a rapid decline in the intermarriage rate. Lipset and Raab base their fears on ideas at least as old as the republic. John Adams long ago wrote that "once [they were]. . . no longer persecuted, [Jews] would soon wear away some of the asperities and peculiarities of their character, possibly in time become liberal Unitarian Christians."

Sources

Lefkowitz, Jay P. "The Paradox of a Great Ethnic Success." *Wall Street Journal* (May 10, 1995).

Lipset, Seymour Martin, and Earl Raab. *Jews and the New American Scene.* Cambridge: Harvard University Press.

Discussion Questions

1) Do American Jews seem likely to lose their ethnic and religious identities? Is this good for America as a whole? for the Jews? Why or why not?

2) How can religious toleration weaken some religions? How might they retain their vitality and strength?

Supplemental Lecture Material
Behind the Veil

Some aspects of Islam sound very familiar to Christians: respect for parents, no adultery. Other rules, however, are less so: a

Muslim should not accept or charge credit, daughters should not marry non-Muslims or live away from home until married.

Perhaps some of that unfamiliarity is best symbolized by Muslim women's wearing of the veil. Though in Saudi Arabia, for example, women may earn college degrees and even run their own businesses, many go out in public only when clad in the *abayya*, a long, black cloak covering them from head to toe. Most also wear a veil from which only the eyes are visible through a slit. And while the dress may strike women in the United States as a symbol of oppression and restriction, many Saudi women defend it, because for them it stands for religious morality, while also providing them with the kind of security they often see lacking in our culture, where divorce or single-motherhood is common.

Since a Muslim man can't kiss even a female cousin, and certainly can't go out with other women, affairs are rare, and divorce never an issue in Saudi Arabia. Also, women wearing the veil are accorded respect, say Muslim women, and they feel protected even in such small things as having to be driven since they are not allowed to operate cars. Men must also provide for women who do not have to work if they choose not to.

Unlike in some other Muslim cultures, Saudi women often make the final decision about whom they will marry, and once they have done so, the home is seen completely as their domain, the place they rule. By Islamic law, men are allowed to have up to four wives, but few choose to do so for financial reasons and because it is difficult to treat all wives equally, as the Koran demands.

While this traditional way of life may be easy in primarily Islamic countries, Muslims living in the United States often feel embattled by the culture around them, some of which clashes with Islamic rules. Even successful and assimilated families feel the strain. To instill conservative social values, the mosque plays a central role. Children attend Arabic classes or other community events there. "Most important, the new subculture offers haven from what many Muslims see as the negative commercial and permissive atmosphere of the larger culture. Parents send teens to mosque activities to keep from dating and from common adolescent temptations." (Marquand p. 11).

Yet, in spite of efforts to counteract negative influences, there is "growing evidence of more divorce, marriage outside the faith, the ignoring of Islamic rules, generational anger, and sibling strife...While Muslim numbers are growing and an Islamic awakening is under way, tensions are also rising in the Muslim community. Many women for example, resist pressure to wear

the *hijab*, a head covering." (Marquand, p. 10).

Sources

Peterson, Scott. "Women Live On Own Terms Behind the Veil." *Christian Science Monitor* (July 31, 1996):1 and 10.

Marquand, Robert and Lamis Andoni. "Islamic Family Values Simmer in a US Melting Pot." *Christian Science Monitor,* January 29, 1996, pp. 1, 10-11.

Discussion Questions

1) Using the various theoretical stances described in the textbook, what is your reaction to the role of women in Islam?

2) In your opinion, why are most religions patriarchal? Is that likely to change? Why or why not?

Chapter 20

Education

I. Education: A Global Survey.
 A. **Education** is defined as the social institution guiding a society's transmission of knowledge — including basic facts, job skills, and cultural norms and values — to its members.
 B. **Schooling** is formal instruction under the direction of specially trained teachers.
    1. In preindustrial societies, formal schooling is usually available only to the wealthy.
    2. Industrial societies embrace the principle of mass education, often enacting mandatory education laws, the legal requirement that children receive a minimum of formal education.
    3. WINDOW ON THE WORLD—Global Map 20–1: Illiteracy in Global Perspective.
 C. In India, many children work, greatly limiting their opportunity for schooling. About half of the Indian population are illiterate.
 D. Japan's educational system is widely praised for producing some of the world's highest achievers. In Japan, schooling reflects personal ability more than it does in the United States, where family income plays a greater part in a student's college plans.
 E. Class differences in Great Britain are more important in determining access to quality education than they are in Japan or most other industrial societies.
 F. Reflecting the value of equal opportunity, a larger proportion of Americans attend colleges and universities than do citizens of any other nation. U.S. education also stresses practical learning.
    1. APPLYING SOCIOLOGY BOX—Following the Jobs: Trends in Bachelor's Degrees. American college students tend to major in fields in which jobs appear to be plentiful.

II. The Functions of Schooling.
Structural-functional analysis looks at how formal education enhances the operation and stability of society.
 A. Socialization: teaching skills, values and norms.
 B. Cultural innovation through research.
 C. Social integration: forging a mass of people into a cultural whole.
 D. Social placement.
 E. Latent functions of schooling.
    1. Child care.
    2. Establishing relationships and networks.

F. Critical evaluation. The structural-functional approach stresses the ways in which education supports the operation of an industrial society, but ignores the persistence of inequality in education.

III. Schooling and Social Inequality

Social-conflict analysis argues that schools routinely provide learning according to students' social background, thereby perpetuating social inequality.

A. Social control. Schools stress compliance and punctuality through the **hidden curriculum,** subtle presentations of political or cultural ideas in the classroom.

B. **Standardized testing** is frequently biased in favor of affluent white students.

C. **Tracking** is the assignment of students to different types of educational programs; in practice, it often benefits students from higher class backgrounds disproportionately.

D. Inequality among schools:
1. Public and private schools. Most private school students attend church-affiliated schools, especially Catholic parochial schools. A small number attend elite preparatory schools. Studies show that private schools commonly teach more effectively than do public schools.
2. Inequality in public schooling. Most suburban schools offer better education than most central city schools, a fact which has led to busing programs. However, research suggests that increased funding alone will not be enough to improve students' academic performance.

E. Access to higher education is limited by several factors, but finances are crucial. People who complete college on the average earn higher incomes.
1. SEEING OURSELVES—National Map 20–1: College Attendance Across the United States. In general, college attendance is highest among adults along the Northeast and West coasts. By contrast, adults in the Midwest and the South are the least likely members of our society to attend college.

F. **Credentialism,** evaluating a person on the basis of educational degrees, is increasingly common in modern societies.

G. Schooling transforms social privilege into personal merit.
1. SOCIAL DIVERSITY BOX—"Cooling Out" the Poor: Transforming Disadvantage into Deficiency.

H. Critical evaluation. The social-conflict paradigm links education with social inequality, but it minimizes the extent to which education has provided the opportunity for upward mobility.

IV. Problems in the schools.

A. Discipline and violence. Almost everyone agrees that schools should teach personal discipline, but few think schools are succeeding.

B. Student passivity is promoted in five ways in large bureaucratic school systems.
1. Theodore Sizer identified five ways in which large, bureaucratic schools undermine education:
   a. Rigid uniformity.
   b. Numerical ratings.
   c. Rigid expectations.

        d. Specialization.

        e. Little individual responsibility.

     2. College: the silent classroom. Passivity is common in colleges and universities. The only voice heard is usually the teachers.

  C. The dropout rate has declined slightly in recent decades; currently about 11 percent of people between the ages of eighteen and twenty-four have dropped out of school.

  D. Academic standards. According to *A Nation At Risk,* the quality of U.S. education has declined sharply and **functional illiteracy,** reading and writing skills insufficient for everyday life, is widespread.

V. Recent issues in U.S. education.

  A. School choice proponents advocate such developments as magnet schools, schooling for profit, and charter schools.

  B. Schooling people with disabilities often involves mainstreaming, or integrating special students into the overall educational program.

  C. Adult education. The share of U.S. students aged twenty-five and older has risen sharply in recent years and now accounts for 43 percent of people in the classroom.

VI. Looking Ahead: Schooling in the Twenty-First century.

  A. Computers and other new types of information technology will be important in the future.

  B. Technology cannot solve all of our educational problems.

  C. CONTROVERSY AND DEBATE BOX—Political Correctness: Improving or Undermining Education?

Chapter Objectives

1) Distinguish between education and schooling.

2) Examine why education has become increasingly important as the world has industrialized.

3) Compare and contrast schooling in Britain, Japan, India, and the United States.

4) Summarize how the structural-functional and social-conflict paradigms direct our attention toward different aspects of the U.S. institution of education.

5) Identify the major social functions of schooling.

6) Define the concept of the hidden curriculum.

7) Explain how standardized testing and tracking have historically worked to the disadvantage of the poor and minorities.

8) Compare and contrast the different quality of education provided by various American private and public schools.

9) Summarize the main findings of the 1966 Coleman Report.

10) Identify factors that lead to differential access to higher education.

11) Define credentialism.

12) Outline the major problems in U.S. schooling, including discipline and violence, student passivity, dropping out, and declining academic achievement.

13) Explore recent issues in U.S. education.

Essay Topics

1) Are there aspects of the British, Japanese, or Indian educational systems which you would like to see implemented in the U.S.? Which? Discuss.

2) Can you think of any additional functions of schooling beyond those outlined in the chapter?

3) What are ways that large, bureaucratic schools undermine education? What steps should be taken to improve schooling?

4) Some people argue that schools ought to teach students how to think critically as well as passing on important skills and knowledge. How well do you feel that U.S. schools presently provide this function? Is this ever likely to be a major function of schooling? Should it be? Discuss.

5) What are the positive and negative aspects of credentialism?

6) Given that standardized tests will always reflect a certain amount of cultural bias, do you believe that we should abolish all standardized testing? Defend your view.

7) Should tracking be abolished? Why or why not?

8) Many Americans believe that access to a good education is all that is needed to overcome inequality in U.S. society. Do you agree? Why or why not?

9) How would you develop a program designed to counter student passivity in high school and college?

10) Many classroom teachers believe that, over the past few decades, the academic performance of most U.S. students has not merely declined but rather has virtually collapsed. What are some of the factors that may have contributed to this problem? How serious do you believe this problem to be? How would you attempt to fight it?

Integrative Supplement Guide

1. **ABC Videos:**
- Dangerous Lessons - Violence in the __'s Schools (*Prime Time Live*, 4/5/95)
- Mismanagement in Schools - Reading, Writing and Rip-off? (*Prime Time Live*, 5/3/95)
- Welfare for U__ Teen Mothers (*World News Tonight, American Agenda*, 2/9/95)

2. **Transparencies - Series V:**
- T-133 Illiteracy in Global Perspective
- T-134 College Degrees in Global Perspective
- T-135 Percentage Changes in Bachelor's Degrees Earned, 1985-1995
- T-136 College Attendance Across the United States
- T-137 College Attendance and Family Income, 1995
- T-138 Educational Achievement for Various Categories of People
- T-139 Functional Illiteracy in Global Perspective
- T-140 How Long Does It Take to Earn a Bachelor's Degree?

Supplemental Lecture Material
Equalizing School Financing

Unlike most other postindustrial nations, the United States has chosen to raise most of the finances for primary and secondary education at the local community level rather than on a national basis. Federal funding for public schools runs about $13 billion annually, just 6 percent of all educational spending. The vast majority of educational funds are derived from local property taxes.

This system keeps most of the power in the hands of members of the local community, which is seen as an advantage. But the consequence of heavy reliance on property taxes is a substantial, sometimes extreme, disparity in the funds available from district to district within any particular state. Poorer districts, lacking higher-income residents and successful businesses, frequently find themselves unable to provide more than a basic level of educational services. This situation flies in the face of the widespread belief that schooling ought to provide an effective avenue of upward mobility for the children of the poor. With more money flowing to schools in affluent neighborhoods, privilege is rewarded and the disadvantaged fall farther behind.

A study based on 1986–87 U.S. census data found that the nation's ". . . ten poorest districts annually spent an average of $2,004 per elementary school student, and the 10 richest spent $6,260. For secondary schools, the average was $3,179 for poor districts and $6,631 for wealthy ones." In Illinois, ". . . the average high school teacher's salary in East St. Louis is $38,000. At New Trier [located in an affluent Chicago suburb], it's $59,000. New Trier offers 18 college-level advanced placement courses. East St. Louis offers none." Urban minorities are seriously hurt by these disparities, but poor white rural children are also at a disadvantage.

Solutions are hard to come by. Court challenges may provide the most hope: since 1989 five state supreme courts have ruled that traditional methods of financing education violate the equal opportunity provisions of their state constitutions.

There is also some interest and some precedent for federal involvement, but there are two big obstacles at this level. For one thing, because only a small percentage of total educational funding is provided by Washington, the federal government lacks both sticks and carrots which might be used to compel or encourage states to equalize funding. More seriously, equalization is unpopular among middle- and upper-income voters, who fear that their children may lose out if available funds are simply shifted to poorer districts. A better solution would be to bring up the bottom without leveling the top. This solution, however, would certainly require raising taxes, which is extremely difficult in the present political climate.

Source

"The Next Education Crisis: Equalizing School Funds," *Congressional Quarterly* Vol. 51 No. 13 (March 27, 1993):749–754.

Discussion Questions

1) What are some advantages and disadvantages of local control and financing of public education?

2) Some argue that not only should school financing not disproportionately benefit schools in wealthier districts, but rather that the reverse should be the case: schools in poor neighborhoods should receive more money than their wealthier counterparts. How do you feel about this proposal? Why?

Supplemental Lecture Material
Recent Issues in U.S. Education

Increasingly, around the country, black parents are finding what they're looking for educationally in the private Christian academies that were opened in the 1950s, 60s and 70s by whites, many trying to avoid integration. Now, however, with declining enrollment and a shrinking economic base, many of these schools have either been taken over by other organizations that have abolished restrictions or have been forced to take in any student who can pay the fees. Some are even recruiting black students, exhibiting a new attitude toward race.

Educators say black parents are being drawn to these schools for a variety of reasons: dissatisfaction with private schools, lower tuition of Christian private schools compared with other independent schools and conservative social values. Jacqueline Jordan Irvine, a professor of urban education at Emory University, points out that "There are a lot of things that go on in these schools that do resonate with many African-American parents and African-American tradition. There is the sense of order and discipline. Segregated black schools were highly disciplined, highly structured schools, and a lot of older black teachers were teaching religion and values".

Across the country, many Christian schools and academies have gone from all white in the early 1970s to nearly all black today. The transitions, however, haven't been smooth at all schools. Some have struggled with introducing multicultural curriculums in conservative school structures and with charges of racism. Dr. Charles Ware, president of Baptist Bible College of Indianapolis and formerly the first headmaster at a Christian school outside of Washington, D.C., notes that "There's a change going on but you still have some residue of the past." Jack Layman, a professor of Bible, history and education at Columbia International University in Colum-

bia, S.C., says "What we're beginning to see is the breakdown of racial stereotypes and racism. It's slow, however, because it's a fortress area. But it is reflected in many of these schools." (It should be noted, that there's great diversity among Christian schools today...they go from one end of the spectrum to the other.)

While some Christian academies still maintain barriers against integration, the diversity in Christian schools is growing along with another trend — a rising number of black church schools. Black private school enrollment is now growing at a faster rate than overall private school enrollment and that of white private school enrollment. According to the National Center of Education Statistics, the overwhelmingly largest share of growth is in the Christian school population.

Originally in the South, many private schools were referred to as "council schools", a term for institutions created by the White citizens Council in the wake of the Brown v. Board of Education decision in 1954. By the late 1980s and early 1990s, however, many private schools opened their doors to African Americans. In addition to declining enrollments, many schools cited changing attitudes toward diversity for their changes in admission policies.

"Some educators argue that the popularity of Christian schools among some African-Americans could be an indication that race is a diminishing factor in the alignment of cultural wars" says David Dent, an assistant professor of journalism at New York University and the author of a book on the black middle class. Not everyone is in agreement, however, on what growing private school enrollment means. David Duke, a professor of education at the University of Virginia sees it as an indication that divisions in American society are now based on orthodoxy and progressivism instead of race or ethnicity. In contrast however, Harvard's Charles V. Willie believes that the popularity of private Christian schools among middle class African Americans is because black parents believe they've been failed by public schools and "therefore, any alternative seems better than what they have."

The changing population of many Christian schools also reflects demographic shifts in communities. From the schools' perspectives, it might also be an economic issue, since many Christian schools would have trouble surviving as an all-white school as whites flee communities that eventually become predominantly African American. Multicultural courses also remain curriculum issue at many Christian academies but as David Barber who is white and the principal at Old National Christian Academy in College Park, Georgia says, "It's not that we've arrived by any means...I'm sure there are still problems, but we're still making a lot of headway."

Source

Dent, David J. "African-American Turning to Christian Academies." *New York Times (Education Life Supplement)* (August 4, 1996):26-29.

Discussion

1) Is it the barrier of race dissolving between two groups with similar values that has led to the popularity of Christian academies among middle-class African Americans or is it more that public education has failed them?"

2) Why do you think that some Christian Academies have been slow to integrate multicultural courses into their curriculum? How do you feel about such a policy?

Supplemental Lecture Material
Public Education: Getting a Good Buy

The funding of public education has long been a source of controversy in America. Contentious debates over the sources and amount of funding have divided communities, states, and even the nation. This conflict has been exacerbated by the contraction of federal, state, and local education budgets across the country. How much should we be paying to educate our children? How can we know if we're spending too little or too much? How can we know if other factors are reducing educational quality?

The factors influencing student performance are a matter of hot debate. The most important predictor of success appears to be the educational level of the student's mother; the educational level of both parents is the next most-important characteristic. Family income correlates with success as well, though it is not certain how closely. School funding levels are important, but they are not the most important way of improving students' academic success. In fact, spending a lot of money on students is no guarantee of high performance.

Comparing expenditures by state shows great variation. While the national per-pupil average was 5,200 dollars in 1991, amounts ranged between Utah's 3,000 dollars per pupil and New York and New Jersey's 8,600 dollars. "Above a level of 4,500 dollars and 5,000 dollars per student, additional money doesn't seem to make that big of a difference" on average in increasing educational quality, according to M. Donald Thomas of the School Management Study Group.

Thomas's statement must be qualified, however, by special challenges a district might face, such as a large inner-city population, numerous non-English-speaking immigrants, a relatively more expensive cost of living and/or wage base, or (as in the case of Alaska) the need to import many books and educational materials. Such districts tend to have relatively high per-pupil costs.

But spending a lot of money doesn't mean that performance will follow. Some of the most expensive per-pupil rates are in districts that also show the worst results. Many observers argue that such a correlation shows that these districts are not using their budgets efficiently. William Bainbridge, the president of a research company called SchoolMatch, believes that in most cases these districts face large numbers of parents with low educational levels who do not value learning. Chicago, Illinois; Hartford, Connecticut; and Hoboken, New Jersey, have all scored badly on educational success as reflected in student test scores and expenses in recent years.

However, some schools have productively combined low per-pupil costs with high-quality education. The Harrison, Arkansas, school district spends only 2,700 dollars per student a year on its 2,900 pupils. Test scores place it in the top 10 percent of the nation. Little money is budgeted for sports or other extracurricular activities, but donations and volunteers make up the difference. A great wealth of community support enriches the schools and encourages the educational goals of teachers and the district. The lack of minorities, low poverty rates, and relative absence of violence in the district make the students easy to teach according to the superintendent.

Although the Little Axe district in Norman, Oklahoma, is also a great buy for its taxpayers, it faces a large proportion of poor students and is made up primarily of Native Americans, with some twenty tribes represented. Joe Work, the head of the district, believes that high expectations make the difference: "If teachers feel good about them-

selves and feel that all kids can learn, then all kids can learn."

Source
Speer, Tibbett, L. "Great Schools, Cheap." *American Demographics* (July 1994):42–47.

Discussion Questions
1) How is school funding related to educational quality? Is it possible to improve quality by lowering funding? Should funding limits be placed on school districts?

2) If you were a school administrator, how might you react to assertions that your district should spend less? Would you react differently if you were a parent, teacher, student, or taxpayer (without children) in the district?

Supplemental Lecture Material
Why Teachers Don't Teach

Almost 90 percent of all teachers belong to a teachers' unions. Originally formed because teachers were poorly paid and subject to hiring inequities, unions are now blamed by many for a decline of quality in our public education system. Why?

Opponents charge that unions hurt education by supporting such practices as a pay scale based purely on years spent teaching or years of education, without regard for excellence. In other words, particularly dedicated and enthusiastic teachers are in no way rewarded for their efforts. Even during a layoff, seniority alone matters. In other words, the most recently hired teachers are let go first, while less capable teachers are retained. This lack of recognition of skill in teaching drives many of the most stellar out of the field and into some other occupation where drive and dedication are rewarded instead of ignored.

Many teachers, on the other hand, are grateful to the unions because they have fought for increased pay, better working conditions and other benefits such as liability insurance and low-interest credit cards.

Unions defend the hiring and firing system based on seniority by warning that without it, some school systems would systematically get rid of more experienced — and therefore more expensive — teachers.

Another complaint raised against teachers' unions is that when jobs are at stake, they support veteran teachers being assigned to subjects outside of their specific field. Therefore, according to the Department of Education, about "a third of high school math teachers, nearly a quarter of high school English teachers and nearly a fifth of high school science teachers are teaching without a college major or minor in their subjects."

Opponents also claim that not only are good teachers not rewarded, but bad teachers are safeguarded. "Astonishing numbers of education graduates fail basic literacy tests introduced in many states in recent years to shore up standards." California administered 65,000 such exams in 1994-95 and gave failing grades to about 20 percent of those tested. But unions haven't made tough standards a priority. On the contrary, the NEA (National Education Association) fought basic skills testing in teacher licensing for years, shifting its stance only after a majority of states introduced the tests. It is also extremely difficult to dismiss an experienced teacher. Union spokespeople, on the other hand, say they are only making sure teachers get a fair hearing.

All these practices, charge some, hurt students by cheating them out of the best possible education by the best possible teacher. Unless reforms are undertaken, our public education system may not survive.

Source
Toch, Thomas et al. "Why Teachers Don't Teach," *U.S. News and World Report* (February 26, 1996):62-71.

Discussion Questions
1) With whom do you agree? Are unions a positive or negative force in education?

2) **Activity**. Research whether cultures with more highly regarded education systems — such as Japan — have teachers' unions. How are hiring and firing decisions made? How well are teachers paid? What is the social standing of teachers?

Chapter 21

Health and Medicine

I. Health is a state of complete physical, mental and social well-being. It is as much a social as a biological issue.

    A. Society shapes poeople's health in five major ways:

        1. Cultural patterns define health.

        2. What is "healthy" is often the same as what people define as morally good.

        3. Cultural standards of health change over time.

        4. A society's technology affects people's health.

        5. Social inequality affects people's health.

II. Health: A Global Survey.

    A. Most historical preindustrial societies were unable to maintain a healthy environment. Problems were particularly serious in cities.

    B. Health problems in poor societies today continue to be serious.

        1. GLOBAL SOCIOLOGY BOX—Killer Poverty: A Report from Africa.

        2. WINDOW ON THE WORLD—Global Map 21–1: The Availability of Physicians in Global Perspective. Medical doctors, widely available to people in rich nations, are perilously scarce in poor societies.

    C. Industrialization has dramatically improved human health. With infectious diseases less of a threat, it is now chronic illnesses, such as heart disease and cancer, that claim most people in the United States. By and large, industrial societies manage to delay death until old age.

III. Health in the United States.

    A. **Social epidemiology** is the study of how health and disease are distributed throughout a society's population.

        1. SEEING OURSELVES BOX—National Map 21-1: Life Expectancy Across the United States. On average, women live longer than men.

        2. Age and sex.

             a. Death is now rare among young people, with the exception of mortality resulting from accidents and from AIDS.

            b. Across the life course, women fare better in terms of health than men.

            c. APPLYING SOCIOLOGY BOX—Masculinity: A Threat to Health?

        3. Social class and race.

             a. Infant mortality is twice as high for disadvantaged children as for children born to privilege.

       b. Poverty among African-Americans helps explain why African-American people are more likely to die in infancy and, as adults, suffer the effects of violence, drug abuse, and illness.

B. Cigarette smoking tops the list of preventable health hazards.

C. An **eating disorder** is an intense involvement in dieting or other forms of weight control in order to become very thin. Eating disorders are much more common among women for cultural reasons.

D. Sexually transmitted diseases:
    1. Gonorrhea and syphilis.
    2. Genital herpes.
    3. AIDS is the most serious of all STDs.
       a. WINDOW ON THE WORLD—Global Map 21–2: HIV Infection of Adults in Global Perspective. Almost 70 percent of all global HIV cases are recorded in sub-Saharan Africa.

E. Ethical issues: Confronting death.
    1. When is a person dead?
    2. Do people have a right to die?
    3. What about mercy killing?

IV. The Medical Establishment.

Medicine is a social institution concerned with combating disease and improving health.

A. The rise of scientific medicine. The American Medical Association was founded in 1847 and symbolized the growing acceptance of a scientific model of medicine. In the early 1900s, state licensing boards agreed to certify only physicians trained in scientific programs approved by the AMA. Both the prestige and income of physicians rose dramatically.

B. **Holistic medicine** is an approach to health care that emphasizes prevention of illness and takes account of the person's entire physical and social environment. These are its foundations:
    1. Patients are people.
    2. Responsibility, not dependency.
    3. Personal treatment.

C. Paying for health: A global survey.
    1. Medicine in socialist societies:
       a. The People's Republic of China. The government controls most healthcare. Traditional healing arts are still widely practiced in China. In addition, a holistic concern for the well-being of both mind and body characterizes the Chinese approach to health.
       b. The Russian Federation. Medical care is in transition. Nonetheless, the idea that everyone has a right to basic medical care remains widespread.
    2. Medicine in capitalist societies:
       a. The Swedish system is often described as **socialized medicine,** a medical care system in which the government owns and operates most medical facilities and employs most physicians.
       b. Great Britain. The British created a "dual system" of medical service.

        c. Canada. Canada has a "single payer" model of health care. But Canada also has a two-tiered system like Great Britain's, with some physicians working outside the government-funded system and setting their own fees.

        d. Japan. Physicians in Japan have private practices, but a combination of government programs and private insurance pays medical costs.

D. Medicine in the United States. Ours is a **direct-fee system** or a medical-care system in which patients pay directly for the services of physicians and hospitals. Medical bills are paid three ways:

    1. Private insurance programs.

    2. Public insurance programs, such as Medicare and Medicaid.

    3. **Health Maintenance Organizations,** organizations that provide comprehensive medical care to subscribers for a fixed fee.

    4. In 1994, the Clinton administration proposed a sweeping reform of health care called "managed competition." But the Clinton reforms were rejected by Congress. Still, public concern about health care runs high, so debate will most likely continue.

V. Theoretical Analysis of Medicine.

A. Structural-functional analysis views illness as a social dysfunction.

    1. Talcott Parsons suggests that people often respond to illness by assuming the **sick role,** patterns of behavior defined as appropriate for people who are ill. The sick role has three characteristics:

        a. Illness suspends routine responsibilities.

        b. A sick person must want to be well.

        c. A sick person must seek competent help.

    2. The physician's role. Parsons saw the doctor-patient relationship as hierarchical. Yet this pattern varies from society to society.

    3. Critical evaluation. Parsons' work links illness and medicine to the broader organization of society, but it also supports the idea that doctors, rather than patients, bear primary responsibility for health.

B. Symbolic-interaction analysis.

    1. The social construction of illness. How people define a medical situation may actually affect how they feel.

    2. The social construction of treatment. Understanding how people construct reality in the examination room is as important as mastering the medical skills required for treatment.

    3. Critical evaluation. This paradigm reveals the relativity of sickness and health, but seems to deny that there are any objective standards of well-being.

C. Social-conflict analysis.

    1. Access to care. The access problem is more serious in the United States than in other industrialized societies because our country has no universal medical care system.

    2. The profit motive. Some conflict analysts argue that the real problem is the character of capitalist medicine itself.

3. Medicine as politics. Scientific medicine frequently takes sides on significant social issues.
4. Critical evaluation. This perspective minimizes the improvements in health brought about by the present system.
D. CONTROVERSY AND DEBATE BOX—The Genetic Crystal Ball: Do We Really Want to Look?

VI. Looking Ahead: Health and Medicine in the Twenty-First Century.
A. The health of Americans overall will continue to improve into the next century.
B. To a significant extent, people can take responsibility for their own health. However, certain health problems will continue to plague U.S. society.
C. The U.S. falls short in addressing the health of marginalized members of our society.
D. Problems of health are far greater in the poor societies of the world than they are in the United States.

Chapter Objectives

1) Explain why health is as much a social issue as a biological one.

2) Examine how health has improved as a consequence of the Industrial and Scientific Revolutions.

3) Examine the health problems currently facing the world's poorer nations.

4) Define social epidemiology and summarize what is known about health in the United States.

5) Be generally familiar with the health risks associated with cigarette smoking, eating disorders, and sexually-transmitted diseases, especially AIDS.

6) Debate the ethical issues surrounding death, including when a person is dead, the right to die, and euthanasia.

7) Trace the rise of scientific medicine and discuss the challenge presently raised to traditional health care by advocates of holistic medicine.

8) Summarize ways in which various socialist and capitalist societies supply health care to their citizenry.

9) Understand the implications and consequences of the U.S. direct-fee system of paying for health care.

10) Explain the three basic ways by which U.S. citizens commonly pay for health care.

11) Compare and contrast how each of the three theoretical paradigms direct attention to different aspects of the health care institution.

12) Describe Parsons' conception of the sick role.

13) Examine how illness and health care are socially constructed.

14) Identify and discuss three major criticisms of the U.S. health care system advanced by social-conflict theorists.

Essay Topics

1) How has society positively shaped your health? Negatively?

2) What factors do you believe contribute to the development of eating disorders? What could be done to reduce these effects?

3) What role, if any, do you think that the economically developed countries should play in attempting to improve health in the poorer nations?

4) Why does the U.S. government simultaneously (a) ban tobacco advertising from the electronic media and issue many anti-smoking public health bulletins, yet also (b) continue to subsidize tobacco farmers with billions of dollars of tax advantages?

5) Some people think that non-smokers, who must risk cancer from breathing second-hand smoke given off by other people's cigarettes, are victims; others argue that smokers are becoming an oppressed minority because their right to smoke in public places is being widely circumscribed. Which position strikes you as more reasonable? Why?

6) Some seek to control the spread of sexually transmitted diseases by educational campaigns advocating safe sex and the distribution of condoms; others insist that only chastity outside of marriage and complete monogamy within it will allow us to conquer these diseases. Which position strikes you as more likely to be effective? Why?

7) Outline what you regard as the principal arguments for and against the right to die and mercy killing.

8) Why do you think practitioners of traditional scientific medicine have been so slow to adopt some of the principles of holistic medicine?

9) Do you feel that the United States needs a system of national health care? How would you structure such a program?

10) Traditionally, physicians were seen as properly having complete and total control over their patients; now the pendulum is swinging and patients are demanding substantially more power in the relationship. What balance do you believe would be ideal in this regard?

Integrative Supplement Guide

1. **ABC Videos:**
- HMOs and Managed Care Guidelines (*World News Tonight/American Agenda*, 11/20/95)
- The Managed Care System & Mental Health Care (*Nightline*, 10/17/96)
- Medical Advertising (*Nightline*, 8/1/96)

2. **Transparencies - Series V:**
- T-141 The Availability of Physicians in Global Perspective
- T-142 Life Expectancy Across the United States, Female
- T-143 Life Expectancy for U.S. Children Born in 1996
- T-144 Cigarette Smoking in Selected Countries
- T-145 HIV Infection of Adults in Global Perspective
- T-146 Types of Transmission for Reported U.S. AIDS Cases, 1997

Supplemental Lecture Material
Physician-Assisted Suicide

Are the attitudes of doctors changing in any way toward physician-assisted suicide, in particular, in regards to HIV infected patients? That's what the authors of an article for the *New England Journal of Medicine* wondered. To find out, they repeated a survey they'd conducted in 1990. The survey consisted of an anonymous, self-administered questionnaire sent to a group of doctors dealing with HIV infected patients in the San Francisco area.

Apparently, *direct* requests for assistance in committing suicide did not change between 1990 and 1995, but physicians in the later survey reported more *indirect* requests.

One large difference occurred in how many physicians said they had actually helped terminally ill patients commit suicide by prescribing narcotics. In earlier surveys, only 7 to 9 percent of doctors complied with such requests. By 1995, that number had grown to 53 percent.

Along with asking the physicians about their real, everyday experiences, the questionnaire also included an hypothetical case vignette about a 30-year old man called Tom diagnosed with AIDS and asking to be prescribed drugs to commit suicide when he decided such a moment would come. The patient was described as intelligent and thoughtful, and not extraordinarily depressed given the circumstances. This vignette was used to create an "intention to assist" score. In 1995, 48 percent of respondents replied they'd be likely to assist, compared to only 28 percent in 1990. They were also less likely to try and talk Tom out of his decision, nor would they condemn another physician granting such a request.

The authors of the study suggest that the increased willingness of physicians to assist in a patient's suicide could be due to a greater societal acceptance of euthanasia and physician-assisted suicide, but four other factors were also associated with a physician having actually assisted in a suicide: 1. having a higher number of patients who had died of AIDS; 2. having received more indirect requests from patients for assistance; 3. the physician being gay, lesbian or bisexual; and 4. having a higher "intention to assist" score as shown by answers to the vignette.

The authors point out that no tracking was done as to how many of the patients the respondents prescribed drugs for actually committed suicide. Also, many physicians view prescribing medication as a way to give a patient comfort "by giving them a sense of control over a disease that tends to rob them of control."

Source

Slome, L.R. et al. " Physician-Assisted Suicide and Patients with Human Immunodeficiency Virus Disease," *New England Journal of Medicine,* Vol. 336, No. 6, (February 6, 1997): pp. 417-421.

Discussion Questions

1) Should terminally ill patients be given the right to commit suicide? Why or why not? Under what circumstances, if ever?

2) Do you think similar results to the ones found in the study above would hold true for other physicians and other terminal illnesses? Why or why not?

3) **Activity.** Write down how you feel about assisted suicide, then watch a documentary about someone dying of a terminal illness. Did watching it change your mind in any way? How? If not, why not?

Supplemental Lecture Material
The Face of AIDS in Asia

The AIDS virus appears to be taking a different path in Asia than it has in Africa or Europe and North America. Because of social changes in many of the rapidly developing economies of Asia, the disease will probably make the continent home to the largest number of HIV-infected people on the planet by 2000, displacing Africa and far outstripping North America and Europe. Estimates suggest that between 30 and 120 million infected individuals will be in Asia at the turn of the century. In 1993, there were about 14 million people infected worldwide.

Research on the spread of AIDS in Asia has been limited. Embarrassed by the problem, a number of governments have stifled or prevented studies to determine the extent of HIV infection. Thailand, however, admitted that it had the potential for a serious AIDS crisis in the 1980s, which has allowed both more-reliable research and the development of the most active intervention programs in all of Asia. AIDS arrived in Thailand in 1984 and has grown at a staggering rate since that time. The infection rate is three times higher than in the United States, primarily via heterosexual transmission and intravenous drug use.

Many high-risk behaviors have exacerbated the infection rate. Intravenous heroin users have a 35 percent infection rate. Many adult men have sex with prostitutes as the culture encourages men to have many sexual partners before and after marriage. Women are expected to be virgins before marrying their husbands and then remain faithful during marriage. In effect, only a small pool of the female population is sexually available for men, which eases transmission. Estimates suggest that about 25 percent of the country's prostitutes are infected. Two AIDS researchers wrote to a Bangkok newspaper, stating that "for Thai women, the most important risk factor for HIV infection is marriage." The worst infection rate is probably among females from thirteen to twenty years old. Unlike Europe and North America, homosexual transmission is not a major source of new infections.

Researchers suggest that other factors in the spread of AIDS are also important. Thailand and other parts of Asia have become the destination of "sexual tourists" from Europe, North America, Australia, Korea, Japan, and other wealthier nations. These tourists seek prostitutes. Pedophilic tourists have increasingly exposed young girls and women to HIV. Also, many unmarried young people are moving from rural areas to cities to take advantage of the booming economy, and young unmarried Thais tend to engage in the most high-risk behavior.

Studying the rate that the AIDS virus is spreading is facilitated by AIDS testing conducted by several important institutions in Thailand. All new military recruits, for example, are tested, and the data from various testing sites show that between 3 and 18 percent are already infected. Pregnant women, tested upon admission for their births, show a 1.4 percent infection rate. Present trends suggest that, out of Thailand's total population of sixty million, somewhere between two and four million individuals will be infected with the AIDS virus by 2000. Health care costs relating to AIDS could consume as much as 10 percent of the gross domestic product by that time. Unfortunately, prevention programs have shown little effect to date. The sex industry, a major source of new transmission across Asia, is often under the protection of organized crime or the local government.

Cambodia, Myanmar, and India have similar forces in play and may be at comparable levels of infection. Indonesia, the Philippines, and China may also become hot spots for AIDS, although they show low levels of infection at this time. Korea and Japan seem to be less at risk and AIDS transmission should proceed more slowly there.

Sources

"Is a New AIDS Pattern Emerging in Asia?" *Population Today* (December 1994):5.

Branigin, William. "Asia Faced with AIDS Catastrophe." *Washington Post* (December 2, 1993):A1, A38.

Discussion Questions

1) Why is AIDS growing so quickly in Asia? How does the spread of AIDS there differ from its transmission in America?

2) Is it reasonable to believe that cultural expectations of women could be changed to decrease the spread of AIDS? Should the behavior of men be changed? Is it ethnocentric to consider such changes? If so, how could changes be made that are not ethnocentric?

Supplemental Lecture Material
Are Hispanics Healthier?

New research by the National Institutes for Health (NIH) shows that Hispanics in America are significantly less likely to die from cancer and heart disease than non-Hispanic whites, even though Hispanics are more likely to be poor and to lack health insurance. These researchers are now trying to determine why death rates for heart disease and cancer are lower for Hispanics.

The results seem puzzling. Many health care professionals have long assumed that access to medical care improved life spans, but for many Hispanics medical care is prohibitively expensive without health insurance. Moreover, Hispanic inordinately suffer from several poverty-related diseases. As Paul Sorlie, an epidemiologist with the NIH, states, "Hispanics are not immune to the detrimental effects of poverty. Our data show that poverty is very detrimental." In fact, Hispanics should not be considered healthier overall than non-Hispanic whites as Hispanics show higher rates of several life-threatening disorders.

The researchers suspect that some aspects in the lifestyle or traditional culture of many Hispanics promotes lower cancer and heart disease rates in particular. Unfortunately, studying the population of Hispanics is difficult as there are numerous differences between the many cultures grouped together in the term.

Several theories have emerged. For instance, people in many Hispanic cultures have a diet based heavily on rice and beans. Both foods are considered to be good ways of obtaining protein and carbohydrates with little fat, and together they work to lower cancer and heart disease death rates. On the other hand, foods that are considered unhealthy because they contain a lot of sugar or are high in fat — such as some milk products and lard — are also a common part of the diet of many Hispanics.

Another theory concerns the family living patterns many Hispanics adopt. Extended families are more common among Hispanics than among other Americans, and the social support such families provide may help their members become less likely to develop certain illnesses and/or to recover from illnesses more quickly and completely.

A third possibility may be connected to data showing that, in spite of having less-regular general medical and prenatal care, Hispanic mothers tend to have low birth-weight babies less often than non-Hispanic white mothers. Perhaps having a better start on life pays off later in some way.

Researchers agree that this area is an important focus for research. Studying the traditional cultures of Hispanics may lead to health improvements for all Americans.

Source

"Why Do Hispanics Have Lower Death Rates?" *American Demographics* (May 1994):18, 20.

Discussion Question

1) How might researchers isolate factors that lead to lower cancer and heart disease death rates among Hispanics?

Supplemental Lecture Material
Backlash Against HMOs

When HMOs (Health Maintenance Organizations) were first formed, many people saw them as the answer to soaring healthcare costs in the United States. As a matter of fact, in 1996, medical costs rose only 2.5 percent, compared to a 3.3 percent rise in all consumer prices. Until HMOs arrived, so-called fee-for-service treatment (also called the direct-fee system) was the norm, which allowed physicians to decide what procedures and medications should be used without concern for cost or degree of need. This, some charge, led to unnecessary treatments and, therefore, unnecessary costs. HMOs, on the other hand, would curtail such abuses and make doctors accountable for what they prescribed. Best of all, HMO premiums would be significantly lower both to individuals and companies. Many people and numerous businesses jumped on the new way of health insurance with its emphasis on prevention rather than expensive treatments. Today, many of them aren't happy.

Not only are premiums and co-payments rising, but complaints about HMOs' handling of patients as well as doctors have become increasingly vociferous. The major complaints include hospital stays that are dangerously short just to save money, gag orders on doctors to prevent them from mentioning expensive treatments, making patients pay for emergency room visits if it turns out the emergency wasn't real after all, and bonuses paid to doctors for keeping their costs below a certain level. As a result, one third of companies now think that the drive to contain costs is hurting the quality of care their employees receive.

Problem is, say some, that many HMOs are for-profit corporations, concerned primarily with the bottom line. . . and keeping its shareholders happy by showing large profits year after year. In addition, executives of HMOs typically receive salaries that are on average 62 percent higher than that of heads of other comparable corporations, accounting for some of the high administrative costs. In fact, the term "medical-loss ratio" that is used to refer to premiums HMOs pay out for patient care, says it all. "The Association of American Medical Colleges reported last November that medical-loss ratios of for-profit HMOs paying a flat fee to doctors for treatment averaged only 70 percent of their premium revenue. The remaining 30 percent went for administrative expenses — and profit." Not surprisingly, this problem is usually far less common in not-for-profit HMOs.

Recent mega-mergers are only likely to aggravate the situation by cutting down on consumer choices and likely raising premiums overall. However, doctors, unions, patients and government are all taking steps to initiate changes. Doctors are forming large physicians organizations to have greater negotiating power with HMOs or even to form their own HMOs. While HMO executives often claim that doctors are only trying to protect their income, which dropped from an average of $172,000 annually in 1993 to $146,000 in 1995, physicians say they are most concerned with the lack of care patients are receiving.

Patients are also organizing to have their wishes heard at ballot boxes. Another major goal is to put together report cards rating the various HMOs, so that people can choose more wisely. In the meantime, government is trying to create a patient bill-of-rights, as well as other legislation forbidding gag orders and other such HMO abuses. While HMOs are not likely to disappear, major changes may well be in the offing.

Source

Church, George J.. "Backlash Against HMOs," *Time* (April 14, 1997):32-39.

Discussion Questions

1) In your opinion, should government become more involved in health care? Why or why not?

2) Do you think HMO abuses have been overblown by the media? Why or why not?

3) **Activity.** Conduct research either on the Internet or in the library to see what new regulations regarding HMOs have been passed since the article was written?

Supplemental Lecture Material
Disabilities

In the U.S., there are an estimated 30 million Americans who have a physical or mental disability. Their struggles to negotiate the demands of day-to-day life have been aided by the passage of the Americans with Disabilities Act (ADA) of 1990. Former California congressman Tony Coelho, one of the primary authors of the legislation, points out that "There is still job discrimination out there, but the tide is turning."

Since the passage of the ADA, the situation has changed for disabled Americans — and for their employers. American businesses have adapted themselves to make the disabled more welcome and productive. Such workplace accommodations often cost little and can be as simple as offering flexible work hours to an employee suffering from chronic depression, or buying a computer keyboard with all the control keys on one side for someone with a missing hand. (IN general, most workplace accommodations cost from $200 to $500/person.)

After voicing initial concerns about the potential cost, U.S. industry has shown an increased willingness to hire people with disabilities despite a tight job market. In 1994 (the latest year for which Census Bureau is available), some 3.7 million people with severe disabilities were at work — up from 2.9 million three years earlier. Still, prejudice, lack of adequate transportation and physical barriers to employment are still common, contributing to a sense of discouragement among the disabled themselves. (While exact numbers vary, experts cite a 1998 Harris survey that found only 30% of adults with disabilities to be employed full or part-time, compared to nearly 80% of adults without disabilities. Nearly 6 out of 10 of those surveyed in a 1997 Louis Harris poll said the ADA had made no difference in their lives.)

In March, 1998, President Clinton created the Presidential Task Force on Employment of Adults with Disabilities. They recommended tax changes to help disabled persons with disabilities pay for work-related expenses, a new program by the Small Business Administration to assist those who want to start their own businesses, a plea for passage of a Patient's Bill of Rights to assist in health care and a call to make the Federal Government a model employer of the disabled. In December, 1998. Vice President Gore announced an Executive Order approving the recommendations concerning the SBA and the Federal Government.

Marriott International of Bethesda, Maryland has been a leader among major corporations in taking a proactive position in aiding the disabled to do their jobs and smaller forms have followed the Marriott example. High-tech firms and computer companies, with their easier access to and knowledge of new technology, are often in the vanguard of efforts to work with the disabled. Both Hewlett-Packard and Kansas City-based Sprint are activist forms that have found minimal-cost accommoda-tion give them a "much richer pool of employees to choose from who can maximize their workplace productivity."

One reason why high-tech firms are more open to the disabled (humane considerations aside) is that the price of accommodating them (at least in some areas) is falling. Henter-Joyce Inc., a St. Petersburg, Florida software company, manufacturers a program for blind and visually impaired people that has come down in price by almost half - $1500 to $795 since its 1988 introduction.

Persons with psychiatric disabilities however, have a much harder time being accepted by corporate America. A major reason is that mental health ailments are often still kept "under wraps." An employer may not even be aware that someone has a mental illness until a difficulty arises on the job. But he biggest problem is the "enor-mous apprehension in hiring people with psychiatric disabilities...will go out of control" according to Ellen Gussaroff, a New York City

psychoanalyst who estimates that about one-third of her patients have had "problems on the job." "But there are people with chronic mental illness who are very capable of doing good work with the right accommodations." Gussaroff adds. To address this, the Equal Employer Opportunities Commission in 1997 issued guidelines under the ADA and provide them with assistance. (For those companies that know how, accommodating employees with recognized mental disability is often easy and cheap. Hewlett-Packard offers workers with emotional problems dealing with the workplace the option of telecommuting.)

While formidable obstacles remain for the physically and mentally challenged, considerable progress has been made.

Source

Koss-Feder, Laura. "Able to Work." *Time* (January 25, 1999).

Discussion Questions

1) Theodore Pinnock, a San Diego civil rights attorney who has cerebral palsy and uses a wheelchair says "Give it about another 100 years. Maybe then you'll see some difference in attitudes." Is he being unduly pessimistic or simply realistic? Explain your answer.

2) What are your feelings about a proactive policy to integrate the disabled more thoroughly into working life? Is it overkill, appropriate, or inadequate tokenism? Explain your answer.

Chapter 22

Population, Urbanization, and Environment

I. Demography: The Study of Population.
Demography is the study of human population.
  A. **Fertility** is the incidence of childbearing in a society's population.
        1. **Fecundity** refers to the maximum potential childbearing ability of the women of a society. It is sharply reduced in practice by cultural norms, finances, and personal choice.
        2. Demographers measure fertility using the **crude birth rate** or the number of live births in a given year for every thousand people in a population.
  B. **Mortality** is the incidence of death in a society's population.
        1. Demographers measure mortality using the **crude death rate** or the number of deaths in a given year for every thousand people in a population.
        2. The **infant mortality rate** is the number of deaths among infants under one year of age for every thousand live births in a given year.
        3. **Life expectancy** is the average life span of a society's population.
  C. **Migration** is the movement of people into and out of a specified territory.
        1. It may be voluntary or involuntary. Voluntary migration may be explained by push and pull factors.
        2. Movement into a territory is termed **immigration** and is measured by the **in-migration rate,** the number of people entering an area for every thousand people in the population.
        3. Movement out of a territory is termed **emigration** and is measured by the **out-migration rate**, the number of people leaving an area for every thousand people in the population.
        4. The **net migration rate** is the difference between the in-migration rate and the out-migration rate.
        5. SEEING OURSELVES BOX—National Map 22-1: Population Change Across the United States. In general, population is moving from the heartland of the United States toward the coasts.
  D. The **population growth rate** is computed by subtracting the crude death rate from the crude birth rate. It is relatively low in the industrialized nations and quite high in the poor countries.
        1. WINDOW ON THE WORLD—Global Map 22–1: Population Growth in Global Perspective. The richest countries of the world have growth rates below 1 percent. In global perspective, we see that a society's standard of living is closely related to its rate of population growth: population is rising fastest in the world regions that can least afford to support more people.
        2. **Doubling time** is another way of expressing a society's growth rate.

E. Population composition.
   1. The **sex ratio** is the number of males for every hundred females in a given population. Sex ratios are usually below 100, because, on average, women outlive men.
   2. An **age-sex pyramid** is a graphic representation of the age and sex of a population.

II. History and Theory of Population Growth.
The growth rate began to increase around 1750 and is presently extremely rapid.
   A. **Malthusian theory.**
      1. Malthus believed that population increased geometrically, while food could only increase arithmetically, leading to catastrophic starvation.
      2. Critical evaluation. Malthus' predictions were not supported in the short run, but they may have some value in describing future demographic trends.
   B. **Demographic transition theory** is a thesis linking population patterns to a society's level of technological development. It entails four stages:
      1. Stage 1, preindustrial: high birth rates, high death rates.
      2. Stage 2, onset of industrialization: high birth rates, low death rates.
      3. Stage 3, industrial economy: declining birth rates, low death rates.
      4. Stage 4, a postindustrial economy: low birth rates, steady death rates.
      5. Critical evaluation. This approach suggests that technology holds the key to population control. It is compatible with modernization theory but not with dependency theory.
   C. Global population today: A brief survey.
      1. The low-growth industrial societies of the North are now close to **zero population growth,** the level of reproduction that maintains population at a steady state.
      2. The high-growth less-developed societies of the South are still in Stage 2 of the demographic transition.
         a. CRITICAL THINKING BOX—Empowering Women: The Key to Controlling Population Growth.

III. Urbanization: The Growth of Cities.
Urbanization is the concentration of humanity into cities.
   A. The evolution of cities.
      1. The emergence of cities led to a specialization and higher living standards. The first city—Jericho, which dates back some 10,000 years, was home to only around 600 people.
      2. Preindustrial European cities began around 1800 B.C.E and flowered in Greece and later in Rome.
      3. By 1750 C.E. a second urban revolution was transforming European cities into an industrial model.

B. The growth of U.S. cities.
    1. Colonial settlement, 1565–1800.
    2. Urban expansion, 1800–1860.
    3. The metropolitan era, 1860–1950.
        a. A **metropolis** is a large city that socially and economically dominates an urban area.
    4. Urban decentralization, 1950–present.
C. Suburbs and urban decline.
    1. **Suburbs** are urban areas beyond the political boundaries of a city. They began to expand in the late 19th century and exploded after WWII. Industrial and commercial activities soon followed population outward.
    2. This trend led to massive problems in the old central cities.
    3. The official response to these problems was **urban renewal,** government programs intended to revitalize cities.
D. Postindustrial sunbelt cities. These cities came of age after urban decentralization began. Sunbelt cities have pushed their boundaries outward, along with the population flow.
E. Megalopolis: Regional cities.
    1. The U.S. census recognizes 384 **metropolitan statistical areas.**
    2. The biggest MSAs are termed **consolidated metropolitan statistical areas.**
    3. A **megalopolis** is a vast urban region containing a number of cities and their surrounding suburbs.
F. Edge cities. Urban decentralization has created edge cities, business centers some distance from the old downtowns. Edge cities have no clear physical boundaries.

IV. Urbanism as a Way of Life.
A. Ferdinand Toennies: *Gemeinschaft* and *Gesellschaft*.
    1. **Gemeinschaft** is a type of social organization by which people are bound closely together by kinship and tradition.
    2. **Gesellschaft** is a type of social organization by which people have weak social ties and considerable self-interest.
    3. Toennies saw the development of modern urban society as a shift from Gemeinschaft to Gesellschaft.
B. Emile Durkheim: Mechanical and organic solidarity. Durkheim described traditional, rural life as mechanical solidarity, social bonds based on common sentiments and shared moral values. Organic solidarity refers to social bonds based on specialization and interdependence. Durkheim optimistically pointed to a new kind of solidarity. Where societies had been built on likeness, Durkheim now saw social life based on differences.
C. Georg Simmel: The blasé urbanite. To prevent being overwhelmed by all the city stimulation, urbanites develop a blasé attitude, tuning out much of what goes on around them.
D. The Chicago school: Robert Park and Lewis Wirth.
    1. Robert Park was the founder of the Chicago School of urban sociology.
    2. Louis Wirth sees a large population, dense settlement and social diversity as the keys to understanding urban society. These traits tend to make human relations impersonal, superficial and transitory, as well as relatively tolerant.

3. Critical evaluation. Research offers only weak support for Wirth's thesis. He ignores how urbanism varies according to class, race, and gender.

E. **Urban ecology** is the study of the link between the physical and social dimensions of cities.

1. This approach helps explain why cities are located where they are.

2. It also generates theories concerning the physical design of cities.

a. Ernest Burgess' concentric zone theory.

b. Homer Hoyt's wedge-shaped sector theory.

c. Harris and Ullman's focus on multicentered cities.

3. Social area analysis studies how neighborhoods differ in terms of family patterns, social class, and race or ethnicity.

4. Work by Berry and Rees ties all of these strands together.

F. Urban political economy is influenced by the thinking of Karl Marx, which sees the city as a natural organism developing according to an internal logic.

1. Critical evaluation. This approach helps explain why many U.S. cities are in crisis, but both urban ecology and urban political economy are not easily applied to cities in other societies or in different eras.

V. Urbanization in Poor Societies.

A. A third urban revolution is taking place because many poor nations have entered the high-growth Stage 2 of demographic transition theory.

B. Cities do offer more opportunities than rural areas, but they provide no quick fix for the massive problems of escalating population and grinding poverty.

VI. Looking ahead: Population and Urbanization in the Twenty-First Century.

A. Controlling global population will be a monumental task.

B. The well-being of the world may ultimately depend on resolving many of the economic and social problems of the poor, overly populated countries.

VII. Environment and Ecology.

A. **Ecology** is the study of the interaction of living organisms and the natural environment.

B. The **natural environment** consists of the earth's surface and atmosphere, including various living organisms and the air, water, soil, and other resources necessary to sustain life.

C. The Global Dimension.

1. Any study of the natural environment must necessarily be global in scope because the planet constitutes a single **ecosystem,** the system composed of the interaction of all living organisms and their natural environment.

D. Technology and the Environmental Deficit.

1. Complex technologies generally pose more threats to the global environment than did the simple technology of preindustrial societies.

2. The world is now facing an **environmental deficit**, profound and negative harm to the natural environment caused by humanity's focus on short-term material affluence. This concept implies three important ideas:

a. The state of the environment is a social issue.

b. Environmental damage is often unintended.

            c. Much environmental harm is reversible.

E. Culture: Growth and Limits.

    1. The **logic of growth** is a widely accepted cultural value which suggests that growth is inherently good and that we can solve any problems that might arise as a result of unrestrained expansion.

    2. The **limits-to-growth** thesis holds that humanity must implement policies to control the growth of population, material production, and the use of resources in order to avoid environmental collapse.

F. Solid Waste: The Disposable Society.

    1. CRITICAL THINKING BOX—Why Grandmother Had No Trash.

    2. Landfills pose several threats to the natural environment.

    3. **Recycling**, reusing resources we would otherwise discard, is one solution.

G. Water and air.

    1. Water supply is problematic in many parts of the world.

D. A special problem is **acid rain**, rain that is made acidic by air pollution and destroys plant and animal life.

        a. WINDOW ON THE WORLD—Global Map 22–2: Water Consumption in Global Perspective.

    2. Polluted water is an increasingly serious concern as well.

    3. A deterioration of air quality was one of the unanticipated consequences of the development of industrial technology.

    4. **Rain forests** are regions of dense forestation, most of which circle the globe close to the equator.

    5. **Global warming** is apparently occurring as a result of the greenhouse effect, a rise in the earth's average temperature due to increasing concentration of carbon dioxide in the atmosphere resulting in part from the decline of the rain forests.

    6. The shrinking of the rain forests reduces the earth's biodiversity.

H. **Environmental racism** is the pattern by which environmental hazards are greatest in proximity to poor people, particularly poor minorities. In part, it is a deliberate strategy by factory owners and powerful officials.

VIII. Looking Ahead: Toward a Sustainable Society and World.

A. We need to develop a **sustainable ecosystem,** the human use of the natural environment to meet the needs of the present generation without threatening the prospects of future generations.

B. This calls for three basic strategies:

    1. We must bring world population growth under control.

    2. We must conserve finite resources.

    3. We must reduce waste.

C. CONTROVERSY AND DEBATE BOX—Apocalypse: Will People Overwhelm the Earth?

Chapter Objectives

1) Define the three basic elements of demographic analysis: fertility, mortality, and migration.

2) Explain how demographers calculate a population's natural growth rate.

3) Explain how demographers study population composition using the sex ratio and the age-sex pyramid.

4) Trace historic trends in the size and growth rate of the world's population.

5) Identify strengths and limitations of Malthusian theory.

6) Explain the theory of the demographic transition.

7) Examine social factors that underlie contemporary population trends in both the industrialized and the nonindustrialized societies.

8) Trace the development of cities around the world and in the United States.

9) Discuss results of urban decentralization.

10) Explain the general approach to urban analysis favored by urban ecologists.

11) Explain the general approach to urban analysis favored by urban political economists.

12) Characterize contemporary urbanization in the world's poor societies.

13) Define the concepts of ecology, the natural environment, the ecosystem and the environmental deficit.

14) Be aware of how technological change, population growth, and cultural patterns collectively impact on the environment.

15) Explain the logic of growth and the limits-to-growth thesis.

16) Discuss the major environmental issues confronting societies around the world today, including solid waste disposal, water supply and pollution, air pollution, the depletion of rain forests, global warming, and declining biodiversity.

Essay Topics

1) Make use of the concepts of push and pull factors to analyze the rapid decentralization of U.S. metropolitan regions that has occurred in recent decades.

2) Is the possibility that the U.S. and other developed nations may fall below the zero population growth point one that ought to concern us? Why?

3) How did changes in the status of women in the developed countries affect their demographic histories?

4) Outline and evaluate some of the steps that nations in the developing world might take to reduce their rate of population growth.

5) Is it possible to revitalize our central cities, or is the trend toward suburban dispersal so strong that the central cities are beyond hope? How would you attempt to reinvigorate the urban core?

6) What do Simmel and Wirth see as the principal advantages and disadvantages of living in cities? Do their analyses correspond with your own observations and experiences with urban life? Discuss.

7) Do you think that we will always be able to find new technological solutions to any ecological problems which arise in the future?

8) How can the logic of growth be modified in order to reduce strain on the environment?

9) How effectively does your community recycle? How might people be convinced to recycle more of their waste?

10) How can citizens work most effectively to promote a cleaner environment?

Integrative Supplement Guide

1. **ABC Videos:**
- City At Peace (*Nightline*, 6/9/95)
- Will There Be Enough Money For Your Old Age? (*Nightline*, 9/18/95)
- Drinking Water Safely (World News Tonight/AA, 6/1/95)
- Environmental Protection Challenged (World News Tonight/AA, 2/28/95)

2. **Transparencies - Series V:**
- T-148 Crude Birth Rates and Crude Death Rates, 1997
- T-149 Infant Mortality Rates, 1997
- T-150 Life Expectancy, 1997
- T-151 Population Change Across the United States
- T-152 Population Growth in Global Perspective
- T-153 Age-Sex Population Pyramids for the United States and Mexico

- T-154 The Increase in World Population, 1700-2100
- T-155 Demographic Transition Theory
- T-156 Urbanization in Global Perspective
- T-157 A Cartogram of the World Population
- T-158 Population Distribution of Industrial and Non-industrial Societies, 1750-2010
- T-159 The Urban Population of the United States, 1790-1990
- T-160 The Internal Structure of Cities
- T-161 Energy Consumption in Global Perspective
- T-162 The Limits to Growth: Projections
- T-163 Rating the Local Environment: A Global Survey
- T-164 Rating the Local Environment: A Global Survey
- T-165 Water Consumption in Global Perspective
- T-166 Air Pollution Across the United States
- T-167 The Formation of Acid Rain
- T-168 Concern for the Environment

Supplemental Lecture Material
The Global Environment: Two Points of View

When it comes to predicting what our environmental future might look like, even scientists disagree as shown during a recent debate of the World Future Society. Here are the points-of-view of both sides, one consisting of "environmentalists," the other of "anti-environmentalists. "

A crisis, what crisis? Ask anti-environmentalists. They happen to believe that forecasts of doom and gloom are inaccurate. Instead, they cite the way trends have been heading: the world's air and water, they say, is cleaner overall; global life-expectancy has risen from 47 years in 1950 to 65 in 1996; the world has been eating better on average because more natural resources are becoming available; economic growth actually leads to less air pollution since people who have a higher living standard start demanding a healthier envir-onment as shown by what has been happening in the United States; and population growth will not impede economic development. Yes, pressure on resources will initially drive up prices, but human ingenuity and business sense will then contribute inventions to fulfill the need or counter ill effects. In fact, non-capitalist practices such as so-called open access commons in some countries, allowing anyone to graze animals on common land, are what create problems since no one has a vested stake in keeping the land productive.

Environmentalists disagree. Those statistics, they counter, are averaged per capita, which obscures the developing poverty gap in the world. In fact, 1.6 billion people now are worse off than they were 15 years earlier, and the ratio between the richest and the poorest has doubled. In fact, the incomes of the poorest 20 percent have actually declined.

The GNP (Gross National Product), which is so often used to assess how well a country is doing, has shown no growth between 1980 and 1993 for most low-income countries, and the same for middle-income countries. In reality, though, the GNP, say environmentalists, is not a very good measurement because it ignores intangibles such as clean air and water and other environmental issues. A better measure for progress is the GPI (Genuine Progress Indicator), which also takes into account the economic toll of such things as prisons or crime on a society, then subtracts those from the GNP. In fact, though the United States GNP has gone up, the GPI has gone down since 1970.

Environmental problems will not fix themselves, and to rely on economics is to pin your hopes on a profession rather than a science, and therefore not held to be accountable or verifiable. The inherent problem is in relying on the market or economy to fix the environmental problems it creates through exploiting resources. Markets always respond and therefore lag behind what is happening. On the other hand, wise government and human ingenuity can use foresight to plan ahead and change environmentally destructive patterns before they create chaos and cause large-scale human suffering.

Source

"The Global Environment: Megaproblem or Not?" *The Futurist*, Vol. 3 1, No. 2 (March--April, 1997): 17-22.

Discussion Questions

1) Where do you stand? Why? Use the three theoretical paradigms you learned about in the chapter of the textbook to underpin your discussion.

2) **Activity**. Take one issue, such as clean water or clean air, and research your state's and your community's environmental laws as well as problems recently encountered.

Supplemental Lecture Material
The Changing Face of U.S. Immigration

The flow of immigrants into the United States has changed dramatically over the past three decades, according to recent Census Bureau statistics. Major changes have occurred in both volume and country of origin of these immigrants.

"The total number of foreign-born people grew only 1 percent in the 1960s, from 9,738,000 in 1960 to 9,619,000 in 1970. It then jumped, by almost half, to 14,080,000 in 1980 and again by half, to 19,767,000 in 1990."

Changes in the country of origin of foreign-born U.S. residents are even more striking. In 1960, two-thirds of this population was born in Europe. Thirty years later, only 20.3% were Europeans. Asians made up 5.1% of the foreign-born population in 1960 and 25.2% in 1990, with the largest numbers immigrating from Southeast Asia (0.1% to 10%) and Eastern Asia (1.1% to 9%).

But the most dramatic increase has been in immigrants coming from Latin America. In 1960, just 9.3% of all foreign-born U.S. residents were born in this part of the world; in 1990, 42.5% were. Native Mexicans alone constituted 21.7% of all foreign-born residents in 1990.

As a result of these trends, demographers expect the ethnic and cultural character of the United States to change markedly in the next century. European-origin citizens will become, for the first time in history, a numerical minority. The transformation will be particularly marked in California, which is the point of entry for very large numbers of immigrants from both Asia and Latin America.

Source

Winsberg, Morton D. "America's Foreign Born," *Population Today* Vol. 23 No. 10 (October, 1993):4.

Discussion Questions

1) Do you feel that the United States ought to encourage or discourage this wave of new immigration? Why?

2) How do you expect that U.S. cultural and social life will change in the coming decades as a result of these demographic changes?

Supplemental Lecture Material
Planting an Orchard in Eden: Saving Madagascar

Located on an island separated from the eastern coast of Africa for tens of millions of years, numerous unique plant and animal species evolved in Madagascar. Some 50 percent of its known bird species, 85 percent of the plant species, 95 percent of the reptile species, as well as many of its mammals are located nowhere else on the planet. But some of the world's most desperate poverty and highest birth rates are located here too. But strenuous efforts to raise the level of environmental awareness and protect the most sensitive areas are competing with empty stomachs and destructive farming practices.

Environmental groups are combining resources in Madagascar with welfare organizations. "What we do sounds like development, and it is. We can't talk about saving plants and animals until basic human needs are met," says Roderic Mast of Conservation International, which has teamed up with the World Wildlife Fund. Literacy training, child vaccinations, agronomy programs, and hygiene and birth control education are all a part of their attempt to help the ecosystem as a whole at the same time as the socioeconomic level of the country's loggers, fishers, and farmers. Tree farms, rice cooperatives, substitutes for the charcoal widely used for cooking, and high-tech research focused on specific problems are all being developed to create a more sustainable economic and subsistence system.

The dual emphasis of conservation and development has been complex and difficult to implement; the Malagasy, for instance, don't always respond to aid the way environmentalists would like them to, and cultural sensitivity is a major factor in the success or failure of any goal. One project brought irrigation to a village, which successfully allowed the farmers to raise more rice. Unfortunately, the villagers sold the rice to buy more zebus, the native cattle, which led to the burning of more sensitive forest in order to create additional pasture for the zebu. Another plan to begin teaching students in one area about environmental sensitivity ran aground when the attendance rate turned out to be lower than 40 percent. In another case, an immunization program almost fell apart when the medics came without warning into a village, which did not understand the purpose of the visit and tried to throw the visitors out. An American graduate student, in the village for different reasons, was trusted by the community enough to able to secure permission to begin immunizations.

The path for Madagascar is brighter because of the end of the communist government in 1993; with luck, democracy will encourage more support for improving the island for all of its citizens, human and otherwise. Some of the new government's officials are beginning to consider encouraging ecotourism as a means both of promoting international support for conservation and of reinforcing conservation programs. The foreign cash will be helpful, too.

The high birth rate may present one of the most dangerous problems that the island faces. Current trends suggest that the island will grow from the current 12 million inhabitants to 24 million within thirty years. Agricultural practices on the island depend heavily on deforestation, and by 2015 only about half of the current amount of forest may be left. The strength and dedication of the current aid workers is impressive, but even more energy must support the beginnings of positive change.

Source

Nash, Madeleine J. "The Making of an Eco-Disaster." *Time* (November 21, 1994):72-73.

Discussion Questions

1) Would the aid workers be more efficient in their conservation programs if they simply commanded the native population to treat their environment differently rather than trying to re-educate them? Would it be faster to bypass them entirely? How? Is the support of the indigenous people necessary or simply the preference of the workers?

2) Do you think the native population understands the long-term effects of their agricultural practices? Why or why not? How might their understanding differ than Western environmentalists? How important are these differences?

Supplemental Lecture Material
Russia's Declining Population

Not so long ago, in Soviet times, having ten children brought tangible rewards to women, because along with "Heroine Mother" status came the privilege of jumping ahead in often long food lines. Today, though, having many children no longer brings benefits, but is more likely to cause financial and economic hardship for a family. Not surprisingly, many Russians are choosing to have small families in spite of the state's push to the contrary.

Russia's population, it turns out, is shrinking at an alarming rate. Not only are birth rates low — an average of 1.4 children per family — but life expectancy has been dipping, particularly for men. In 1985, men on average lived to be almost 64, women to 74. In 1994, that had dropped to 57.7 years for men and 71.3 years for women. Suicides, murders, alcoholism, and tuberculosis account for a large proportion of early deaths.

In fact, in 1996, 1.7 more Russians died than were born. If this trend continues, Russia's population will shrink by almost a million annually. In 1994, the population was 148,400,000. It is projected to be only 115,000,000 by 2015, and 58,000,000 by 2040-2060.

Some politicians are calling for the reinstatement of the Heroine Mother award, but would such an award be enough in a country where economic conditions are tough, families live in tiny apartments, and working women are likely to put off having children? In fact, hundreds of thousands of Russian women have abortions every year or use contraceptives in spite of the Russian Orthodox Church's prohibitions.

Radical politicians blame the intelligentsia and the media for fostering an unhealthy emphasis on individualism and non-family attitudes. This makes moderates fear that a more dictatorial approach to birth promotion might be coming. But Russian sociologists point out that Russian women have been choosing to have fewer children for more than 100 years, nor are women necessarily buying the rhetoric. Instead, they often see a generally overpopulated world that doesn't need more children. They also see a lifestyle where families are more conscious about making sure they can support the children they have before they decide to do so. After all, even if they ultimately decide to have children, the state no longer provides any tangible support to outweigh the costs of having a family.

Source
Meek, James. "Russia Strives to Reverse Population Shrinkage, *Washington Times* (September, 22, 1996):A8.

Discussion Questions
1) Do you think the dire predictions for Russia's population will come true? Why or why not? What will it mean for the country if they do?

2) Given the overpopulation of the world, is Russia's dilemma the world's benefit? Why or why not? In what way is the declining population of particular countries of concern globally?

Chapter 23

Collective Behavior and Social Movements

I. Studying Collective Behavior.
Collective behavior is defined as activity involving a large number of people, often spontaneous and sometimes controversial.
    A. Studying collective behavior.
        1. The study of collective behavior is difficult to study for three reasons:
            a. Collective behavior is wide-ranging.
            b. All collective behavior is complex.
            c. Much collective behavior is transitory.
        2. All collective behavior involves the action of a **collectivity**, a large number of people whose minimal interaction occurs in the absence of well-defined and conventional norms.
            a. There are two types of collectivities, localized and dispersed.
            b. Collectivities differ from social groups in three ways: limited social interaction; unclear social boundaries; weak and unconventional norms.

II. Localized Collectivities: Crowds.
    A. **Crowds** are temporary gatherings of people who share a common focus of attention and whose members influence one another. There are five types of crowds:
        1. Casual.
        2. Conventional.
        3. Expressive.
        4. Acting.
        5. Protest.
    B. Mobs and riots.
        1. A **mob** is a highly emotional crowd that pursues some violent or destructive goal. Lynch mobs are the best known example.
        2. A **riot** is a social eruption that is highly emotional, violent and undirected.
    C. Crowds, Mobs, and Social Change.
        1. Ordinary people typically gain power only by acting collectively.
        2. Because crowds have been able to effect social change, they pose a threat to elitist's power.
    D. Explaining crowd behavior.
        1. **Contagion theory** argues that crowds exert a hypnotic influence on their members, turning them into irrational automatons.
            a. Critical evaluation. This theory is not entirely incorrect, but research suggests that it overemphasizes the irrationality of crowd behavior.

2. **Convergence theory** views crowds as assemblages of like-minded individuals who are drawn together because of their common attitudes and interests.
   a. Critical evaluation. This theory is reasonable, but ignores the ability of the crowd to intensify sentiments.
3. **Emergent-norm theory** suggests that distinctive patterns of behavior develop within the crowd as it interacts.
   a. Critical evaluation. This theory stresses the rationality of crowd behavior and accommodates the fact that not all crowd participants behave in the same way.

III. Dispersed Collectivities: Mass Behavior.
Mass behavior refers to collective behavior among people dispersed over a wide geographical area.
A. Rumor and Gossip.
   1. **Rumor** is unsubstantiated information spread informally, often by word of mouth. Rumors have three essential characteristics:
      a. Rumor thrives in a climate of ambiguity.
      b. Rumor is unstable.
      c. Rumor is difficult to stop.
   2. CRITICAL THINKING BOX—The Rumor Mill: Paul Is Dead!
   3. **Gossip** is rumor about people's personal affairs.
B. Public Opinion and Propaganda.
   1. **Public opinion**, widespread attitudes about controversial issues, is another example of highly dispersed collective behavior.
      a. SEEING OURSELVES—National Map 23–1: Support for Public Broadcasting Across the United States.
   2. It is often influenced by **propaganda**, information presented with the intention of shaping public opinion.
C. Panic and Mass Hysteria.
   1. **Panic** is a form of localized collective behavior by which people react to a threat or other stimulus with irrational, frantic and often self-destructive behavior.
   2. **Mass hysteria** is a form of dispersed collective behavior in which people respond to a real or imagined event with irrational, frantic, and often self-destructive behavior.
D. Fashion and Fads.
   1. **Fashion** is a social pattern favored for a time by a large number of people.
   2. A **fad** is an unconventional social pattern that people embrace briefly but enthusiastically.

IV. Social Movements.
Social movements are organized activities that encourage or discourage social change.
A. Social movements may be characterized in terms of the breadth and depth of the change they are seeking. Combining these variables results in four types of social movements:
   1. **Alternative social movements,** which pursue limited change in certain individuals.

2. **Redemptive social movements,** which promote radical change in certain individuals.

3. **Reformative social movements,** which seek moderate changes in the whole society.

4. **Revolutionary social movements,** which promote sweeping transformation of an entire society.

B. Explaining social movements.

1. **Deprivation theory** holds that social movements arise among people who feel deprived, compared to others. **Relative deprivation,** then, is a perceived disadvantage arising from some specific comparison.

    a. Critical evaluation. Since most people experience some deprivation most of the time, this approach does not adequately explain why movements only arise some of the time. It also has a tendency to be circular and to focus more attention on the setting in which a movement emerges than on the movement itself.

2. **Mass-society theory** traces the origin of social movements to rootless individuals seeking a sense of membership and purpose.

    a. Critical evaluation. The concept of a mass society is difficult to operationalize. In addition, this approach minimizes the legitimate political discontent which underlies many movements. Empirical research sometimes supports and sometimes challenges mass-society theory.

3. **Structural-strain theory,** developed by Neil Smelser, argues that six factors promote the development of a social movement:

    a. Structural conduciveness.

    b. Structural strain.

    c. Growth and spread of an explanation.

    d. Precipitating factors.

    e. Mobilization for action.

    f. Lack of social control.

    g. Critical evaluation. This theory recognizes the complexity of the factors underlying movement development and is distinctly social in focus, but it is circular and incomplete.

4. **Resource-mobilization theory** focuses on the resources available to a movement.

    a. Critical evaluation. This approach ignores the fact that even without extensive resources, groups of poor people who are committed and well organized can sponsor effective social movements. It also may overstate the extent to which powerful people (with resources) are willing to challenge the status quo.

5. **Cultural theory** developed from the recognition by sociologists that social movements depend on cultural symbols.

    a. Critical evaluation. This approach reminds us that not just material resources but also cultural symbols form the foundation of social movements. However, powerful symbols support the status quo.

6. **New social movements theory** notes the importance of quality-of-life issues to recent movements.
    a. Critical evaluation. This approach may overstate the differences between "traditional" and "new" social movements.
C. Gender and social movements: Because of patriarchy, men have generally been more active than women in social movements:
D. Stages of social movements.
    1. Emergence.
    2. Coalescence.
    3. Bureaucratization.
    4. Decline, which may occur for four reasons:
        a. The movement may have succeeded.
        b. It may succumb to poor organization.
        c. It may be co-opted.
        d. It may be repressed.
E. Social movements and social change.
    1. Social movements exist to encourage or to resist social change.
    2. Social change is both the cause and the consequence of social movements.
    3. CONTROVERSY AND DEBATE BOX—Are You Willing to Take a Stand?

V. Looking Ahead: Social Movements in the Twenty-First Century.

A. While social movements have historically brought about change, new issues ensure that social movements will continue to shape our way of life.
B. The scope of social change is likely to increase for three reasons:
    1. Historically excluded categories of people are gaining a greater political voice.
    2. The technology of the Information Revolution has drawn the world closer together.
    3. Social movements are now uniting people throughout the entire world.

Chapter Objectives

1) Define collective behavior and social movements.

2) Identify reasons why collective behavior is difficult to study.

3) Distinguish between collectivities and groups.

4) Describe the main types of collective behavior, including crowds, mobs, riots, rumor, public opinion, panic, mass hysteria, fashion and fads.

5) Compare and contrast the main points of contagion, convergence, and emergent-norm theories of crowd behavior.

6) Identify and describe four types of social movements.

7) Compare and contrast the main points of deprivation, mass-society, structural-strain, resource-mobilization, cultural social movements, and new social movement theories to explain social movements.

8) Identify and discuss four stages in the life cycle of social movements.

Essay Topics

1) What are some examples of riot behavior in U.S. history? What social injustices were the riots a reaction against?

2) What are some examples of propaganda you have experienced? Did it sway you toward some viewpoint?

3) What theory do you think best explains social movements? Why?

4) Research one social movement and describe the stages in the life of that movement.

5) What is the subjective experience of being a part of a large expressive or acting crowd like? Draw on your personal experiences.

6) How well does the discussion in the text explain the spread of some rumor with which you are personally familiar? Discuss.

7) Early sociologists tended to analyze collective behavior as irrational. From the position of the individual participant, would you regard participation in a riot as necessarily highly irrational? How about involvement in a rumor? In a panic? In a fad?

8) Why do fads appeal especially strongly to adolescents?

9) Demonstrate your understanding of Smelser's structural-strain theory by using it to analyze the large-scale rioting in South Central Los Angeles following the Rodney King verdict.

10) Is it possible for a social movement to be a permanent feature of a society, or must it inevitably decline? Discuss.

Integrative Supplement Guide

1. **ABC Videos:**
- The Law and Gay Rights in America (*Nightline*, 10/9/95)
- Million Man March on Washington (*Nightline*, 10/16/95)

2. **Transparencies - Series V:**
- T-169 Support for Public Broadcasting Across the United States
- T-170 Four Types of Social Movements
- T-171 Relative Deprivation and Social Movements
- T-172 Stages in the Lives of Social Movements
- T-173 Political Involvement of Students Entering College in 1996: A Survey
- T-174 The Environment Versus the Economy, 1995

Supplemental Lecture Material
Lynching

In September 1892, several members of the white Woodruff family of Quincy, Mississippi, became ill and suspected that the water in their well had been poisoned. A number of white residents of Quincy decided that a black man named Benjamin Jackson may have poisoned the Woodruffs' well. Jackson was promptly arrested by police, along with his wife and his mother-in-law.

Before his trial could begin, a crowd of some two hundred whites demanded that Jackson be released to them so he could be lynched. The police complied, and Jackson was promptly hanged. A formal investigation was held to determine the possible involvement of Jackson's wife and her mother in the alleged poisoning. The investigation found no evidence that they (or Jackson himself) had been involved in a crime of any kind, and a jury ordered that the two women be released. When they returned to their home, however, they too were seized by a mob and promptly hanged. At this point, the mob began a search for another black man, Rufus Bigley, whose name had been mentioned during the legal investigation. Within a short time, he was hanged as well.

This account is typical of thousands of lynchings in the United States. The term *lynching* is derived from the activities of Charles Lynch, a Virginia colonist who attempted to maintain law and order before the establishment of formal courts. As applied in the 19th and 20th centuries, however, the word meant terrorism and murder outside the legal system.

Lynchings such as those described here were chronicled by Ida B. Wells, a black woman who courageously opposed lynching in her newspaper *The Free Speech* in Memphis, Tennessee. Her efforts served only to provoke local whites into forcing the closing of her paper. As Wells noted, the tragedy of widespread lynching was surpassed only by the apparent indifference of whites to this perversion of justice and basic human decency.

Sources

Wells-Barnett, Ida B. *On Lynchings*, (New York: Arno Press and the *New York Times,* 1969; orig. 1892), pp. 48–49.

White, Walter. *Rope and Faggot* (New York: Arno Press and the *New York Times,* 1969; orig. 1929).

Discussion Questions

1) Why do you think that lynchings, very common in the 19th and early 20th centuries, have virtually ceased today?

2) What would be some of the difficulties that a 19th century sociologist interested in studying lynching might have experienced?

3) How would contagion, convergence, and emergent-norm theory differ in their analysis of a lynch mob?

Supplemental Lecture Material
Disaster Research

One of the most interesting fields of study in collective behavior is the area of disaster research, which focuses on individual, organizational, and community patterns of response to fires and explosions, tornadoes, hurricanes, earthquakes, airplane crashes, train wrecks, and the sinking of ships.

Researchers have discovered that people commonly behave very differently in disaster situations than most of us would expect. Enrico Quarantelli discusses two of the most widely held misperceptions under the headings "the image of panic" and "the image of dependency."

The image of panic suggests that during and shortly after disasters most people respond in highly emotional and nonadaptive ways. During the disaster itself, "people may lose the ability to speak coherently and their behavior may appear random and ineffective. . . [alternatively], terror may cause people to act on the basis of naked, short-term self-interest. . . . Gripped by such terror, disaster victims have no inclination to cooperate with others or to give aid to those who are suffering" (Miller, p. 176). Immediately after the disaster, according to this view, people exhibit symptoms such as "spatial and temporal dislocation and helplessness" (Miller, p. 176).

In reality, such behaviors do occur, but they are atypical. "During disasters, people usually exhibit a remarkable degree of composure and concern for family, friends, neighbors and strangers" (Miller, p. 177). For example: flight attendants are trained to help passengers from their seats, down escape chutes, and away from the plane in the vital moments following air crashes. Attendants have carried out these activities while injured, being showered by flying glass and metal, and facing the very real danger of violent explosions (Miller, p. 177). Overall, research suggests that fewer than 2 percent of all disaster victims display "highly or mildly agitated states involving uncontrolled behavior" (Miller, p. 177).

Panic flight away from the disaster scene is also rare; in fact, convincing people to evacuate, either in the face of an impending disaster or just after one has struck, is a much more common problem for the authorities. "Substantial numbers of people refuse to evacuate, evacuate slowly, or leave for locations other than those specified by authorities.... Often, people attempt to re-enter the community before all danger has passed" (Miller, p. 177).

Finally, research suggests that post-disaster emotional shock is usually much less severe than many people might expect. A series of studies showed that the largest percentage of any population studied that experienced such shock was 14 percent — 22 percent of the women and 5 percent of the men. "There are no documented instances in which a majority of a population exhibited shock reactions after a disaster" (Miller, p. 178). Survivors do commonly report "experiencing grief, depression, despair, headaches, loss of appetite, sleeplessness and nightmares in the weeks following disaster" (Miller, p. 178), but these symp-

toms only rarely interfere with effective coping behavior.

The image of dependency suggests that victims are usually so stunned in the immediate aftermath of a disaster that they are unable to assist their fellows in need of aid. Further, "after being officially guided to safety, the victims will, it is thought, be so shocked, discouraged, apathetic, and lacking in initiative that everything will have to be done for them" (Quarantelli, p. 143).

In reality, "characteristically, the first rescue and recovery efforts are made by members of disaster-struck communities. These efforts are usually quite direct and effective, partly because of the survivors' familiarity with their community" (Miller, p. 178). Victims work together in small informal groups to rescue their fellows.

Relations with formal relief agencies are often quite strained. "Residents [often] resent the curfews, traffic rerouting and parking restrictions imposed by authorities to maintain order" (Miller, p. 178). In fact, far from passively depending on organizations like the Red Cross or Civil Defense, many disaster victims call on such sources of assistance only as a last resort. Thus, "the temporarily homeless either avoid the shelters altogether or use them only for a short time. If the option exists, survivors usually prefer to sleep in a real bed and have hot meals at the home of a nearby relative rather than sleep on an army cot and eat peanut butter sandwiches in the high school gym" (Miller, p. 178).

Another interesting aspect of individual reaction to disasters is the considerable degree of altruism normally demonstrated by immediate bystanders. The following account of the behavior of Iowa farmers following the 1954 crash of a Braniff airliner is typical:

[The farmers] risked their lives to remove survivors from the gasoline-drenched wreckage. . . . Many farm women carried their family's warmest blankets to the crash site with little concern that the blankets would be permanently soiled with bloodstains, mud, and oil. Few blankets in which survivors were sent to hospitals were ever returned. In the days following the crash, warm meals and hot coffee were provided, around the clock, to state police and aviation officials. Finally, farmers provided tractors, loading equipment, and labor during the removal of the wreckage. Families received little reimbursement for their efforts, although reimbursement seemed to be of little concern to these people. They took pride in their generosity. (Miller, p. 183)

Why are survivors and bystanders frequently so altruistic? Some attribute this to the fact that survivors can "look around them and see the capricious nature of what has happened. . . . [They] initially tend to underestimate their personal losses and to feel that others have suffered greater loss. Given this, survivors experience initial feelings of anxiety and guilt as to why God or circumstance has spared them. . . . Giving assistance to others substantially reduces these stresses" (Miller, p. 184).

Sources

Miller, David L. *Introduction to Collective Behavior.* Belmont, CA: Wadsworth, 1985, pp. 171–214.

Quarantelli, E. L. "When Disaster Strikes," in Helen M. Hughes, ed., *Crowd and Mass Behavior.* Boston: Holbrook Press, 1972, pp. 139–146.

Discussion Questions

1) Why do you think that erroneous images of panic and dependency are so widely accepted by people unfamiliar with the actual behavior typical in disaster situations?

2) Why do you think that victims often resist and even resent the assistance that is offered them by formal relief agencies?

3) Can you think of any additional reasons why many people at disaster scenes act in highly altruistic ways?

Supplemental Lecture Material
Women and Democracy in Latin America

All across Latin America, women have been important catalysts in the transition from dictatorships to democratic states. In many countries, women's groups have been closely affiliated with pro-democracy, anti-poverty, and human rights groups, and frequently their participation in these groups led to changes in their view of themselves and their roles and social status. According to Peruvian sociologist Gladys Acosta Vargas, the process of pressing for freedom for all citizens often started very personal self-examinations and was an end to the "domestic imprisonment" many Latin American women had been limited to.

Some of the most widespread types of transformative pro-democracy groups women have formed and joined in Latin America were not explicitly political in nature. In Chile, special programs meant to ease severe unemployment and deprivation during a military dictatorship exchanged labor for food. In some cases, the programs directly benefited the participants and organizers, but sometimes the programs were intended to help others. The Glass of Milk Program in Peru, for instance, distributed milk to children in Lima. While such programs were not radical in intent, they gave many women widespread creditability to effect social change and the practical experience of organizing and leading a group.

Moreover, women have proven to be especially important as the "living memory" or conscience of many pro-democracy movements. The Mothers and Grandmothers of the Plaza de Mayo, Women for Life, the Widows of Guatemala, and other groups all tried to prevent the passage of laws that would allow the new democracies to legally "forget" and forgive past crimes of repression and corruption under autocratic regimes. Their voices became the consciences of democracies and seemed to bridge traditional roles of women and the new context of leadership.

Somewhat less frequently, Latin American women became some of the most visible and outspoken opponents of dictators, typically because male leaders of pro-democracy groups faced violent repression, death, and incarceration. The simple absence of men in these groups forced women to assume roles formerly unavailable to them. Female leadership was often quite radical in spirit because in almost every relevant Latin American country women had little or no precedent for political leadership.

All kinds of participation in organizations that were directly political (such as human rights groups) or indirectly political (such as charitable organizations) seeded the mental earth of men and women for true women's rights groups. The establishment of democracies did not mean the end of women's activism. Many Latin American constitutions and laws contain passages guaranteeing equal rights and prohibiting discrimination based on gender, all of which were the result of feminist groups that were building on victories they had won in other areas of political life. In some parts of Latin America, women have encouraged their governments to support international statements by the United Nations and other groups in favor of improving the welfare and status of women across the globe.

Vargas argues that the adoption of political leadership by women in Latin America often occurred when other institutions were weakened or fell away, freeing women to act in new ways. In effect, when the traditional means of keeping women in politically irrelevant or subordinate positions were removed, women tried to and often did rise in the vacuum. But as Vargas also points out, women have not typically built on these new roles once democracies were established. And the paucity of participation has not always been as a result of the reestablishment of traditional authority by men. In many cases, women have returned of their own will to their homes and familiar paths as periods of crisis have ended.

The future political participation of women in Latin America seems more complicated than a few decades ago. Traditional female roles continue in good health, but new kinds of roles have been established, and an infrastructure of women leaders has been built. Additional change in these societies will bring new opportunities to their female members.

Source

Vargas, Gladys Acosta. "The Latin American Women's Movement and the Construction of Democracy." *SSSP Newsletter* (Summer 1994):7–11.

Discussion Questions

1) Do you know of any parallels in American and Latin American history between the increase in the membership of women in human rights' groups (such as anti-slavery groups) and in the birth of the feminist movement?

2) Does the participation of women in charitable organizations in Latin America seem to have significantly contributed to women entering political organizations? Why? Are there similarities with contemporary American charitable organizations?

Supplemental Lecture Material
Sex Gum and a Missile

It was a plot. Palestinian officials and the public were sure. Bubble gum spiked with sex hormones sold for only a penny to unsuspecting school children. Why? To drive women sexually mad enough to be willing to become prostitutes and spies, while at the same time making them infertile and so slowly killing the Palestinian nation. What about those children? Chewing the gum would turn them infertile as well, a diabolical long term plot. The perpetrators? The Israelis.

The unlikely tale of bubble gum rushed to a lab where it supposedly was discovered to have been laced with progesterone, one of two female hormones, spread like wildfire. What tipped off officials? Both the sultry image of Pocahantas on a sticker inside and the accidental words "for adults only" put on the outside by the Spanish manufacturer.

Not that food tampering is unheard. Spoiled flour found its way to the West Bank and the Gaza strip in 1996, and baby food sent to Gaza turned out to relabeled and expired soy formula.

The Palestinian Supply Minister said "the authority seized 154 pieces of the suspect gum. By the time the story reached Hebron in the West Bank, local health official Mahmoud Batarna was saying he had captured 200 tons of the stuff in this city alone."

An independent test commissioned by the Washington Post of the gum found no trace of the hormone. In addition, while the instruments they used were capable at detecting as little as a microgram, it would actually take 300 micrograms for the hormone to have any birth control effect. In reality, progesterone would be highly ineffective in that capacity anyway, since the body inactivates it quickly after it is taken orally. For that reason, birth control pills normally "rely on synthetic compounds known as progestins or progestogens that are similar but not identical. These oral contraceptives diminish female libido rather than increase it, although the effects in either direction are not dramatic." On the other hand, these hormones do indeed impair men's sperm production and ability to maintain an erection.

Nonetheless, science seems to have had little effect on the story. Most Palestinians continue to believe in a plot.

This could never happen here, you say? What about the persistent story that TWA flight 800 was shot down by a missile shot from a U.S. naval vessel? A photo surfaced purportedly showing the flash of a missile in the sky above where the plane crashed. Trouble is, the flash was actually taken North, away from where the plane crashed. Nor have any credible eye witnesses surfaced, and a plot to keep the accident secret would involve a conspiracy between hundreds of sailors, flyers, divers and government officials. Would there really be no leaks when so many know about something?

And why shoot down flight 800? Because Kissinger was supposed to be on it.

Only problem is. . . he never was. Never mind, though. As in the Palestinian incident, rumors are tenacious, in this case especially so, since no certain explanation for the crash has ever been given. So the tales continue to grow on the Internet where this one started through a private e-mail that found its way onto the Net.

Sources

Gellman, Barton. "Pop! Went the Tale of the Bubble Gum Spiked with Sex Hormones," *Washington Post,* (July 28, 1997):A14.

Lacayo, Richard. "Shot in the Dark?" *Time*, Vol. 148, No. 24 (November 25, 1996):44.

Discussion Questions

1) Using what you've learned in the chapter, discuss what elements of collective behavior are at play in the stories above. Why did the latter sound plausible to so many of us when the former strikes us as far-fetched?

2) **Activity.** Search the Internet or newspapers for rumors similar to the one above that have swept this country. Can you find certain commonalities among these tales?

Chapter 24

Social Change: Traditional, Modern, and Postmodern Societies

I. What Is Social Change?
Social change is the transformation of culture and social institutions over time. It has four general characteristics:
   A. Social change is inevitable.
   B. Social change is sometimes intentional but often unplanned.
   C. Social change is controversial.
   D. Some changes matter more than others.

II. Causes of Social Change.
   A. There are three important sources of cultural change:
      1. Invention.
      2. Discovery.
      3. Diffusion.
   B. Tension and conflict within a society can also produce change.
   C. As Max Weber demonstrated in his analysis of the origins of capitalism, ideas may promote social change.
   D. Demographic factors such as population growth, shifts in the composition of a population, or migration also influence social change.
      1. SEEING OURSELVES—National Map 24–1: Who Stays Put?: Residential Stability Across the United States.

III. Modernity.
Modernity consists of social patterns linked to industrialization. **Modernization** is the process of social change initiated by industrialization.
   A. Peter Berger notes four major characteristics of modernization:
      1. The decline of small, traditional communities.
      2. The expansion of personal choice.
      3. Increasing diversity in beliefs.
      4. Future orientation and growing awareness of time.
   B. Ferdinand Toennies interpreted modernization as a loss of community, or the decline of *Gemeinschaft* and the rise of *Gesellschaft*.
      1. Critical evaluation. This approach synthesizes the various dimensions of change, but says little about cause and effect and may be seen as romanticizing traditional societies.
   C. Emile Durkheim stressed that modernization involved an increased division of labor (specialized economic activity, and a shift from mechanical to organic solidarity).

1. Critical evaluation. Anomie does seem to be a problem in modern societies, but shared values and norms have by no means disappeared in modern societies.
   D. Max Weber analyzed modernization as the replacement of tradition with rationality.
      1. Critical evaluation. Conflict theorists would argue that the real problem is social inequality, not rational bureaucracy.
   E. Karl Marx analyzed modernization as the ascendancy of industrial capitalism. He anticipated a socialist revolution that would lead to an egalitarian society.
      1. Critical evaluation. Marx underestimated the significance of bureaucracy in shaping all modern societies, capitalist or socialist.

IV. Theoretical Analysis of Modernity.
   A. Structural-functional theory: Modernity as mass society. A **mass society** is a society in which industry and an expanding bureaucracy have eroded traditional social ties. This occurs for two principal reasons:
      1. The scale of life has increased greatly in mass society.
      2. The state has also expanded tremendously. These two developments leave people with little control over their lives.
      3. Critical evaluation. Mass-society theory romanticizes the past and pays little attention to problems of social inequality.
   B. Social-conflict theory: Modernity as class society. A **class society** is a capitalist society with pronounced social stratification. This approach sees social revolution as necessary to eradicate the social inequality that results from capitalism.
      1. Critical evaluation. This approach overlooks the ways in which modern societies have become more egalitarian. It is unlikely that a centralized economy could cure the ills of modernity.
   C. Modernity and the individual.
      1. Mass Society: Problems of identity.
         a. According to David Riesman, modernization brings on changes in **social character,** personality patterns common to members of a society.
         b. Preindustrial societies are characterized by **tradition-directedness,** rigid personalities based on conformity to time-honored ways of living.
         c. Modern societies reflect **other-direction,** a receptiveness to the latest trends and fashions, often expressed in the practice of imitating others.
      2. Class society: Problems of powerlessness.
         a. Herbert Marcuse condemns modern society as irrational because it fails to meet the needs of many people.
   D. Modernity and progress. Whether people see change as progress depends on their underlying values.
      1. GLOBAL SOCIOLOGY BOX—Does "Modern" Mean "Progress?" The Case of Brazil's Kaiapo.
   E. Modernity: Global variation. While it is useful to contrast traditional and modern societies, the old and the new often coexist in unexpected ways.

V. Postmodernity.
Postmodernity refers to social patterns characteristic of postindustrial societies.
   A. Postmodernity encompasses the following five themes:
      1. Modernity has failed in important respects.
      2. The bright promise of "progress" is fading.
      3. Science no longer holds the answers.
      4. Cultural debates are intensifying.
      5. Social institutions are changing.
   B. Critical evaluation. Modernity has raised living standards despite its failings. What are the alternatives?
   C. CRITICAL THINKING BOX—Tracking Change: Is Life in the United States Getting Better or Worse?

VI. Looking Ahead: Modernization and Our Global Future.
   A. In global context, modernization theory argues that poverty is caused largely by traditionalism.
   B. Therefore, intervention in the economies of the poorer societies by the advanced nations is necessary.
   C. Dependency theorists respond that the economic reliance of poor societies on rich societies and on multinational corporations means that poorer societies are unlikely to be able to duplicate the experiences of the developed societies.
   D. CONTROVERSY AND DEBATE BOX—Personal Freedom and Social Responsibility: Can We Have It Both Ways?

Chapter Objectives

1) Define social change and describe characteristics of the process of social change.

2) Examine causes of social change: culture, social structure, ideas, the natural environment, and demographics.

3) Define modernity and identify four characteristics of modernization.

4) Compare and contrast the theories of Toennies, Durkheim, Weber, and Marx on modernization.

5) Distinguish between mass and class analyses of modernity.

6) Discuss David Riesman's notion that modernization brings changes in social character.

7) Identify and describe five major themes of personality.

Essay Topics

1) What do you see as the most positive social change in your lifetime? The most negative?

2) Do you think that modernity has failed? Why or why not?

3) Do you agree with the notion that postmodernity is a postmaterialist era, in which issues like social justice and environment

and animal rights, command more and more public attention?

4) Some groups, like the Amish, attempt to minimize the amount of social change that they experience. What are some strategies that might promote this goal? Is it possible to completely avoid all social change?

5) How might a sociologist explain and interpret the fact that a steadily increasing amount of the social change that takes place in the world today is planned rather than accidental? What are some consequences of this trend?

6) Do you think humanity will ever get to the point where the natural environment is no longer an important source of social change?

7) Do you think the changes that have resulted from modernization have improved or degraded human life? Defend your position.

8) Do you think life in the United States is getting better or worse? Defend your position.

9) Do you find mass or class theory more useful in trying to understand the problems of contemporary U.S. society? Discuss.

10) Do you think that it is either desirable or possible for a single, relatively specific value system to be held by the sizable majority of the citizens of a modern mass society such as the U.S.? Discuss.

Integrative Supplement Guide

1. ABC Videos:
- Middle Class - The Family Dream (*Nightline*, 1/6/95)

- Changes in the Workplace (*World News Tonight/American Agenda*, 12/27/95)

2. Transparencies - Series V:
- T-175 Who Stays Put? Residential Stability Across the United States
- T-176 Support for Science: A Global Survey

Supplemental Lecture Material
Brazil's Kaiapo Resist Assimilation

Only a handful of societies around the world have been able to continue living as hunter-gatherers or horticulturists. Prominent among these are the Kaiapo, who live in a protected area in the center of Brazil's vast but shrinking Amazonian rain forest.

Most traditional cultures have been shattered through ". . . decimation by diseases spread by contact with whites and cultural extinction through assimilation." But the Kaiapo and seventeen other tribes, a total of about five thousand individuals, have found a refuge in the Xingu National Park where they continue to live much as their ancestors did, hunting, fishing, and gardening in the jungle and using the jungle as a pharmacy.

With the assistance of the Rainforest Foundation, established by British rock star Sting, the Kaiapo are currently pressuring the Brazilian government to expand their reserve to over 44,000 acres, nearly the size of New York State. But the continued survival of the traditional cultures is far from certain. "From the air, one can see the geometric patterns of encroaching change: cow pastures, soybean fields, and red dirt roads stretching to the edge of the park boundary." And the cooperation of the government of the state of Para may be hard to obtain: its largest single source of revenue is a sales tax on lumber harvested in the rain forest.

Source

Brooke, James. "Rain Forest Indians Hold Off Threat of Change," *New York Times International Edition* (December 3, 1990).

Discussion Questions

1) Is it possible, or even desirable, to preserve preindustrial cultures such as those of the Kaiapo?

2) What role can citizens of the developed societies play in this effort?

Supplemental Lecture Material
America Then (1900) and Now (1999)

"Sometimes the facts get in the way of nostalgia about the ☐good old days' " writes U.S.A. Today reporter Haya El Nasser.

Changes in American life in the 20th century, from comparisons between the earliest data available in 1900 and the 1999 "Statistical Abstract of the United States" reveal that in 1900:

- Men were the breadwinners. Women worked and raised children but couldn't vote. Children as young as 6 worked instead of attending school;
- At the turn of the century 60% of Americans lived in rural areas where families were bigger and life in farm towns was quiet and monotonous;
- The "one-room school house", where children from ages 8-14 would attend school in the same classroom (although attendance was not compulsory in many states);
- By 1900, 95% of Americans lived within 5 miles of a railway depot where trains offered easy access (often a two-or three-day ride) to large cities where industrialization promised steady work and a chance to join the middle-class;

- Race was defined as black or white. Blacks were poorer and died younger (at an average age of 33);
- Daycare wasn't a problem — if children could work; they could stay on their own when parents were away.
- Poverty was widespread. There were no social welfare programs. Labor protests were taking shape. And retirement didn't exist because most people died young (men at 46, women at 48); and
- While most people didn't have indoor plumbing, the excitement of change was pervasive. The automobile, telephone and electricity promised as much change as the Internet or genetic research does today.

In marked contrast, in 1999:

- The Protestant work ethic that dominated our value system in 1900 was alive and well — corporations just called it "peak performance";
- Americans were working long hours. Life was intense. And both adults and children lived a much more structured life than they did in 1900;
- for many, the 40-hour workweek was on its way out yet almost one-third of those employed worked more than that;
- close to 60% of women worked outside the home and about 30% of them were mothers. Divorced parents were at an all-time high, as they juggled work and family on their own;
- nearly everyone lived in a metropolitan area. A typical household had fewer than three people and was located in the suburbs;
- there was less poverty, more social welfare and better health care. Childbirth was no longer a killer. There were vaccines for polio, tuberculosis and the measles. People lived longer — so long that many were able to retire from one job and them begin a second career;

- more people than ever owned their own homes, had more than one car and one TV, and were using cell phones, computers, and CD players. Educationally, 83% of Americans completed high school and 24% finished college;
- while women still make less money than men, the gap continued to narrow. And women had enough political clout to shape election results;
- race was no longer an issue of black and white. The most recent wave of immigrants were from Latin America and Asia, not Europe. Hispanics were the majority in Los Angeles, more than 150 languages were spoken in L.A. schools, and interracial marriages were increasing; and
- recreation had become a major industry. (In 1996 Americans spent $431 billion – 8.3% of their annual earnings – on recreation. The figure has only gone up since then thanks to a booming economy.)

El Nasser concludes:

Despite the dizzying changes in this century, the prospect of more scientific discoveries promises to alter American lifestyles even more.

Source

El Nasser, Haya. "Living in America in ...1900 and 1999." *U.S.A. Today* (December 13, 1999):3A.

Discussion Questions

1) What are the scientific discoveries that you project will alter the lifestyle of Americans living during the twenty-first century?

2) What change, invention, or discovery during the twentieth century has had the greatest effect on your life?

3) What factor(s) do you think will shape and/or determine the major social changes that will occur during the twenty-first century?

Supplemental Lecture Material
The Lonely Crowd

Chapter 24 outlines two distinct types of social character as identified by Harvard sociologist David Riesman in his classic 1950 book, *The Lonely Crowd.* The **tradition-directed person,** most characteristic of preindustrial societies, conforms rigidly to time-honored ways of living. In contrast, **other-directed people,** typical of late industrial or postindustrial societies, are strongly guided by their perceptions of what people around them expect them to do and be.

Riesman also identified a third type of social character, which he terms **inner-direction** and is most commonly found in societies undergoing the early and middle phases of the Industrial Revolution. In the United States, the latter half of the 19th century and the first half of the 20th were the heyday of inner-direction.

If the tradition-directed learn what is expected of them by observing the unchanging norms of their culture and the other-directed develop a sort of internal "radar" that allows them to keep pace with the ever-changing expectations of their peers, the inner-directed person is fitted during the socialization process with a mechanism that Riesman compares to a gyroscope. This mechanism spurs the individual toward success in pursuit of certain somewhat generalized goals, usually economic, but recognizes the faster pace of change in industrial societies by allowing the individual considerable flexibility in pursuing his or her goals in order to adapt to changing external circumstances. Thus the inner-directed person is far more flexible than the tradition-directed type, but considerably more committed to specific goals than is the typical other-directed person.

Childrearing in the era of tradition-directedness is mostly a matter of providing unambiguous models of expected behavior. Other-directed parents mainly stress how important it is for their children to get along with their peers and not stand out in a crowd. In contrast, the inner-directed child is subjected to a good deal of formal character building, whose purpose is to instill an inner drive to success. Chores and self-discipline are emphasized. A strong superego forms. An inner-directed home is rarely comfortable — the child is not necessarily expected to like or be friends with his or her parents — but it does produce strong achievement-oriented individuals. Riesman suggests that "the tradition-directed child propitiates his parents, the inner-directed child fights or succumbs to them, the other-directed child manipulates and is manipulated by them."

In school, the inner-directed child is held up to high expectations. He or she is taught that what matters is what he or she can accomplish, not how nice his or her smile is or how many people like him or her. The system is harsh on failures. During the other-directed era, the classroom becomes more focused on the child's social and psychological adjustment and somewhat less concerned with formal academics. The teacher serves less as a taskmaster and more as an opinion leader.

Inner-directed children, as one might imagine, are not especially tightly bonded to their peers. They cannot cite the failings of their friends as a defense against adult ex-

pectations: "But Dad, everyone else flunked the test too," is of no interest to the inner-directed parent. Inner-directed children commonly pursue solitary hobbies such as reading or stamp collecting. Other-directed children are deeply involved in the peer group and almost totally vulnerable to its demands. Children devote enormous energy to following the preferences of their fellows in styles of dress and music. If the inner-directed child is learning to be a hard-working producer, the postindustrial other-directed child is learning to be a discriminating consumer. If the greatest sin for the inner-directed is to fail to achieve his or her pre-set goal, the greatest failing for the other-directed child is to be rejected because one is too different. "The proper mode of expression requires feeling out with skill and sensitivity the probable tastes of others and then swapping mutual likes and dislikes to maneuver intimacy."

Riesman suggests that the shift from inner-direction to other-direction strongly affects many other aspects of a culture. Consider, for example, the media. The dominant media in the era of inner-direction are books, newspapers, and magazines. Designed to be read alone, the print media of this period frequently reinforced the child's need to achieve. Horatio Alger-type stories and the biographies of great men served as what Riesman terms "the whip of the word," pushing their readers toward ever more exertion in pursuit of their goals. Other-directed children still sometimes read, but they characteristically prefer stories that help them understand what others expect of them. The adult equivalent is the flood of self-help and pop psychology books that currently fill American bookstores. However, the most characteristic media of the modern era are television and films, which are generally watched collectively. For these media, the popularity of a particular program amongst one's peers is of crucial importance — consider the remarkable contemporary success of programs like "The Simpsons" or "Twin Peaks."

Take as a final example the worlds of work and leisure. The inner-directed worker thinks of his or her job mostly in terms of impersonal categories. In the industrial era, many people worked directly with physical objects. Those who worked with other people tended to treat them impersonally. You were expected to do your job; getting along well with your co-workers was secondary. Leisure was sharply separated from the world of work and often solitary. Successful people were commonly quite eccentric in their choice of leisure activities, having no one to please but themselves. On the other hand, in the era of other-direction, the work environment is viewed mostly in interpersonal terms. The ability to effectively manipulate others becomes the most crucial job skill. The worker does not seek to stand out, but rather to gain the admiration and affection of his peers. Work and leisure are less separated, and a central concern with the views of others emerges here too. Inner-directed diners eat what they like whether or not others agree: other-directed "gourmets" follow the current trend in restaurants — this week Thai, next week Cajun — and worry about whether or not they enjoy a bottle of wine as much as they ought to.

Discussion Questions

1) Most people who read *The Lonely Crowd* come away with the impression that the author feels that we may have lost more than we have gained in the transition from the inner-directed to the other-directed character type. Do you agree? In what ways are inner-directed people poorly suited to live in a postindustrial society?

2) Generate a discussion among the students to determine whether their childhood experiences prepared them to be primarily inner- or other-directed. This would be especially appropriate if your class includes both older and college-age students.

3) Most of America's political and business leaders were raised in the inner-directed period, whereas most people in the society today are other-directed. What problems does this create? How do you expect to see politics and business changing as other-directed people gradually take control of these institutions?

Supplemental Lecture Material
America in the 1950s: The Way We Used to Be?

The decade of the 1950s has become a period viewed with nostalgia by many social conservatives and with disdain by many liberals. Especially for those who idealize the period, the 1950s have become a way of gauging the "decline" of America. Negative and positive myths of the 1950s cloud a fair assessment even if more accurate views won't necessarily resolve any arguments.

Observers frequently focus their arguments on the family of the 1950s. Families of this period were overwhelming nuclear families; 79 percent of families were married couples in 1950 and 74 percent in 1960. Fifty-five percent of American families were married couples in 1991. So-called nontraditional families, such as households run by a woman or a man alone, were only 11 percent of all families in 1950 but 15 percent in both 1991 and 1940.

Most couples married quite young in the 1950s relative to other decades this century. The median age of marriage reached its low point in 1956: 20.1 for women and 22.5 for men. In 1900, the ages were 26 for men and

22 for women, quite close to the 1991 medians of 26 for men and 24 for women.

Marriage rates themselves were not particularly high in the 1950s, but the lower age of marriage gave that impression to many people. Additionally, birth rates rose to pre-Depression levels for a brief period as women began having children earlier and with less space between births. During the baby boom period of 1946 to 1964, the birth rate rose above 100 per 1,000 women aged 15 to 44. The rate fell quickly afterwards and has stabilized between 65 and 70 per 1,000 women.

Some current myths about the decade suggest that women didn't work much or at all in the 1950s, especially married women. In fact, many women were employed outside of the home, totaling 34 percent in 1950 and 38 percent in 1960; the rate is over 60 percent now. Married women have historically worked outside of the home in smaller numbers than unmarried women — about 25 percent in 1950 and 59 percent in 1991. The higher percentage of working women in the 1990s reflects decreased buying power. Two incomes are usually necessary to maintain a standard of living that could be held in the 1950s with one earner.

Many myths also concern the lack of few visible "deviant" groups. Homosexuality was widely frowned upon, and few homosexuals dared to come out in any public forum. Certainly homosexuals existed, but there are no accurate surveys to estimate how much of the population they made up. For that matter, such percentages are still a matter for broad debate today.

Illegitimacy, too, was highly frowned upon, and perhaps as many as half of all out-of-wedlock teen pregnancies resulted in marriage before delivery. During the late 1970s, more women began choosing to avoid such marriages, and now about two-thirds of all teen pregnancies occur outside of marriage.

Crime levels appear to have been genuinely lower as well, even after accounting for crimes that weren't reported, such as sexual abuse, or that were probably very underreported, such as rape or spousal abuse. Criminal activity was much higher in the 1920s and 1930s than during the 1950s, but crime was an important issue during the 1950s as crime rates rose rapidly in larger cities across the country.

Source
Crispell, Diane. "Myths of the 1950s." *American Demographics* (August 1992):38–43.

Discussion Questions
1) Why might conservatives view the 1950s as a high-water mark for American society? Why might liberals find the period repressive? How do you feel that the decade compares to the 1990s?

2) How have politicians in recent elections discussed the 1950s? What qualities of the 1990s might future conservatives and liberals emphasize as they look back in forty years? How realistic or meaningful are such idealizations?

3) Is there a period in American history or in your own life that you view with nostalgia? Why? How well do you think that this interpretation would stand a careful assessment of its accuracy?

Supplemental Material
The Evolution of Despair

You would think evolution's role is to prepare us for the world. Mostly, it has done just that, and admirably, too. But what happens if our environment changes so quickly, evolution doesn't have time to act? That is what has occurred, say evolutionary psychologists, and the result is a dramatic rise in depression and anxiety disorder and suicide. Why? Because according to an emerging field of study called "mismatch theory," the human mind — our emotions, our wants, our needs — evolved in an environment where there were neither telephones, nor cars, nor planes, nor computers. In other words, our minds are floundering in an alien world, stressed and confused.

To imagine what   called   environment might have been like, evolutionary psychologists look to remote hunter-gatherer societies or those with primitive agriculture. "Because social cooperation improves the chances of survival, natural selection imbued our minds with an infrastructure for friendship, including affection, gratitude and trust." In fact, hunter-gatherer societies are typified by intimate relationships, such as friends and family, that are stable. Probably because life in such an environment is far from private, child abuse in preindustrial cultures seems to have been virtually unknown possibly for two reasons: unwanted children were killed at birth, and childrearing was a public process where the child was always under the watchful eyes of many. Thus, the nuclear family idealized in the 1950s has serious drawbacks by isolating family members and putting the raising of children behind closed doors where abuse can be hidden.

Urban living, too, has increasingly added to our isolation. Once, even in big cities, neighborhoods were close-knit, almost small towns, but suburbanization brought those communal ties to an end. Mothers, in particular, were more and more left on their own devices and cut off from support, ushering in the feminist movement.

When it comes to technologies, television has been perhaps the most isolating of all. Instead of visiting friends or neighbors for a chat, we now sit for hours, silent and absorbed by what happens on a screen. "When you are watching TV 28 hours a week — as the average American does — that's a lot of bonding you're not doing." Television also sets up unrealistic standards for us to compare ourselves to. Once we might have striven to be more like a real person; Nowadays, we aim to become as perfect as a fictional character. Who could possibly live up to that in the long run?

While some see the Internet as a way to   new communal bonds, others maintain that   lacks the tactile and visual contact we thrive on while at the same time adding to informational overload, another stressor.

So what about the notion that civilization restrains our anim... are, socializing us into kinder, gentler creatu. s?

"This points to the most ironic of evolutionary psychology's implications: many of the impulses created by natural selection's ruthless imperative of genetic self-interest aren't selfish in any straightforward way. Love, pity, generosity, remorse, friendly affection and enduring trust, for example, are part of our genetic heritage. And, oddly, some of these affiliative impulses are frustrated by the structure of modern society at least as much as the more obviously 'animal' impulses. The problem with modern life, increasingly, is less that we're 'oversocialized' than that we're undersocialized — or, that too little of our 'social' contact is social in the natural, intimate sense of the word."

Capitalism acerbates our modern dilemma. Not only does the free market keep adding new antisocial technologies, it also drives our vocational specialization and our mobility, all of which decrease our social bonds. Yet we seem unwilling to spend money — such as taxes — on institutions (workplace-daycare, public parks, good public schools) that might counteract these isolating forces.

The result? More and more, we are alone, and more and more, we are feeling the negative effects in a growing sense of dissatisfaction and awareness that the material things we crave and buy still leave us hungering for more. Still leave us feeling empty, because our primitive mind still yearns for the good old days of community.

Source
Wright, Robert. "The Evolution of Despair," *Time* Vol. 146, No. 9 (August 28, 1995):50-57.

Discussion Question
1) What might be a sociologist's response to the theory above? Use one of the theoretical stances on social change in your discussion.